Reviewers' comments on Ss:

—— On *Astrology, Psych*

"...it's stupendous — just v
of modern astrology in the face of its excessive complication and fragmentation by others."
— Kenneth Negus, Ph.D.
Rutgers University

"You have presented so eloquently, so practically, the only new approach to astrology in a generation."
— Dr. Arthur D. Cain

"...a *thinking* book that is warm, practical, beautiful, and holistic without losing sight of the 'real' problems that are the daily concern of man. A student will be safe from the inflexible, unfounded, limited, and limiting cook-book descriptions that are flooding the market. Arroyo's presentation is simply superb."
— Lore Wallace
Astrology Now

—— On *Astrology, Karma & Transformation* ——

"Arroyo's new book reflects a real depth of comprehension and ability to integrate humanistic astrology with Jungian psychology and Eastern philosophy. The simplicity and clarity of his treatment of complex ideas is remarkable; it makes accessible even to the beginner a wealth of understanding...giving meaningful psychological grounding to astrological interpretation."
— *Library Journal*

"This is straight, clean astrology, in modern terms, very well and concisely written. One of the best modern works we have seen."
— *CAO Times*

"You have done a superb job on *Astrology, Karma & Transformation*. It is the kind of book that is going to raise the level of consciousness in the astrological field. I salute you for the depth of consciousness and the insight that is shown in your book."
— Isabel Hickey
Author of *Astrology: A Cosmic Science*

"I find it to be superior to any other astrology book I have ever read. It is a remarkable work of extremely meaningful material that is written in a very lucid and practical style, and that is why I tell my students that I consider it to be an absolute 'must'."
— Robert S. Kimball
Astrological Researcher & Teacher

NOTE ON COVER PHOTO:

The photograph on the cover was taken by Robert Ishi from the top of Twin Peaks in San Francisco on the day of an exceptionally spectacular sunset. In astrological language, the Sun was then conjunct the cusp of the seventh house, the house traditionally associated with relationships. Since the Sun is always *setting* when located at this position in the sky, one might also say that this photo is symbolic of the need to subdue the individual ego in order to make one's relationships vital and radiant.

RELATIONSHIPS & LIFE CYCLES

Modern Dimensions of Astrology

STEPHEN ARROYO

CRCS PUBLICATIONS
Post Office Drawer 4307
Vancouver, Washington 98662
USA

Library of Congress Cataloging in Publication Data
Arroyo, Stephen.
    Relationships & life cycles.

    Bibliography: p.
    1. Astrology. 2. Interpersonal relationships.
I. Title.
BF1711.A77   133.5   79-53979
ISBN 0-916360-12-1

FIRST EDITION
INTERNATIONAL STANDARD BOOK NUMBER: 0-916360-12-1
LIBRARY OF CONGRESS CATALOG CARD NUMBER: 79-53979
Published simultaneously in the United States
& Canada by CRCS Publications
Distributed in the United States
by CRCS Publications
Distributed in the United Kingdom
by L. N. Fowler, Ltd. and Thorsons Publishing Group
Cover photo by Robert Ishi

Dedication

To my fire-sign parents,
whose way of being has taught me
so much about flowing with the
cycles of life and about simple faith
and courage.

Acknowledgements

I want to express my special gratitude to both Diane Simon and Joanie Case for taking on the tedious work of transcribing hours of tapes into a typed manuscript with which I could work. The fact that they approached such a task with enthusiasm and without any complaint or delay makes me feel particularly indebted to them. In fact, I am amazed at and admire the perseverance, dedication, and intelligence that they have exemplified on this and other projects.

I'd also like to thank Joanie Case and Barbara McEnerney for their editing and proofreading, which—as on previous books—they performed with extraordinary skill and insight. To be fair to them, I must point out that I told them to be especially tolerant of the informal nature of the transcripts. Hence, any grammatical errors or lapses in punctuation remain because I personally insisted on maintaining the original character of the workshops, including my sometimes erratic way of speaking.

Contents

Key to Outline & Illustrations

Prologue

> Science is the art of creating suitable illusions which the
> fool believes or argues against, but the wise man enjoys for
> their beauty or their ingenuity, without being blind to the
> fact that they are human veils and curtains concealing the
> abysmal darkness of the unknowable.
>
> —Carl Gustav Jung

The above quotation from Jung expresses how I often feel about
all attempts to explain astrology or to "interpret" the many factors
used in astrology. The practice of astrology is such an individualized
art that each person necessarily evolves his or her own way of approaching and expressing it. And this leads, therefore, to a tremendous diversi-
ty of ideas, theories, and philosophies that are presented to the public
under the general label "astrology." Indeed, I often feel that much of
the talk, many of the books, and most of the theories that attempt to
deal with "astrology" lead one to run around in circles, always remaining distant from the center of the circle. In other words, I often feel
that the essence of astrology is inexpressible in words; it more nearly
approximates a form of celestial music. At most, one can hope to point
the reader of an astrology book in such a direction that he or she can
begin to trust feelings, to rely on personal perceptions and experience,
to bring forth insights spontaneously, and occasionally to gain a fleeting
glimpse of this transcendental essence.

I have tried to do this in my previous two books*, and the response from readers seems to indicate that—at least in part—the attempt has met with some success. This book has some of the same objectives as my previous ones, but the approach and format are completely different. First of all, unlike the other books, this one was not *written*. This book (with the exception of two brief sections that were originally written as articles) is comprised of three transcribed workshops, and the style is therefore more in the form of "blips" of information than a systematic, organized treatise.

In addition, one of the ideas underlying the publication of such informal workshops as these is that one should be able to *enjoy* astrology. Not all truths are discovered through theoretical, logical, or statistical analyses. Sometimes one must concentrate more on tuning in on the *living* nature of ideas by having fun with them, and this can often be more significant for students of astrology than systematic and dry attempts to be deep and meaningful.

My previous books go into more detail and depth than does this book. This work, on the other hand, gives an added perspective which many readers of the manuscript have enjoyed. Although temperamentally I prefer to write more systematic, in-depth sorts of things, people whose judgment I trust have urged me to have this material published, especially since I no longer do many in-person talks or workshops. I simply find myself unable to accept the vast majority of requests for public appearances that I receive. This book is therefore the next best thing to attending a workshop, and it is actually much less expensive than attending even one in-person presentation. Ideally, then, readers can get from this book at least some of the flavor of an informal talk, and I hope that readers of my other books will not be too surprised at the necessarily more informal, less comprehensive nature of this work.

I do, however, want to explain a few things about this book and about the workshops that are transcribed in this volume. These workshops were frank, informal, and often humorous (although much of the humor does not come out clearly in print), and most people attending them had taken my classes for some time. The fact that we were familiar and comfortable with each other allowed more flexibility, spontaneity, and freedom of expression than would have been the case

---

*Cf. *Astrology, Psychology & the Four Elements* and *Astrology, Karma & Transformation*.

in a formal lecture with complete strangers. Questions and comments from the audience often started us on tangents, but I've been told by many students that such tangents and examples from personal experience can elicit insights and understanding that can't easily be found in books. Sometimes, something significant can be expressed spontaneously through a tone or gesture that can't easily be put on paper. I've tried to indicate such nuances by my method of editing the transcripts, but some subtleties still get lost now and then. All in all, the rules of grammar and punctuation have been sacrificed to spontaneity. The workshops were informal, and so therefore is this book. Some editing was done, but no attempt was made to radically alter the character of the transcripts themselves.

Also, because of the need in a workshop to cover many ideas in a short time period, the reader should understand that I use less qualifications when speaking than when writing. So, some statements may occasionally seem too abrupt, harsh, or one-sided. But when I say something rather specific about a particular astrological factor, it is not a *judgment* of people who have that factor in their charts. It is not to be viewed as "good" or "bad." I'm simply citing some qualities that have been repeatedly observed in personal experience and "calling a spade a spade" so the listeners will get the point. Despite the drawbacks of this simplified method of expression, it's still quicker, better, and more interesting for the audience than endless rationalizations, repeated qualifications, and overly abstract theories that most students cannot relate to.

More than half the material in this book deals with relationships and compatibility. I urge the reader to refer often to the *Systematic Outline of Synastry* in Section I as you read the first three sections of this book. This outline was handed out at the workshops, and it gives some sense of the order and structure of the workshops that might not otherwise be immediately apparent.

Finally, many people have inquired about the availability of my next scheduled book, *Person-to-Person Astrology*, which was originally planned for 1979 publication. I have decided to change the entire concept of that book, which will delay its publication until at least 1981. Once that book is published, however, it is my feeling that the informal tone of this book will complement the more structured quality of *Person-to-Person Astrology*.

I — The Individual's Capacity for Relationship

This is the beginning of a series of two workshops on relationship, and this part is part one and deals primarily with the individual natal chart. We'll spend most of the time going over things related to the Moon, Mars, and Venus in relation to your own chart and anybody else's chart, and also miscellaneous other factors that have some ramifications in trying to analyze relationships—like the seventh house, and so forth.

There are so many things you can put into this kind of a workshop; it's set up like this. Part 1, this workshop, primarily deals with analyzing the individual chart; but we'll mention some things about chart comparison in passing. The second part, the second workshop of this series will deal with the actual technique of doing a chart comparison, and that is even more involved in some ways than just looking at the natal chart because you have two sets of factors to look at.

The idea with this outline* is—on one page—to put all the basic factors that you can (and really should) look at in a thorough analysis of any person's relationship potential, relationship capability, and specific types of compatibility shown by a comparison, which we'll get to at the next workshop.

---

*See Outline in this chapter. This outline was handed out to workshop participants. This outline is referred to periodically in the following material.

SYSTEMATIC OUTLINE OF SYNASTRY

Part I

1.-*The Individual's Capacity for Relationship*

a) General study of the individual charts, focusing on each person's primary needs, desires, and orientations; "affinities" & "disaffinities"; general energy attunement of each person; what vibrations and qualities "color" or "tone" the personal planets by sign, house, & close aspects.

b) Capacity for close relationship, as indicated in each individual chart: the 7th house; aspects to the Sun (especially for women) and Moon (especially for men); the sign and aspects of Venus—what each person looks for in close relationship, friendship, marriage, love, etc.

c) Emotional & sexual needs and orientations: look at Mars, Venus, & Moon—their signs & aspects; examine *overall elemental balance of chart* to see "where the person is coming from."

d) Study all relevant houses, especially the 7th, 5th, 11th, 8th, 1st, and that house which corresponds to the person's Sun sign.

e) Examine all close transits & progressions that might relate to important developments, new awareness of personal needs, or new types of self-expression.

f) Note especially any indication of "shared experience"—that is, all "interaspects" that are within 2° or so of exactitude which will be simultaneously activated by a transit.

SYSTEMATIC OUTLINE OF SYNASTRY

Part II

2.–*Techniques of Chart Comparison*

a) How will the energy fields of the two people interact? Look first at all close "interaspects" (i.e., interchart aspects within 4° or so of exactitude). How will the two people "feed" each other?

b) Then look at more general "interaspects" indicated by harmony or discord between the two people's planets according to the elements (this shows the overall energy blend in the relationship). Look especially at harmony or lack of it between the people's Suns & Moons, both persons' Mercurys, and between Venus/Venus, Mars/Mars, Venus/Mars, Venus/Moon, and Sun/Mars.

c) Note that any close interaspect involving at least one "personal planet" or the Ascendant or Descendant is most important!

d) Any *conjunction* of either person's Ascendant, Descendant, or the 1st or 7th ruling planets to one of the other person's planets will be important in indicating the overall long-term tone of the relationship (although be aware that this can evolve over time and express itself in a variety of ways in a single relationship).

e) Next, place each person's planets in the other person's chart by zodiacal degree, and note which houses in each chart are enlivened or activated by doing so. Houses wherein the other person's Sun, Moon, or Ascendant (or their rulers) fall are especially important. Houses where the outer three planets fall are not usually important, unless a close *conjunction* is formed with either a planet or an angle or unless the people are of vastly different ages.

f) Any interaspects that are repeated twice are *always* indicative of a major type of energy exchange between the two people. This is called a "double whammy" by some clever souls. (Example: A's Moon conjunct B's Jupiter & B's Moon trine A's Jupiter.)

g) Likewise, if there is a great predominance of a certain type of aspect with one particular planet (for example, many harmonious aspects with either person's Jupiter, this tone of energy exchange colors the entire relationship.

h) After examining all the major factors, what kind of impression predominates? A good balance in most ways? Too much emphasis on excitement and stimulation? Too much focus on security? Does either person provide what the other lacks and, if so, are the people too different or can they handle each other's differences and even appreciate them? What is the common goal and/or ideal of the two people?

My favorite book of all on chart comparisons (it doesn't really show you how to analyze the individual chart, but it's very good on chart comparisons) is that little pamphlet by Lois H. Sargent. It's been around for years; it's one of the cheapest books and it's still about the best for chart comparison.* There are very few books that deal in any detail with the individual relationship needs of the person. There's one by Ebertin called *The Cosmic Marriage*; there's something in there about the individual chart, and *Astrological Compatibility* by Palmer has quite a bit on Venus and Mars in the signs; it's more complete than most of the others. I don't agree with everything said, but you can definitely learn from it.

So, I'm doing this workshop first because, before you can do anything with chart comparison—people are always wanting to know "am I compatible with George, am I compatible with Mary" and all that stuff—you've got to look at the individual chart first because it may be that the person is compatible with nobody. To put it more specifically, it may be that the person is really hard to get along with, or very demanding, or kind of insensitive, or at times even cruel, or whatever. . . . So the individual chart is the first thing, because so often I've done chart comparisons or made an appointment to do a chart comparison and the person comes, and I'll look at the natal charts, and I'll spend most of the time saying "it's kind of difficult for you to deal with anybody very well." So compatibility isn't the only thing; it's also "are you able to tune in on any compatibility or harmonious energy flow that might come your way; are you capable of relating to it, or relating to somebody who's attuned to you in a compatible way?"

THE MOON

I think I'll talk about the Moon first, and then we'll get into Venus and Mars, because Venus and Mars will take a lot of time. Naturally, you have to look at all kinds of things, but I'll try to isolate some of the specific details that are major. Whatever sign your Moon is in represents some kind of mood, some kind of tone or vibration, that you're attuned to all the time, and so it has, of course, much to do with domestic-type of needs, in other words, what kind of person would you like in your home; what kind of behavior do you want to feel free to express all the time. In other words, if your Moon is in a very

---

*Reference here is to Sargent's book *How to Handle Your Human Relations*, published by the AFA, Inc., and available from the publisher of this book.

independent sign like Aries, Aquarius, Sagittarius, Gemini, you're not going to want a home life that is oppressive, or where your partner is always dragging you down or making you stay at home; you're going to want to feel free and independent. And of course the Moon sign, for men, has particular relevance to the type of female mate that they might feel comfortable with.

The Moon has so much to do with *comfort,* inner comfort, domestic comfort, what feels good to you, what feels natural to you. I know a man—he's about sixty years old—who has the Moon in Capricorn; he retired early, and ever since he was about fifty, he's felt comfortable with, you might say, Capricorn-type behavior. He feels comfortable with old age. He's cultivating getting old. He's really not very old; and he's very healthy, very moderate—he smokes twice a day. He drinks two beers, that's it. No immoderate behavior in any way, and he'll probably live to be a hundred, but he's *cultivating* old age. Because, with Moon in Capricorn, he feels really comfortable in the Capricorn role, regardless of what the sun sign is. Naturally, you'd have to look at the Moon aspects to see if that role was easy to express. One of my favorite astrological laws is that the planets in the signs show your urges and your needs—what urges towards self-expression do you have, what needs for fulfillment do you have. And everybody who has, say Moon in Capricorn, has certain basic archetypal needs, similar needs.

Q: How does he deal with not working, though?

A: He feels comfortable in the old age role of being retired. He putters around the yard; he's a professional putterer—loves it.

But once you have the planets in the signs, you could look at anybody's chart with just the planets in the signs and identify the primary urges, the primary needs. The aspects are the crucial thing, because they show how readily, how easily, or in what way the person is seeking to express those needs or to deal with those urges. For example, say you have the Moon in Capricorn and you want to—whether you consciously want to or not is beside the point—play certain Capricorn roles, to fit into a Capricorn mold or lifestyle, to have a fairly conservative domestic situation, or at least very secure. Moon in Capricorn's always very security-oriented, as is Moon in Cancer, and Moon in Scorpio.

Q: Is it more or less true what they say, like Moon in Capricorn the same as Sun in Capricorn, the Capricorn is old when they're young and young when they're old?

A: I find that true in most cases, yeah. I think I've seen a few exceptions, but most people with Capricorn Moon or Sun, and Capricorn rising too, that's often true. But not in every case; say somebody's chart is packed with six planets in Gemini—which is extremely youthful, you know, then the Capricorn part of them might not be obvious. It will still be there, but it won't be obvious.

So, anyway, the aspects show you the plot in the big drama of your life; they show all the intricacies of the plot, how are you going to try to satisfy those needs, or express those urges. So say your Moon is in Capricorn, or really Moon in any sign with a challenging aspect to Saturn—conjunction, square, or opposition; there you have a very Saturnian Moon. Your Moon, you might say, would then be colored by Capricorn and/or Saturn. With a Capricorn Moon also in aspect to Saturn, a double Saturnian impression, you might say, would be made on the Moon; therefore your need for inner security and for inner tranquility would be very much tied in with Saturn types of vibration: security, or authority, or worldly recognition, or some other kind of Saturn or Capricorn quality. And anybody who has Saturn in close aspect to the Moon, especially a challenging aspect, takes things very seriously, and takes themselves very seriously. They take marriage, partnerships, relationships very seriously. And any man with Moon in Capricorn, or Moon aspecting Saturn (and somebody with both, it would be especially strong) would take anything with the wife seriously and be extremely oversensitive. With Sun and Moon aspects to Saturn, you're oversensitive to anything. You take everything personally; you take everything wrong, usually. There's a tendency toward negativity, obviously in Capricorn and Saturn—toward a negative reaction, particularly if the Moon is aspecting Saturn or in Capricorn. Well, I'm going off on a bit of a tangent here. . . .

The Moon shows your security needs and your nurturing needs. The Moon, of course, is the Cancer planet and everybody needs some amount of nurturing. If your Moon is in Sagittarius, you'll feel nurtured by somebody who says "Let's go to Yosemite!" and they'll jump in the car and whip you off to Yosemite. And you'll feel nurtured by that. But if your Moon is, say, in Cancer or in Scorpio or in Pisces, you'll feel much more nurtured by somebody who says: "How'd you like a back rub and a nice cup of herb tea?"—you know, something that gets to you emotionally. And so, everybody needs some kind of nurturing.

You can even chart a kind of life cycle that everybody goes through wherein there are times that you regress; you know, everybody has growth spurts and then they'll have plateaus and sometimes they'll have brief regressions, especially during intense growth periods. They'll feel like regressing to something secure because everything is in flux. This is especially true if your current cycles shown by progressions and transits are mainly Uranian or Neptunian or Plutonian—big, big change times that leave you very uncertain and up in the air and *spacy*—confused, you can't get your feet on the ground because all the outer planets are making your whole body vibrate—you're "Gee, where am I going?"—then, you'll often try to regress to older patterns, or with another person, try to find some degree of grounding or security or nurturing.

I learned something just this week about that because transiting Pluto is opposite my kid's Moon now. The Moon, of course, has to do with all this stuff anyways—the early childhood, security, and all this—Pluto brings things to the surface; when it's transiting something in your chart, it transforms and brings to the surface the old stuff to be changed or to be eliminated. *But* often before you can eliminate the old, you've got to go back into it, and it's even sometimes like descending into the depths during a Pluto cycle. So my kid's done some interesting kinds of regression lately. Until now he pretty much grew very steadily and was very confident and didn't seem to be very clinging, but recently things have changed—he got a little bit ill, too. And for those who have kids, it'd be useful to know, if you don't already, that in a kid's chart the Moon has a lot to do with health and if his or her Moon is stressfully aspected by transiting Saturn, Mars, Pluto, Neptune, or Uranus, there can be some kind of health problem. It's different in every case. Mars to the Moon especially tends toward fever; Pluto tends toward eruptions. He's recently gotten this rash, never had any skin trouble before (he's three and a half); he's got this rash, but also he's done some little regressive things, like he's wet his pants a couple of times.

Last night he dropped a toothbrush down the drain. He pulled out the drain plug and dropped it in; you know, drains are ruled by Pluto; Pluto deals with all drainage, all eliminative channels. (And if you don't believe it, I heard this summer that someone asked, "What happened to you when you were about two years old, because Pluto crossed your midheaven?" And the guy thought and thought and said, "Oh yeah, I fell in the cesspool!") And you wouldn't have believed his reaction to dropping his toothbrush down the drain. He was heart-broken; he just cried, "Oh, my toothbrush!" His toothbrush was some kind of security thing. So anyway, luckily I've got this needlenose pliers and just reached down there and pulled his toothbrush out. He was like one reborn, you know, laughing and crying simultaneously in ecstasy because his toothbrush had been brought back from the depths. I mean, that's a very ridiculous analogy, but to me it was really symbolic of something he's going through with his Pluto aspect. And he's been much more clinging toward his mother, too; he's usually very independent—Aquarius Jupiter in the first house, a lot of Gemini, Moon in Aries, but with this aspect he's regressing, playing more lunar roles, dependency roles.

So, anyway the Moon sign is really important, and all the astrological books over-emphasize the Sun sign and don't talk about the Moon sign very effectively. To me, among all these other things, the Moon sign shows what mode of self-expression, what mode of living, what lifestyle is *comfortable* to you, feels natural to you, feels like "this is me, this is home, this is how I'm supposed to be, this is how I'm supposed to live." And, again, if you have challenging aspects to the Moon, you might find that living in that way may not come too easily, or you might feel particularly compelled to work at living in that mode. You might even over-emphasize your Moon sign qualities if it's in challenging aspects because you'll feel like "I've got to make some kind of adjustment here." The very word "adjustment" is the best word I know of for explaining square aspects. They're not "bad" aspects; they show where you have to make adjustments in your self and in your life.

Richard Ideman, the astrologer, says that the Moon—not maybe for everybody, but for most people—is closely related to what they call love. You know, there are different kinds of love; there's Venus love, Neptune love, there's also Moon love, there's definitely Sun love, as in Leo—supportiveness and vitalization. For many people, especially men, the Moon has to do with feeling mothered by some woman, feeling nurtured. All you ladies here, does the Moon in your chart show anything about whether you feel loved or not; can anybody relate to that? It's definitely true for men, I think.

Audience: My Moon happens to be in Capricorn. For me there's "Papa" kinds of things too that are connected with Saturn, and lots of what I label "good Papa characteristics" are important, almost corrective, in ways, but at the same time, you know, like "you can do it" support. . . .

Yeah, I remember somebody I know with Moon in Capricorn—but her Sun is conjunct Uranus in Cancer and so she's got the polarity of Cancer-Capricorn highly activated, both of which are very security-oriented signs; they're parent signs, father-mother, they both deal with the past, with the security of the past. But she has all this Uranus, so she likes boyfriends or live-in mates who are somewhat paternal, who take care of her, but then her Uranus can't stand it. So she'll try to have that going, and then she'll sneak out and run off with other people for a week-end now and then or something else just to get her Uranus going. Uranus always wants excitement, always wants change.

Q: What about aspects between Neptune and the Moon? What does that do?

A: Again, it'd be somewhat different with men and women in relation to relationships. With anybody, in principle, it could show a tendency toward some sort of escapism. But also tremendous psychic sensitivity, a lot of imagination, a strong romantic nature—the Moon is kind of romantic, anyway, and so is Neptune. It could be a very artistic or imaginative type of person. With relationships though, there could be a constant feeling of things being up in the air, especially in a man's chart with the main woman in his life, or with his mother—something unclear, something up in the air, something that's always making him feel a little awkward, a little uncomfortable, that he'd like to avoid or evade. Many times when transiting Neptune is conjunct, square, or opposite the man's, any man's, Moon, he'll go through a period of about a year and a half or so of—say he's married—his marriage being totally vague, like he'll have an urge to get out of it, to escape from it. . . .

Audience: Nebulous.

Yeah, and he'll be unable to relate to his wife in a realistic way because he'll be projecting a lot of stuff onto her. Neptune is always your dreams, positively or negatively. But of course Neptune squares and conjunctions and oppositions are the best aspects you can have (to any number of planets) for spiritual development, because it gives you a very strong urge to transcend the mundane affairs of life. You've got to somehow try to escape. But you can escape, naturally, through booze and drugs and dissipating things or you can escape through meditation or spiritual things or service to humanity or whatever. . . .

Q: What kind of effect would transiting Neptune have in a man's chart if it was eventually going to form a conjunction to the Moon, a square to Neptune, and then later on an opposition to Mercury which are all involved in a T-square in the first place?

A: That's too much to answer. That would take too long to go into. But, you know, the more I do astrology the more I don't separate things like I used too. Neptune hitting any number of planets will mean that there's a kind of Neptune vibration in that person's life. It'll *center* on the area of life shown by the planet being aspected and to some extent the house, but—astrology's really simple; there's only twelve basic principles, and once you understand those, you can simplify and synthesize. Say Neptune's aspecting something or other; immediately you know that there's a kind of Neptunian vibration in that person's life, in that person's consciousness; even if they're not fully aware of it or can't identify it, they'll feel discontented. Neptune is *the* planet of divine discontent.

But back to relationship, this Neptune-Moon interchange—say some man has Neptune aspecting his Moon, he may want to marry a Pisces, which would fit real nicely, or he may marry someone who's real spaced out or be very committed in a relationship to somebody who's always up in the air and kind of dreamy, and thus that fits his kind of Moon pattern. I've seen one guy, his Moon was in Taurus, which normally, in a male's chart, means he will want and feel comfortable with a woman who is sort of Taurean: slow, security-oriented, liking cooking and all this. But his Moon's conjunct Uranus and, in his behavior and relationships, it's almost like his Moon's in Aquarius, because he can't stand slow, Taurean type women. He likes real jumpy types, like Aquarians, real lively, eccentric ones.

"AFFINITIES" & "DISAFFINITIES"

Let me go through some of this outline and see what we come up with. Okay, first there's a general study of the whole natal chart; anything in the natal chart can relate to relationships, even though it doesn't specifically deal with Venus, Mars, Moon, or seventh house. Anything could. Because, say in your chart you have six different aspects that relate to tremendous willfulness, a real domineering personality, you know right there that it's going to take a particularly adaptable person to live with that kind of person. Because their entire chart shows that they are this kind of person—ruthless, domineering, willful, whatever. Or say they're real wishy-washy—say you have some man's chart that is really passive and not into asserting himself at all, not any of the usual cultural roles for men. A lot of women won't be able to like him, won't be able to respect him. And so right then, there's a kind of key insight into what kind of relationship possibilities are appropriate for him.

In number 1a here on the outline, there's a term that I should explain, "affinities" and "disaffinities." That's a term that was used by Kenneth and Joan Negus at a talk I went to at the Las Vegas AFA convention. This term "affinities" is something that you don't see much in chart comparison books; most chart comparison books say "A's Moon trine B's Sun" and so forth. Affinities are something you cannot discover without looking at the individual chart in some depth. Say Mars is conjunct Uranus in your chart and you're a real energetic type and you want lots of change and you have a super-high sex drive and you're very independent, in fact you don't like to cooperate with anybody, ever; then you may have an *affinity* with somebody whose chart has something similar. Perhaps somebody else with a Mars-Uranus square or even a trine, somebody else who is attuned to that and who can therefore understand that in you.

An affinity can be a very good thing, even if the aspects aren't particularly harmonious. Many times looking at the aspects *between two charts* won't show you this affinity *between the people*. Say you're doing a chart comparison and you say, "Gee, the aspects don't look that obvious, and there's all kinds of stressful aspects and you guys have been married for twenty years and you like each other." Look then to the affinities. The charts may be totally different except in one or two crucial ways. Like one specific type of aspect, or a tremendous emphasis on Uranus, or Neptune, or Pluto in each chart, but in different ways and by different aspects. Say one person has Sun conjunct the Moon in Scorpio, and the other person has Mars conjunct Pluto on the Ascendant; they're both going to be very Plutonian types. They may get along. Because, you know, two Scorpios are wary of each other. They know how to defend themselves. Scorpio-Scorpio marriages are incredibly common; probably more common than any other marriages between the same Sun sign.

Another thing is, say you have Mars conjunct Saturn, and you're always a little bit frustrated, and you're always having to blow off steam in some way. Now, if you live with somebody who's real passive, and doesn't feel that way, and you have your explosion, they might take it personally. Or they might think "What's wrong with you, anyway? Why don't you just go in the back room and kick a door?" But, if the other person has Mars square Saturn and has that same kind of constant inner frustration, they might be able to very much identify with that tone of your being. When you start throwing your shoes against the mirror, they might be able to do it with you and laugh about it. Channeling frustrations and channeling aggressions is really important in relationships, and especially for people with strong attunement to Mars, Scorpio, or Aries.

A "disaffinity" is just the opposite. Say your whole chart has a dominant theme of strength and willfulness, independence, assertiveness, and initiative; you live with somebody or marry somebody whose whole chart is dominated by just the opposite themes—you know, passivity, clingingness, possessiveness, all these things. You can see how the people might have been attracted, in a general way, because opposites attract; but opposites also repel! If the opposites are really opposite, if they're too different, the people might get really sick of each other and might get sick of not having anything that they can really share. So that is what you might call disaffinity.

You'll find it in many specific ways, in certain aspects, too. Say one person has Mars conjunct Jupiter conjunct Venus in Leo; they're real generous with everything—their money, and their feelings and energy. They're very dramatic; they're very demonstrative. And the other person's planets are all Taurus and Scorpio, all self-contained and hidden, secretive, retentive, and stingy. Those two people are going to have definite conflicts, no matter how many harmonious aspects are in their chart comparison. There's going to be conflict there because of the distinct disaffinities in the two personalities. That's not to say they can't work it out; that's not to say they can't learn from it. But an awareness of those differences is absolutely necessary for any positive development to take place within the relationship, should it reach some kind of impasse.

Q: What if you've got those same conflicts within the same person, in your own natal chart? Like, self-contained, limited, and also. . . .

A: Most people have some of that, yeah.

Q: But a really strong emphasis on that kind of. . . .

A: The only thing I can say is, in terms of partnership, either marry or pair off with somebody just as complicated, have a relationship with somebody who's just as complicated. *Or*, do without a kind of full feeling in relationship; very few people have a relationship, especially a marriage, with somebody that they can share *everything* with. And that's almost an absurd demand to make of a marriage, especially if you're an exceptionally complicated person. Well, everybody first knows what she's asking, right? Say she has a whole lot of emphasis on outgoing things like Leo and whatnot, but then there's also a whole lot of, say, Cancer and introversion and so forth. In many cases, a real complicated person will often attach themselves to someone who's simple in nature, because it's a soothing sort of thing for the complicated person to be with someone simpler and less challenging.

Q: It's also boring.

A: It can be. It can be. Yeah. The best example I know of—you see that all the time in artists and writers. Like James Joyce, who was a very egotistical, arrogant, very complex writer; his wife was almost illiterate, an extremely simple person. But of course, maybe his ego was just too big for him to live with anybody who also had much of an ego. That's something you often find. All I can say is—I suppose the *ideal* thing would be dealing with somebody who was fairly complicated also. 'Cause otherwise it does get boring, no doubt about it. But again you have to look at the individual charts: what do you want? Some people aren't very demanding of relationships. Some people don't know how to relate and don't care about it. Other people have a great many planets in their seventh house, and their whole life is *who they can get close to*. So that's a crucial thing. If you're so relationship oriented . . . say there's a whole lot of stuff in the air signs in your chart, or in the seventh house, or Venus on the Ascendant—something like that, you know, Venus conjunct the Sun, also will emphasize relationship more. Then it's more important that the person find somebody they're compatible with. 'Cause they can't just live in a shell, you know. They can't just live out a social *role*, which many other people can. Other people *can* do that.

I learned quite a bit, I think, from watching my parents, who are still married after more than 3½ decades. Their chart comparison is incredibly compatible; I must say, I've hardly seen anything more compatible. You know, one's an Aries, one's a Leo; my father's Moon is in Aries conjunct my mother's Sun in Aries, and their rising signs are exactly opposite, so that each Ascendant is conjunct the other's seventh house cusp, which is the partnership house. . . . They have all kinds of things. But, they both frankly say that the reason it has lasted is that both of them, being very independent and fiery type critters, could handle that in the other person and they often go weeks without seeing much of each other. My father will go off on a business trip, or he'll go off hunting or fishing. Or she'll drive down to the Bay Area from the mountains where she lives and go shopping and to plays for a week or so, and visit all the kids. They sometimes hardly see each other; that's why they get along. You know, fire needs room to operate, fire always needs space to express themselves, and hardly ever can they do it all with one person. Fire signs, in fact, aren't known for relationship. Fire signs are known more for dynamic self-expression. But of course, if there's a lot of emphasis on Venus or the Venus signs, it will emphasize relationship more.

Q: I was going to ask you, going back to affinities, would affinity be considered, say one person's chart had Moon conjunct Saturn and another person's chart had Venus conjunct Saturn? Is that a sort of similar quality?

A: Yeah, as an overall tone, there'd be a particular emotional cautiousness and security orientation. Often a lot of loyalty you find with Saturn-Moon or Saturn-Venus aspects.

Q: But that is, that's considered an affinity?

A: That's an affinity, definitely. You can also find it, like, one person's Venus will be in Capricorn and the other person, no matter where Venus is, might have Saturn closely aspecting Venus, and that will make their Venuses, you might say, more compatible—even if they're not in signs that you think of as compatible.

LEO, THE 5TH HOUSE & THE FIRE ELEMENT

Q: But if, um, like Leo's a sign . . . (inaudible);

A: Leo *women* are much more, as a rule, capable of relating to other people in a one-to-one way. Leo men often find it very difficult to come down off their kingly throne, to relate to the peasants. I mean, there are Leo men who are more humble, and more able to relate. But Leo men and Leo women are on totally different trips when it comes to relationship.

Q: Well, a lot of times Leo men are very chauvinistic.

A: Right.

Q: Well, wouldn't you say Leo, being sort of dramatic, that they sort of dramatize romance and love?

A: Yes, that's what I meant; it's kind of like the drama and the playing, love affairs and wooing and all that, intrigue Leo. It's dramatic and a game. And Leos love games. It's speculative, you know, they love speculating. You can't have a love affair without taking some risks. You risk something in yourself, you know. I think that's the connection with Leo, a kind of letting go and . . . and it's also entertainment. One of the main things about love affairs that intrigues people is that it's entertaining.

Q: The conquest.

A: Well, I was thinking more of just the game of it. You're talking about men, or women, or both?

Q: Just really specific types of both. Some just never can really relate to any one particular person for a long time.

A: I think *fire* signs can identify with the conquest part of it more than say water or air. In fact, the fire signs can easily get into the conquest part, particularly Aries and Leo. Oh, but the other thing too is that Leo is a sign that craves some kind of recognition of their identity, some kind of confirmation of their identity and really, I think if you really analyze what motivates people in many—not all of course—"love affairs" (I'm separating that from a relationship that is enduring for quite a while; a "Love Affair" is the Leo thing; it's a fling.), part of the motivation behind it for many people is that they get their identity confirmed. They're playing this love game, and there is this kind of vibration that makes them feel "in love." Like, *"falling in love."* Falling means like (sound effects here)—you fall. You're becoming somewhat unconscious voluntarily. Because if you're too conscious, how can you be romantic? You've got to be a little bit unconscious and try to let some mystery stay there.

But anyway, in a love affair with somebody, the other person is paying a lot of attention to you, they want to do things for you, they're complimenting you; so your ego gets a real nice boost and of course Leo is *the* sign of ego. I think that's a very important motivation in a lot of fifth house things—confirming your ego. Whether it's through your children, through love affairs, through creating things. . . .

The seventh house is "I relate to you one-to-one as a person," on a personal level. It's not playing roles. The fifth house is more playing roles, the drama, the big love game. The seventh house is: "I'm actually relating to you as a person." Now, some people can't relate too well at all. They'll have maybe a big inhibition, in some cases Saturn in the seventh house, and they'll kind of hold back in relationships, they'll be very cautious relating; they'll be afraid of the intimacy of relationship. In other cases, though, you'll find Saturn in the seventh house to indicate somebody for whom it's so *important* to relate to others. You can either run away from something or you can work at it more. Those seem to be two alternative modes of dealing with stressful things in your chart. The fifth house deals also with physical, emotional, and sexual comfort—how comfortable you feel with somebody. So often you'll find the fifth house relationships emphasizing this kind of comfort. This is especially common when Jupiter's transiting the fifth house, which is, by the way, a very common time to have love affairs. I know Jupiter transiting the *first* house *or the fifth* are two of the best times in life for most people.

Q: What if Saturn's transiting the seventh at the same time?

A: I don't know, you might just be working harder at defining where you're at in relationships if Saturn's transiting the seventh. I don't really have a negative attitude towards Saturn. Sometimes when it's aspecting certain *planets*, I'll be glad when it's over, but with Saturn through the houses, you learn so much. Like when it goes through the fifth house, you learn so much about love in a deep way, a practical way—because duties and responsibilities are always tied in with any love attachments that you have then, and any that you had even before, like family and children. Their needs become very immediate when Saturn is transiting the fifth house.

When Jupiter goes through your fifth house, there's an abundance of creative and playful energy, at least in most people's lives. I'm sure you can have exceptions, if certain negative things were present, or certain aspects were present. In most cases, though, there's an abundance of creative energy when transiting Jupiter is in the first or the fifth houses. And that's true to some extent for the ninth house—the fire houses, in other words. But the first and fifth seem to be—when Jupiter's there—particularly enjoyable times for expansion, for self-expression, for more confidence. That's the key to it. The fire signs are all confident; *the* key to the fire signs, I think, is confidence. You have, somehow, this inner faith. But sometimes you'll find fire signs who don't have it, but the rest of the chart will show something about that, as will talking to them about how they were raised. Say you have a Leo with Moon in Aries and the parents were both Cancers or Taureans or some energy that was holding the kids down and wanting them to stay at home. That fire sign person may not develop self-confidence until they're thirty years old, or thirty-five, or forty. And, seeing as how women are an oppressed group throughout the world for the most part, many, many women don't come into their own, in terms of confidence, or in terms of even an awareness of their creativity, until they're past thirty-five or forty. I've seen so many times, you know, guys will come in for consultations, and their whole chart will be full of all these creative things and emphasis on some sort of creative activity—and they're in touch with it. They feel that urge toward it. So many women will have the same aspects, but not all are in touch with it. More and more younger ones, particularly, *are* in touch with those same feelings. But it seems so many women have put their energy, and in many cases it's been necessary, into raising kids. I often think that nature conspires to keep women *unaware* of their creativity until their kids are older. Naturally, I'm not against motherhood. I mean, what is more creative than helping some human being to grow. In fact, the fifth house *is* children and creativity—there's no difference.

THE 7TH HOUSE, SATURN & PLUTO

(Referring to outline.) The capacity for close relationship as indicated in each individual chart. Naturally, you look primarily to Venus things. Close relationship meaning one-to-one sharing type things. You look to the seventh house, which is a Venus house. You look to all Venus aspects and anything in a Venus sign, too. If you have, say, Mars in Libra or Taurus, there's a drive to have a kind of emotional sharing experience be a major part of your life. The seventh house—you can look at any old textbook and read about the various planets in the seventh house, but the astrological tradition is worth clarifying here. Traditionally, most of the old books say, "look to planets in your seventh house to see what kind of partner you attract," or some such theory. And sometimes it works like a charm. But other times it doesn't at all. I think a more fruitful approach to astrology in general, than to say the chart shows what's going to happen to you, or what kind of person you're going to meet or whatever, is that the chart is a blueprint of your mind-set; it's a blueprint of your attitudes, your feelings, needs, you might say your *karma*.

So seventh house planets show you what you're looking for in a relationship *and*, most importantly, they show what parts of yourself you will get in touch with through close relationship, and what parts of yourself you'll have to confront. Because remember the seventh house is opposite the first house. The first house is that which you're doing spontaneously yourself and you're often spontaneously conscious of it. The seventh house tends to be, according to the planets there and the sign on the cusp of the seventh house, something that you project on other people. You don't see it in yourself too often, but that's not always true. People are at different awareness levels, and so sometimes you'll be very much in touch with your seventh house indications. But in many cases, the person will project the seventh house stuff on somebody else.

So say you have Saturn in your seventh house. You might marry a Capricorn; I've seen that repeatedly. But what does Saturn in the seventh house really show? You might say it does show that you might marry a Capricorn, but it could mean other things too—that your attitude toward close relationship, especially any kind of legal contract like marriage, is really, really serious, very cautious, and you're prone toward a lot of anxiety in that area. Whatever house Saturn is in can show where you've got anxieties. Things are real important to you there, but they're often *too* important. They're so important, you wind yourself in knots. You know, Saturn is rigidity. You tie yourself in knots and you get rigid in the area of life shown by the house where Saturn is. All these books about Saturn in the seventh house meaning you might not get married, or it delays marriage . . . it's true, it delays marriage sometimes, but what does delaying marriage mean? All kinds of people are delaying marriage nowadays. Some people are delaying it permanently, even though they may live with the same person for twenty years. So, what does that mean nowadays? Delaying marriage? I suppose in the old days it meant that you might not get married until you're thirty, but nowadays it's essentially meaningless in that regard.

Same with Saturn in the fifth house. All these books keep saying that this means—you know, that you won't have any love affairs, or you won't have any children, or disappointing love affairs, disappointing children—crimeny sakes! Those are utterly meaningless statements—totally meaningless! Anybody who has a few love affairs is going to be disappointed once in a while; anybody who has a couple kids is going to be disappointed here and there, in some way. But Saturn in the fifth does not at all mean that it's going to restrict your love affairs. It might mean, in fact, that love affairs are so important to you that you'll spend most of your energy trying to have love affairs! Or, in some cases, it means that you'll have lots of love affairs, but they'll all be really important—no light, playful things; all really deep, and something that you learn from in a very immediate way. Because wherever you have Saturn, whether it's in a house, in a sign, or aspecting some planet, there's always an indication, then, of some kind of importance. Something in that house is really important to you, something about that sign and it's qualities is *important* to you. Or, something about the planet. Say Saturn is aspecting Mars, it's important for you to assert yourself. If it's aspecting Venus, it's important for you to have some kind of closeness. Whatever is *important* often becomes your big problem, because you're too attached to it. You know, you have intensity—"it's just really *important*, I've got to have it"—so you blow it. Wherever you have Saturn is where you're not letting things happen, not letting things flow, and you're trying to control too much. Like Capricorn, you know, what is the basic meaning of Capricorn?—trying to control and manage nature, inside themselves, self-discipline, and getting some authority so they can make things more manageable in the outer world. So, Saturn in the seventh, Saturn in the fifth ... I don't think I've ever seen any textbook that is very accurate about those positions of Saturn.

But, I think what one can say that will be true in most cases is that, with Saturn in the seventh or the fifth, the person will approach relationships, love affairs, children (whichever house you're talking about) with a tremendous sense of responsibility. And therefore, they might be wary of those involvements, because they'll feel so responsible for what happens. Again, they're not letting things happen. They're taking it on themselves; they're taking everything on themselves. "Well, if I get married, I want it to last *forever*." That's the kind of attitude you can have with Saturn in the seventh, or Venus in Capricorn in many cases: "I gotta make it last. I know my husband hits me, beats me, I hate him, but I've got to make it last." And of course, then if you throw in money, you know, Venus in Capricorn is very conscious of material security . . . .

Q: Also Saturn in Libra?

A: Saturn in Libra to some extent, but it's not quite so dramatic because that's more of a whole generational thing, it's not quite such an individual factor. *Basically* that's true, Saturn in Libra indicates a kind of person that takes relationships seriously; they're more wary of commitment to a partnership, because they feel it as a big important thing. Like I say, if something is *too* important you may postpone it forever. You may be afraid of facing it, of taking on those responsibilities. Saturn in the fifth, too—if you have kids, they're a heavy responsibility. But you can either look at it and face it and really learn from it, or you can do what one lady told me: "I have Saturn in the fifth and that means I have more children than I wanted and I have two, and they're both bummers." She complains about everything; she's a very unhappy person, so naturally she interprets her whole chart in an absolutely negative way.

Q: What about Pluto in the seventh house? What kind of effect would he have in your seventh house?

A: Is Pluto a he? I think Pluto's bisexual. In this article I wrote about Pluto, I wrote what I feel about Pluto ... it's such a unique thing; it's like Scorpio. It's at once an outgoing, extremely powerful force, yet it's sensitive and it's psychic. And it's the same thing with Scorpio. So many beginners in astrology think that Scorpio is a fire sign, you know; I've heard that so many times, because Scorpio is so dynamic. And you don't think of them as very sensitive. They don't show it; they don't show their sensitivity. Pluto is the same way. But I'll tell you one thing though, Pluto in the seventh is really hard to interpret in the abstract. If I *talk* to somebody about their life, I can get a feel for it. In some cases it means that you'll have some kind of *incredible* kind of relationship; very often it's a marriage, with somebody who is extremely powerful—sometimes extremely willful—and, in many cases, somebody who dominates a good deal of your life. Not to say that that's a negative thing. Like one guy I know that's been married to the same person thirty-five years, very happily, has a bunch of kids and all—his wife is extremely strong-willed, a super-duper Aries, and even a bit ruthless, she can even be kind of cruel; and he has Pluto in his seventh house.

Q: Couldn't the person, say with Pluto in the seventh house, couldn't it be just the opposite? The person himself would be willful and strong toward the marriage partner?

A: That's just what I was going to say. Pluto always shows some kind of compulsion. If you look at it and you analyze it, it doesn't make any sense. You just do it, compulsively. But remember the seventh is the Libra house, and Libra always wants to be fair, and to give the other person their fair share, and their individual freedom. Pluto in the seventh, in some cases, shows somebody who gives other people a great deal of freedom—in fact, who has such a compulsion to give other people freedom that they can't *relate* to other people. No matter what you ask them, trying to relate personally they just say, "well, you can do whatever you want." And so how can you relate to them? But the other side of the coin, the other manifestation that you sometimes see with Pluto in the seventh is like you mentioned. Somebody who's attitude toward relationships is really compulsive and domineering. Pluto in the fifth can show it too. Sometimes you'll attract people who are very Plutonian, really powerful lovers, for example, or very powerful children. In other cases, you'll be kind of ruthless in your attitude toward lovers or children. . . .

Q: Then it can go either way, dominate or be dominated?

A: Yeah. And really, in all of astrology, there's that kind of duality. Sometimes you will experience things as coming to you from the outer world, and sometimes you'll experience it as an inner thing. Say Pluto is in your fifth house, and everytime you go walking down the street, you run into real passionate Scorpios. Okay, now there your Pluto in the fifth house is manifesting as something coming to you from outside. It's still coming into your life though. And it's forcing you to deal with certain issues. In other cases, natal Pluto in the fifth house will mean that you put power trips on people, that you act kind of Scorpionic in love things. You're always overpowering people—conquest. It can always be either way, sometimes it's even both. You put out something and you get it back. But of course, sometimes what we get back, we put out in past lifetimes, if you think of things in terms of reincarnation.

COMMENTS ON URANUS & OPPOSITIONS

Q: (Inaudible.)

A: Even the trines of Mercury to Uranus of which many books say: "this is very smart, and brilliant, and insightful"—that's often true, but that same aspect also inclines toward eccentricity in thinking and extremism in your ideas, though not in quite such an obvious way as the opposition. But often a person with a Mercury-Uranus opposition (and you'll find it too in other Uranus oppositions with the personal planets) will be somebody who's hard to talk to because they're so *fast*; they're so speeded up. They can't sit down and wait for your ideas; they keep interrupting you. Or you sit there and you try to talk with them in a systematic way, and you can see they don't want to be there. They want to jump up and run around, or . . . they want something exciting. And the only thing that excites Uranians is themselves. Uranus is the most self-centered planet. You can really see it. This is something most textbooks don't emphasize either. Wait til transiting Uranus hits something in your natal chart. You don't want to cooperate with people anymore. You want to just do your thing, and do it quickly, and in some way that excites you, and you don't want to have to accommodate anyone else.

Uranus aspects, especially the stressful ones, always show a tendency towards willfulness, insistence on: "I've got the right to do it, and the heck with you." Well, anyways, this opposition is in the chart of a guy who's been in jail three times for violence. (Here referring to chart on blackboard with Venus in opposition to a Mars-Uranus conjunction.) He gets into fights and he bashes somebody's head with a chain or something. Like a motorcycle type of person. So I did his chart one day.—I was a little bit hesitant to be too honest with him too. (laughter) That's one advantage of Libra, you can tactfully tell the most violent person that they're really a clod, and they won't even take it as an insult. Anyway, this guy here, needless to say, has some difficulty in relationships. Other things in his chart also repeat the same theme, but what the old books call "afflictions"—the stressful aspects to Venus, especially the opposition, with Uranus or Saturn really are indicative of definite relationship problems. With the opposition though it's especially true—it tends toward being very *demanding.* Everybody here has probably heard the old thing about Mars-Uranus combinations being *violent,* and in some cases they are like this one; in some cases it works out in a totally different way.

This guy here (back to example on blackboard), his only marriage was a big flop. And then his wife remarried, and she has the only kid they had. So this was his situation. Well, first I asked him why he thought he kept getting in trouble with the law, and all these fights and he says: "Well, I never start them, I just kind of go into these bars and start drinking, and pretty soon somebody starts a fight with me." Naturally, it wouldn't occur to him to go into bars of a different sort than the bars he goes into, where all the motorcycles are out in front, and chains. . . . So with Venus oppositions, you'll find a tendency toward projection—toward projecting your problems on the other person. In this case, Mars conjunct Uranus opposite Venus. What he projects is his own violence—he projects this onto these other people. He sees *them* as troublemakers. Of course it's not *him.*

With Moon oppositions you'll also find a lot of projection, but it's a bit different: you project your subconscious needs or subconscious problems onto the other person. *Any* opposition with a personal planet can relate to projection—towards finding your problems in somebody else. Richard Nixon is the best example—Sun opposite Neptune.

Neptune oppositions with the personal planets are very inclined toward scapegoat kind of behavior. You see your own problems in everybody else. Neptune can also relate to evasion and to refusing to face the facts, to refusing to face the reality of the situation. We'll get into that more later today when we talk about Neptune aspects to Venus and Mars.

But back to this guy, so then I asked him, well, why do you think your first marriage didn't work out too well? And he says: "Oh, gee, she just didn't have any understanding. I mean, I'd leave the house, you know, and gee, she'd ask me where I was going! And you know, I like to be able to leave 3, 4, 5 days, whatever I want." Mars-Uranus! —very *"self,"* me, me, me, *I do what I want,* freedom, and the heck with anybody. And Uranians and Aquarians hate any restraint for the most part. That's a generalization that won't fit all Aquarians, but it's a general characteristic of Uranus and Aquarius. So, his ex-wife had the gall to ask him, for example, even things like "when will you be back?" So, obviously, his relationships—Venus—were incredibly upset by his insistence on his own will and his own way of doing things. Any opposition with a personal planet can relate to relationship hassles and also to projection.

ASPECTS WITH THE SUN & MOON

Another thing is aspects to the Sun for women and to the Moon for men. Now this is something that used to be a fairly reliable indicator (in individual charts) of things about the potential husband or potential wife. In other words, the old books say things like: "The Sun in a woman's chart relates to the husband and the Moon in a man's chart to the wife." In a general way it's still true, but you have to be much more careful now, because more people are more complete. More people are living out their totality. More, many more women are expressing their Sun, you know, their individuality, their ego needs, their need for recognition, achievement, and so forth. And therefore, those particular women don't project it, at least not nearly so much, on the husband.

And likewise with the Moon. The Moon for men is still a little more reliable an indicator than the Sun for women. It seems that women are changing much more rapidly than men are nowadays. But in a general way, the Moon in the man's chart, its sign, as I mentioned before, but also, even more importantly, its aspects, have to do with the *attitude* toward the mate or wife, and any stressful aspect with the

Moon often shows a kind of energy you have difficulty expressing with your mate (if you're male). See if there is any stressful aspect to the Moon and if there is, look at the planet making that aspect to the Moon; and in many cases it will show that the person has a hard time expressing that energy with his wife, or with his female mate. Say Venus is square Moon, or Mars is square Moon—it could be difficult, with Venus, for that particular man to express his emotional, caring feelings. If it's Mars, it could be difficult for him to express his assertiveness or his sexuality. And all the old books say Mars square Moon means you're irritable. Of course you're irritable if you can't express what you *want* (Mars) with the person that you're with. And so you get irritable. But the main thing isn't that they're irritable, the main thing is that there's some difficulty in expression there.

And even more, *much more* than the sign position of the Sun in a woman's chart, much more important are the aspects to the Sun—not so much that it predicts the type of husband, although it does in some cases; but it tends to symbolize something that the woman has to experience with either the husband or the father, or both. And the term "husband" here, you can also stretch it to mean if you live with somebody for quite a few years, so that you start playing somewhat of a married kind of role with each other, kind of depending on each other.

The Sun aspects are really crucial—I think what it comes down to is, if the woman expresses the Sun energy herself, there's going to be certain things that happen. Say a woman has Uranus aspecting the Sun, by conjunction, square, or opposition. That's a traditional aspect of "divorce." Okay, well why does it manifest, in many cases, not all by any means, why does it manifest as divorce? Because the Sun-Uranus aspects in anybody's chart, male or female, show somebody who's incredibly insistent on their freedom, who's very self-centered, and who is very much their own person. And they will not stand, or want to tolerate, any restraints. So you find some woman with Sun-Uranus stressful aspects, and naturally she won't at all fit into the usual social role of being the passive female—and she won't accept the authority of her husband, either, which most males will try to assert. So, it's not some kind of magical indication—"oh, that's a divorce aspect!"—it's a need for freedom, and for freedom of self-expression that many men cannot handle. One thing I've found—you know we live near quite a few air force bases in this area, and I've done lots of charts for women from Travis Air Force Base, and I think nine out of ten of them have

Uranus aspects to their Sun. Not only does Uranus traditionally rule aviation, but also, these women like that kind of marriage, because their husband's gone half the time; he's flying off some place. And a number of them told me that their marriage couldn't have lasted, or put it this way, they couldn't have tolerated being married, if it weren't that the husband was splitting every once in a while, for quite a few weeks at a time.

Q: Going back, just like what you were saying, like going back to, say, Pluto in the seventh house. Supposing the woman's Sun in her chart is aspecting Pluto. And say the person that she's living with or married to has Pluto in the seventh house. Would that aspect in her chart, Sun sextile or trine to Pluto, sort of fall in with his Pluto being in the seventh house?

A: Yeah, you see those kinds of things a lot. Sometimes they're very subtle to pick out; other times they're real obvious. Sometimes you'll see some woman's Sun opposite Saturn, say, and she'll marry a Capricorn. Or, she'll marry a real, real, practical man, very conservative, very authoritarian. But what does it mean? The Sun aspecting Saturn in a stressful aspect, in a woman's chart, generally means that she'll have to *work* (Saturn) to express herself. And she'll probably have to overcome quite a few obstacles, starting with the father. The father, with that kind of aspect, is often oppressive, *or* the father spoils the kid rotten, so that the woman doesn't have a *real* relationship with him as a fallible human being. She's always in a kind of role in relationship to the dominant male in her life. There are so many things like that. Anyway, the main thing is, in a woman's chart, the major aspects to the Sun always show what she wants to express. (The major aspects to *anybody's* Sun show something about how they have to express themselves, what that urge is.) But then, these aspects also manifest, in many cases, as what kind of male they will deal with, or what kind of thing in that relationship will be a problem. Say Pluto is square the Sun. They'll often have to deal with a very domineering husband. They might marry a Scorpio, or someone with that temperament.

Q: Or she might be domineering to her husband. Couldn't it work?

A: Oh, undoubtedly she'd be domineering just because that's the aspect in *her* chart. But it might work the other way too. You get back what you give out, consciously or unconsciously.

Q: All right, so with a sextile, then the Sun in sextile to Pluto would be in harmony, although it still is strong will power and everything?

A: What I find is that the squares, oppositions, and conjunctions are the strongest aspects in all cases. If you look to the aspects of the Sun for these kinds of considerations, you maybe should look to those aspects more than to sextiles or trines.

Q: Supposing there isn't any, or you only have one aspect to look at?

A: Well, you use whatever you've got.

Q: Do you want a testament? To what you just said?

A: What?

Q: Okay, I'm Scorpio; I married an Aquarian, and it was a sheer disaster. I have Sun and Uranus in opposition.

Q: I'm wondering if you're going to mention, talking about the seventh house, what if there are no planets in the seventh house?

A: That relates to a kind of general question of what about empty houses in general. And, to me the thing that makes the most sense is that an empty house means that, in this lifetime, there's not particularly a lot of special attention required in that area. It doesn't mean you won't deal with it. To almost everybody, loneliness is a problem, if they don't have a relationship. So, for one thing, you always look at Venus in everybody's chart. If the seventh house is empty, the dominant thing would usually be Venus when it comes to relationship, marriage, and so forth. But also if the house is empty, the ruling planet of the seventh house. The planet that rules the sign on the seventh house cusp will sometimes give you some clues. Even though, from my experience, it's not nearly so good as looking at Venus. There's so many old astrological rules that people adhere to rigidly that don't make a lot of sense when you really look at them. The ruling planet of a house, though, in many cases, will give you useful information. But even more so, in the case of relationships, would be Venus. Or any planets *in the Venus signs.*

Back to the aspects to the Sun in a woman's chart, say Pluto's square her Sun. And to make it really powerful we'll put Sun in Scorpio, and square Pluto, so you have a double Plutonian emphasis, somebody who is really willful. Now, for one thing, they may not get married at all, because they may terrify men with their power. But that person, whether it's a male or female's chart, with that configuration, then it's somebody who's very willful, and often, very manipulative. So, say the person marries somebody who is equally strong willed, problems often start developing, the problems often will develop as the woman is getting older; when she's more conscious of what she is and thus what she wants, and what she wants to express. Well, say some woman with a Pluto-Sun square marries a Scorpio—a very strong willed guy. Then there may be no problems at first, as long as she is projecting all this strength onto him: "oh, I'm married to a very strong man." When she starts feeling her own strength, that's when the problems can start happening.

You've got to confront everything shown in your chart. If you don't confront it within yourself, then you'll confront it in outer experience. In fact, it seems to me that the least conscious people have to experience the grossest kinds of things, just to make them learn something. Whereas, if you're a very inward person and quite reflective, you'll often go through periods of tremendous changes, and cycles and transits and so forth that show a lot of stress, and you'll feel that stress, but a lot of it you'll work out on an inner level, emotionally and mentally. Not in every case. But I don't know any way of predicting somebody's level of consciousness from a chart, no matter what some people say. Some people say, "Oh, if you have this aspect and this aspect, that means you're a highly advanced soul." I think that's really a lot of rot. Because, you know, you could have two people born at the very same moment, and one might go off in an ashram and meditate his whole life, and the other person could be a criminal, you know, never think of anything spiritual. To me, your consciousness is more like electricity flowing through a particular light bulb, and you could have a 10 watt consciousness flowing through your chart, and you'll have somebody who's at a low level of consciousness and they'll express those energies in a not very evolved way. Or you could have a 10,000 watt consciousness flowing through your chart, and you could have the higher manifestations of the potentials shown in your chart.

THE 11TH, 8TH, & 1ST HOUSES

A couple of other things about houses too. We mentioned the 7th and 5th. Now the 11th house—this relates to chart comparisons too—in a chart comparison it's sort of nice to have some planet in the other person's chart, one of the personal planets preferably or the ascendant, falling in your 11th house. Because the 11th house is friendliness and it's nice to be in close relationship to someone you feel friendly toward; especially if it's a marriage, it's nice to have some friendliness there too. The 11th house, and Aquarius, are future-oriented, progressive. So planets falling in your 11th house from somebody else's chart indicate that that person may help you toward expression of your sense of purpose, what you want to do in the future. All the old books say it's the house of hopes and wishes and objectives. It is the house of future hopes, future wishes or objectives you personally want, not so much in a career sense which is more the 10th house, but what you personally want to *be*.

The 5th and the 8th houses are both related to sex. The 5th, like we mentioned before, is more playful sex, sexual comfort, sexual playfulness. The 8th house is more sexual intensity and it represents, among many other meanings, the urge to be healed and to have a catharsis—to have a release from psychic tension through sexuality. It's a much more profound kind of sharing than in the 5th house, which is much more of a dramatic role playing.

The 1st house also, by polarity with the 7th, has a big impact on relationships. For example, I suppose everybody here knows that any planet conjunct the ascendant affects your whole being, your whole approach to life—and any planet in the first house also, but the closer it is to the ascendant the more powerful it is. That also goes for planets that are *technically* in the 12th house that are close to the ascendant within even 10 degrees. I still interpret that as a 1st house planet, even if it's usually considered to be in the 12th. But say your 7th house is empty and say your 1st house has something pretty powerful in it. The 1st house is the Aries house; it's initiative, it's doing things yourself, doing things alone. And so you'll need a lot of "alone" activity. One common thing that is problematical is when you find Libra rising. There you're putting Libra, the partnership sign, on the house of independence. It tends to show that you can't feel independent unless you've got some kind of partnership. And yet if you've got the partnership, how can you be so independent? It's a totally unresolvable thing. Not that it's bad, not that it *has* to be experienced as a problem, but invariably Libra rising people are very dependent upon a partnership to motivate them to express themselves. It's like they have to express themselves through a partner. Sun in the 7th house is somewhat like that too; Sun in Libra is somewhat like that. To tune into your own individuality you need a partner to bounce off, to relate to and to reflect who you are. You get to know yourself by relating to someone else. You might even add, especially in a woman's chart, the Moon in Libra or in the 7th house; they will have that same kind of thing. There's a whole huge dominant part of your nature that you can't quite contact unless it's through relationship. It doesn't have to be done through marriage or living with somebody. It could be done through becoming a counselor, psychologist or someone who does one-to-one activity, a consultant of some sort.

Another thing—if you have planets in opposition between the 1st and 7th houses, right there you've got the same kind of duality or potential hassle between independence and dependence. "I may be independent but I sure would like some company." It's not necessarily a problem, but very often if you have an opposition between 1st and 7th houses, the person can identify with the feeling of an inner pull between "I would really like some more companionship" and "I'm really independent and I've got to do my own thing and I don't want anyone telling me what to do," which is the first house Aries quality.

THE "SHARED EXPERIENCE" CONCEPT

Let's skip down to f for a second here, on the outline. It says, "Note especially any indication of shared experience." This kind of gets into chart comparisons also, but I couldn't leave everything until the second workshop because it's going to be quite a challenge as it is to cover everything in that workshop. "Shared experience" is related to close "interaspects;" that means aspects between one person's planet A and the other person's planet B. That's technically called an "interaspect."* Some people call it an interchart aspect. It's simply the angle between some planet in your chart and some planet in the other person's chart. Any close interaspect within 2 degrees or so of exact (including the quincunx) will mean that both planets involved will be simultaneously activated by any transit. That's what "shared experience" relates to. It's just something to look for and be aware of, because the closest aspects between two people's charts are always extremely indicative of major themes in their relationship.

The "shared experience" concept is so important—say your Moon is conjunct somebody's Venus, which is a nice aspect, really pleasant, usually very affectionate feelings toward one another, very comfortable with each other. OK, say those planets are in Scorpio and Uranus is now in Scorpio. Say one person's Venus is in 7 degrees Scorpio and the other person's Moon is 6 degrees Scorpio. Within about the same time period when Uranus goes through 6° and 7° Scorpio, both are going to have a Uranian vibration in their lives. And since they have that

---

*The terms "shared experience" and "interaspect" are derived from the excellent work on relationships and chart comparisons done by Joan and Kenneth Negus, as presented in a workshop at the 1976 AFA Convention.

mutual interchange of energy anyway, shown by the close aspect in the comparison, it's very likely that they will share quite a bit of intense change at that time. Not that all changes then will be a shared thing or will relate to the partnership, but whatever happens then is likely going to make an impact on the other person too. Let's see how this might manifest.

Uranus hitting Venus generally means that your closest relationships are going to be radically transformed in some way. In some cases, you'll meet some new person and you'll split from the old person. In other cases, if you're married and you want to stay that way, you'll have a fling with somebody and after the aspect is over you'll emotionally go back to your marriage partner. Say Venus is in the woman's chart and the Moon is in the man's chart. Uranus hits her Venus, she might go out and have a fling with somebody. Simultaneously it's hitting his Moon, the domestic situation, the security; so all of a sudden his life is up in the air, uncertain. "Gee, what's she doing? She might be going off with somebody. Is she ever going to care about me any more? Gee, I better look around for new possibilities in my life." So he might start looking for some kind of action, another woman maybe or maybe thinking, "We're not too compatible if she doesn't like me enough to want to stay with me." It can be any number of things and every aspect is different, but the whole concept of shared experience is a pretty good one. And in chart comparisons you'll find so often, in most long term relationships, there will be at least one and usually two or three really close aspects between the two charts. And when those degrees are activated by some transit, especially of the outer four planets, there will often be something that will affect both people.

Q: Couldn't that transit also rejuvenate the feeling between the two people? Rather than separate?

A: Oh, definitely. It could do *both*. It could make her go and have a fling. See, Uranus is the awakener. So it could awaken her to the emotional needs and possibly the sexual needs that she wants satisfied. It could awaken him to some of his wife's needs. It could be a *crisis* period for them. "Crisis" comes from the Greek word meaning to take a new course in your life. It could start on a whole new course. I'm not saying that it's a bad thing, but particularly the shared experience concept can help you pinpoint major things the two people went through *as a couple*.

Q: As to compatibility factors, whether this would be disruptive or whether it would be a rejuvenation of the relationship. . . .

A: It could be both, like I said. Nowadays it's more and more both because more and more people are getting a kind of psychological awareness of the fact that the ideal life is not to have everything under control. The notion of each person growing individually is becoming more and more of an ideal for more and more people. And as that happens, then when big changes come, even though it may upset them emotionally, maybe make them feel insecure for a while, the people can detach themselves from it and look at what's happening and what it means. In my experience, the most intense learning experiences always come from crisis, things that were very disruptive, and often very jarring.

Have I made it sufficiently clear how a planet might be colored by a sign and aspect? It's a kind of double thing. Let's take Venus; what sign is it in and what planet rules that sign? If Venus is in Capricorn, you've got a Saturnian coloration or tone to Venus activities in your life—to relationships, love, etc. A similar thing can happen with Saturn closely aspecting Venus—that seriousness, that loyalty, caution, wanting to make sure it's safe. Any time you find both, it's a "double whammy." Say you take Venus in Capricorn and aspecting Saturn. You've got two things telling you the very same thing. Venus is colored or toned by Saturn in a very dominant way, and therefore you've got something that's going to be a major, major indication of the whole way that that person approaches, in the case of Venus, relationships.

RELATED PROGRESSIONS & TRANSITS

It says (referring to outline) under e here, "examine all close transits and progressions that might relate to important developments, new awareness of personal needs, or new types of self-expression." Of course, just about any *transit* of the outer four planets, especially when they hit your personal planets, Jupiter, or Saturn, can indicate big changes that can have an impact on relationships. But I thought I would mention some of the most common things to be aware of, especially some specific progressions. If the progressed Sun or Moon aspects Venus, especially by conjunction, there's a strong likelihood of some kind of important development of your awareness, of your emotions and your feelings, and in some cases your sexual needs too. Sometimes it indicates a major relationship. Sometimes it indicates a fling. Sometimes it indicates a very short-term thing but still something that's a major experience.

One woman I've seen is a Mormon, and Mormons consider the worst sin of all—worse than murder—is having sex outside of marriage. And she has never been married. She is real big, almost 200 lbs., so she's not too popular given this culture's fondness for skinny ladies. As the progressed Sun conjuncted her Venus, she went on a vacation to the Middle East where a lot of guys like big women. She had all these guys after her constantly. She had this big crisis; she really wanted to mess around but she had this Mormon thing. She finally slept with a couple of people, and she had a tremendous guilt feeling. On the surface, the old interpretation would have fallen flat because the old interpretation (traditionally) is: progressed Sun conjunct Venus—"a very wonderful and happy time. You'll be filled with love" and so forth. She was filled with guilt and remorse. But at least she learned something about her emotions, her emotional needs, and what she had been neglecting, ignoring, or not fulfilling.

I've seen the progressed Moon conjunct Venus—only the conjunction is reliable with the progressed Moon. Sometimes a sextile of the progressed Moon will indicate something; most of the time it will pass by and nothing will happen. Any conjunction of the progressed Moon, in my experience, is always important, but—for relationships—especially when it hits Venus. There's almost always a relationship that's important. It's not always a love affair as such. Invariably there's some kind of fondness, or some kind of awakening in you to emotional experiences.

The progressed Venus hitting the Ascendant very often will also manifest like this. One of the best rules for interpreting transits or progressions conjunct the Ascendant is: whatever hits the Ascendant comes to your attention immediately. When progressed Venus hits your Ascendant, what comes to your attention?—Venus, very often some kind of love experience. Venus can relate to other things too, but in most cases it will be some relationship. In some other cases it could even be money or some kind of gift from somebody, or you might start some artistic projects; but in many cases it will be relationships. I clued into that one time when this one lady with a husband and two kids fell in love with somebody and was thinking of getting divorced, and the transits showed nothing. I did the progressions and her progressed Venus was exactly conjunct her Ascendant, and she was just gone! As soon as progressed Venus got just a degree away from the Ascendant, the whole relationship ended. But it awakened her to a lot of things in herself that were important, and she got quite a bit of positive feedback.

You can also progress the Ascendant or the Mid-heaven, and if either of those two things come to a conjunction of natal Venus, there will often be some kind of relationship activity. The general rule in progressions is that the most marked things tend to happen when an angle hits a planet or when a planet hits an angle no matter which is being progressed. Because it's the angles of your chart that tend to show your life structure; those are the points where your inner self meets the outer world. That's why very often when, for example, Jupiter or Saturn transits the Mid-heaven or Ascendant something will happen not just inside you but outside too—a move, a new job, whatever—something relating to your outer life.

A couple of other things are worth noting. Transits and progressions are particularly useful for counseling because often people who want a chart comparison are either thinking of defining their attitudes about a certain relationship, or sometimes they're thinking of getting married or thinking of getting divorced. The transits and progressions will often show you whether this current feeling is a long-term thing or a short-term thing, and what the meaning of this time period is, why are they feeling like that. The chart *comparison* itself will tend to show the potentiality of the relationship in terms of various developments in learning and compatibility.

The *cycles* of transits and progressions are important to look into. Until last year, I used to think that having a transit of Uranus conjunct, opposite, or square Venus was not too good a time to get married, because that's when all the old-school teachers and old books told me, "Don't do anything under Uranus because it's likely to be impulsive." As if impulse is bad, as if the only way you should do anything is in a Saturnian way of making sure that everything is safe! What a boring way to live! So it occured to me that the old rule might be wrong, after seeing so many people getting married when Uranus was aspecting Venus. And often they are very good marriages, and often long lasting. It does not at all mean that someone is going to be jumping into a stupid marriage if Uranus is hitting Venus, like some people say. The old rule just doesn't work. But it means you'll be awakened to some kind of emotional excitement—that you can count on for sure. Whether the relationship is going to be long-term will depend more on the overall comparison than on that particular aspect.

Likewise, if someone is already committed to somebody, married to them, living with them, male or female, when Uranus hits Venus or Mars by conjunction, square, or opposition, the tendency will be to become dissatisfied with the status quo—often a lot of sexual dissatisfaction too and the need for adventure and excitement emotionally and sexually. But if you're counseling somebody who has that kind of aspect, and they're freaking out, "Gee I can't stand to be around my spouse anymore," you might just tell them to wait awhile. If they think that the marriage is very good, they may want to move out for a while. They might want more freedom for awhile, and that might be good for them. If the relationship is solid and not just based on artificial, rigid roles, then it will still be there after the person has developed a perspective on things.

But what often happens under Uranus, Pluto, and Saturn transits is that the person will come to an awareness much more clearly of the fact that the relationship was never really very good, or at least they'll confront what is really frustrating about it, and thus they can act on it. They can either work on it, or demand of their partner that they work on it with them, or they can split. Saturn aspects will confront you with things. They'll say, "look, you've got to do this, this is necessary, you have no choice." Uranus aspects will awaken you to the true state of affairs, except you do have to be a little cautious with Uranus because it does tend to make you want a change for its own sake. It does give you the *urge* to just blow apart everything, to get rid of any oppression and make a change. Pluto tends to be a little bit similar, an urge toward a drastic transformation, towards drastically transforming your life by often ruthlessly leaving behind old patterns. But I'm not valuing this as either good or bad. Any aspect can be a very positive thing. Sometimes it's seen as a positive thing only in retrospect, because during it you're often going through a lot of stress. And most people like pleasure and not pain, and stress is felt as pain most of the time. But it's refreshing to me to see some people go through some of these difficult things positively.

I remember one woman, transiting Pluto conjuncted her Mars and her husband died. According to what she said, and there's no reason to doubt it, they had a really good marriage. It was a really neat marriage and he supposedly understood her and encouraged her to express herself and to be more confident, and she just felt it was the greatest. (Of course people sometimes tend to idealize things also.) They met, had a fling, got married, and he died—all within two years of when Pluto hit Mars. Now Mars in her chart is in her first house. Anything in the first house is really important. Transiting Pluto was conjunct Mars. The old astrologers, the traditional, event-oriented ones, would say: "Oh yes, of course, Pluto is the planet of death and Mars indicates the men in your life. The man in your life died." But in most cases when Pluto hits your

Mars, you *don't* have the man in your life die. The deeper meaning was that through that relationship and through the confidence she got from the relationship, Pluto brought about a kind of rebirth of her own Mars—her own assertiveness, her own self-sufficiency, ambition, and within that period she was radically changed. She got much stronger, much more ambitious, much more confident of her artistic talents, which were considerable, but she had never had any faith in her ability. So sometimes there will be outer events that just click with the aspects, but other times it's a much subtler thing than what many books say.

TRANSITING JUPITER & SATURN IN THE 5TH & 7TH HOUSES

We mentioned before Jupiter and Saturn briefly. In the 5th house there's a big emphasis on love. Saturn there is a real serious emphasis on what love really is. You start seeing other people and other relationships that you might be involved in much more practically. You know how Capricorn and Saturn are detached and a little bit aloof. You start getting a little detached from your children, from your lovers, or from anything or anybody that is shown by the 5th house. You start seeing what's really there. And if there's any love there, you start seeing it in a much deeper way and understanding it much more deeply. The usual thing for most people is, when Saturn goes through the 5th house, they feel unloved. They feel "nobody likes me, nobody loves me, nobody appreciates me; you know I do all this work and nobody does anything for me. I've got to find somebody else who will appreciate me for what I am." And then if they go out and try to find that ideal lover when Saturn is in the 5th house, what kind of person do you think they would find? A Capricorn or somebody who's sort of parental, somebody they can lean on. Saturn through the 5th house is an excellent period for becoming practical about how you can fulfill your love and sex needs. And so at that time you just might want to find yourself a Capricorn and say, "well look, I need these things, you need these things, let's have some kind of rendezvous here." And, in a very cold and detached way, start taking care of each other. I'm not advising that everybody do that, but it's something that happens. If you have relationships then, it tends to be with older people or with people who are kind of Saturnian.

When Jupiter goes through the 5th, it also very much inclines toward love affair type experiences, but they're usually much more happy, much more expansive, much more pleasant and exuberant than with Saturn. Jupiter is more like falling in love and playing a whole lot. When Jupiter was in my 5th house the last two times, I also had tremendous creative energy. Within one year when I was twenty-one I did more creatively than I had ever done before—writing plays and making movies, and all sorts of things. I had an abundance of creative energy. Jupiter in the first house is a lot like that also.

Then take transiting Jupiter and Saturn in the 7th—with Saturn through the 7th, the old routine is, "this is a bad time for your marriage." It's only a bad time for your marriage if your marriage is not worth evaluating, or if your partnership won't stand up to a realistic examination; then it's going to be a bad time for that relationship. But if it's a very solid, deep thing, when Saturn goes into the 7th house, you'll at *first* probably start to hang back and be more detached, saying, "I better look at this again; I'm not so sure about this." But if it's *really* solid, then over the time period that Saturn is in the 7th house (which is about 2½ years in any house), you'll tend to more and more see the deep values in that relationship. It's the same with Saturn in the 5th—if you stick it out, you'll more and more see the deeper love values in any deep relationship that you have, with your children as well as with anybody else.

Jupiter in the 7th—some people talk about that as "wonderful, wonderful, you've lived 35 years now and never been married; well Jupiter is going into your 7th house now, and you'll get married." Of course, that's not necessarily true. Some people do have opportunities to get married with transiting Jupiter in the 7th. A few people I've seen have actually had multiple proposals with Jupiter in the 7th, like three different people wanting to marry them within that one year. But basically what Jupiter means—like Saturn in the 7th shows the urge to define the state of any relationship that you're in and, in general, to define what kind of relationship needs you have—so, on the other hand, Jupiter in the 7th gives an urge to expand the horizons of your relationship activities. Now, that can radically improve an existing relationship, too, if that relationship is pretty viable and improvable. If it's not, though, if that relationship is rigid and it can't or doesn't grow, then Jupiter in the 7th often means that you'll have the urge to expand your relationship activities beyond the boundaries of that existing relationship. Jupiter always wants to expand beyond the boundaries, like Sagittarius, never wants to stay inside any little boundary; they want to expand all the time.

Comment from audience: I just did a chart for a woman that has Jupiter transiting the 7th house and is in the process of getting a separation. . . .

Personally, I have seen more people start divorce proceedings with Jupiter in their 7th house than any other indication, which I bet you money you won't find in any astrological book. The traditional books say Saturn in the 7th is really divorce prone. Uranus going across the 7th house cusp or the Ascendant *is* very divorce prone, because there is a urge for radical change and freedom. But I've seen more people get divorced or start that process with Jupiter in the 7th. Why is that? It's because whatever house Jupiter is transiting in is an area of your life where, during the time Jupiter is there, you've got this urge to understand it more completely, to improve it, to improve the existing situation, and—if the existing situation is unimprovable—you'll often not want to do it anymore. Like many people change jobs when Jupiter goes into the 10th house. They'll often do it even though their old job was secure and paid them good money; but they will often quit their old job, as Jupiter goes into the 10th, with nothing on the horizon that can give them any money, with no other job. Why are they doing that? They feel the urge to improve the whole thing. Also what else is Jupiter related to? It's prophecy, the future; when Jupiter goes into the 10th, you want to get into something with a *future* in it. Jupiter in the 7th too—if there's no future in that relationship, Jupiter in the 7th will show you that, and you'll want to start a life style that has more of a future in it.

VENUS & MARS IN THE ELEMENTS & SIGNS

The first thing I might mention is one thing you might keep an eye on in dealing with *any* chart in relation to relationships, sexuality, emotional ease: look at Venus and Mars in relation to each other in the natal chart, because very often you'll find a Mars-Venus square, a Mars-Venus opposition, or a Mars-Venus quincunx, which are indicative of a certain inner discord in the way that the person is trying to get what he wants. In other words, Mars represents the urge to go out and get what you want, to go out and assert yourself. Venus has a lot to do with what your emotional needs are, so you can feel satisfied. If Mars and Venus are not in harmony, there is often an inner emotional discord or frustration, and by "in harmony" I mean if they're in elements that aren't compatible. And if they're in a real close stressful aspect, it's much more dominant still. Say Mars in fire and Venus in water—there could be *some* problem there, but *especially* if Mars were in Leo and Venus were in Scorpio, both fixed signs and in square to each other.

Q: Do you have any suggestions for resolving this aspect?

A: Prayer. Awareness. Just be aware of what you're doing and why you're doing it. Especially with Venus or Mars in water signs, it's particularly important to be aware of what's motivating you, because otherwise you're always a little bit compulsive. The main thing is awareness. That's the whole purpose of astrology, I think—to get some awareness of what you're like and to get some perspective on it. Basically, most psychotherapy is oriented toward fostering some kind of awareness. Whether it's awareness through screaming, or through yelling your anger, or through talking to an analyst or whatever.

When Venus and Mars are in stressful or "challenging" relationship to each other, one thing that often manifests is that you're impatient (Mars) with people you like, or with people you're close to (Venus). There's a kind of irritability you express that people you're close to will feel.

The natal Sun-Moon relationship is also very important when it comes to dealing with the opposite sex, as well as just expressing your whole entire self. One often finds problems particularly with the squares and oppositions, but the most problematical is the square between the Sun and Moon. Even if they're in signs that are in square to each other but the aspect isn't close, there's a kind of inner discord between your conscious self (Sun) and your subconscious needs (the Moon). It's like your subconscious needs (shown by the Moon) are always getting in the way of or interfering with your self-expression (the Sun), the solar, ego-type of expression. And then in dealing with the opposite sex, there's often conflict felt in the sexual roles (between *active* and *passive*) when you have the Sun-Moon square and to some extent with the opposition.

I'll talk about a couple of things about Venus and Mars first and then talk about them in the elements and then go through the signs. One of the best ways I find of thinking of Venus and Mars is that Venus shows the "female ego," Mars shows the "male ego." If you think of it in terms of the cultural images and social patterns that are true for *most people*, in men the Mars sign will show how you'll want to assert your masculinity, your strength, impress somebody, impress some woman too. In women, the Venus sign has so much to do with the female ego, especially how she seeks to make herself look and feel good with various and sundry adornments. For example, take Mars in Leo in a man's chart. How might someone like that try to impress somebody else? In a Leo sort of way! "Look at my big car," or some kind of generous, dramatic demonstrations.

Q: How about in a woman's chart?

A: I'll get to that. It's all coming. I'm talking now about Mars in a man's chart, that is, in the chart of a fairly average, hetrosexual American man. It has to do with the male ego and the Mars *sign* has to do with how he seeks to project his strength and masculinity. If you get Mars in Taurus or Scorpio (retentive signs), you have an inner reserve, a silent inner strength. If you have some guy with Mars in Sagittarius, Aries, or Leo (the outgoing signs), you'll find somebody who's trying to impress you with demonstrative, overt type of behavior. Mars in air signs—very verbal: "Look how smart I am. See all these things I've done because I'm so clever." With Mars in earth—"See how competent and responsible and disciplined I am." Get the picture?—the male ego.

On the other hand, women are very much tied in with and identified with their Venus sign qualities, in terms of how they want to feel feminine and express that femininity (the "female ego"). Venus in Aries—you get someone like these glamour girls in Hollywood, like Marilyn Monroe. I believe Elizabeth Taylor does too. Because they're assertive and able to express and project their Venus forcefully.

Comment from audience: Elizabeth Taylor has Uranus conjunct Venus in Aries.

Yes, I don't even know how to describe this quality. It's kind of show-offy and gaudy. It's pretty masculine too. Aries is a masculine sign.

Q: What effect would Mars and Venus retrograde have?

A: I have no idea. I personally don't find retrograde too important in most cases. The only thing I've ever noticed is that men who have Mars retrograde are often more gentle, less pushy. And I suppose women with Mars retrograde would also have less tendency to assert themselves very dynamically. Other than that, I've never noticed anything about Venus or Mars retrograde. There are all kinds of theories I could spiel off that I've read, but it's never impressed me as that remarkable a behavioral difference.

Q: Doesn't a planet retrograde just mean that that planet just isn't working quite up to par?

A: No. I don't believe that at all. That's what I mean about theories I could repeat but which I don't believe. For example you can find fantastic writers with retrograde Mercury and professional athletes with retrograde Mars. I think that if a planet is retrograde—if it means anything different at all—it's something more self-contained and more inward, and the person has more control over it. It's like they mull it over more before they do it, or *say* it (in the case of Mercury). Occasionally, Mercury retrograde will be found in charts of people who stutter and stumble and normally can't verbalize, but usually there's something *else* in the chart that indicates that difficulty. The retrograde issue has, to me, never seemed too important. In fact I don't agree with what many people say about when you have planets retrograde at birth and then when they turn direct by progression—there's all these theories about how big a change that brings into your life when your progressed Mercury, for example, goes direct. I know a lot of people who have hardly noticed anything. But that's a whole other subject entirely.

Mainly I want to convey that thing about the male ego with Mars and the female ego with Venus. It should be clear later when we go through Venus through the signs. Another thing is Jung's concept of the *animus* and *anima*. The idea is that within every male there is a female side that he's usually not in touch with, and he projects it onto women—which would be his *lunar* and *Venus* nature. And then in all women there's the male side, which would be the Sun and Mars, which they project onto men. In Jungian psychology, the more in touch you are with your other side, the more conscious you are, the more able you are to relate to people of the opposite sex in a *real* way instead of just through projections. So Venus and Mars can be seen as *anima* and *animus* too. In other words, in most men's charts Venus will show the *anima* according to its sign and somewhat its aspects. Venus in a man's chart has to do with what kind of woman turns him on. It's a certain romantic *image* that's stimulating to him. Mars in a woman's chart symbolizes her kind of *animus*; her male qualities, most evident when projected onto some man, would be somewhat like her Mars sign. If she has Mars in Taurus, someone who is very Taurean might appeal to her. And therefore where her Mars is and the aspects to it have to do with what kind of man she attracts, on a physical level primarily, on a kind of instinctual level. Venus in a man's chart also has much to do with what kind of woman will appeal to him emotionally, on the instinctual, sensual level. It's not necessarily communication or a *profound* type of sharing.

Q: (Inaudible).

A: If you just go by archetypal factors, Venus is the feminine of the two, the Mars-Venus pair; *traditionally* that's how women get what they want—not being up front but *attracting* it. If they like some guy, they don't usually say, "Hey, you want to go out somewhere?" That's not the tradition, not the archetype. Things today are changing a little bit as people are getting more daring. Usually there's all these little games and wiles used to magnetically attract somebody, which is Venus. Again, on the archetypal level, men (Mars) are supposed to go out and get what they want. They're *supposed* to be more up front and all that. But you know when we talk about Venus and Mars in these ways, a lot of it is on the archetypal level, and every person is a different mixture of male and female.

Well, for *everybody*, Venus shows how you give affection and how you receive it, whether you're male or female—how you sense affection, how you sense appreciation and closeness. These generalizations should get clearer as we go through the signs. Venus also shows your tastes—what aesthetically seems good to you. The Sun also shows your tastes, but they're broader, more *total* tastes. Venus is more your emotionally-colored tastes—what feels nice to you, what looks balanced to you, what is pleasing to you. Venus has to do with pleasure. What sign your Venus is in will always give you a clue about where you get pleasure out of life. Also, the sign and the aspects show your attitude toward love, relationship, and all social interactions. So if you put Venus in one of the more private signs, like the water signs, you'll be less inclined to socialize too quickly, whereas Venus in air signs tends to be very social, easily dealing with different kinds of people.

Mars for *everybody* shows how one expresses desires, how you go about getting what you want. Mars is your *method of operation*, how you try to get what you want. Mars' sign also shows how you assert yourself, how you express "I want this"—an ambition you have, sex, or whatever. Mars also shows the attitude toward sex and the basic attunement of sexual energy—in other words, according to your Mars (the sign and aspects), how the sexual energy is stimulated. Is it very controlled like it is in Capricorn or in aspect to Saturn, or is it super excitable all the time like when in aspect to Uranus or in Aquarius, or is it vague and you don't know quite what you're doing with it like when it's in aspect to Neptune or in Pisces? And Mars also shows the actual mode of release of the sexual energy.

To differentiate between men and women in terms of what Venus and Mars show, first of all it should be said that, according to my experience and according to everyone I've talked to in counseling (males and females), female sexuality is much more complicated. Venus and Mars are much more *intermingled* in women than in men. Also, the Moon in women's charts—being a very receptive planet—has a lot to do with sexuality also. For example, someone with Moon in Scorpio usually has very strong physical and emotional needs, no matter where her Venus and Mars are. (The position of Venus and Mars then either amplify or moderate the tendencies shown by the Moon.) So you have to tune into the Moon too.

For women then, as well as showing the "female ego" (how she seeks to be attractive), Venus is also closely related to sexuality—specifically, how she *approaches* any *relationship* that might eventually *lead* to sex. Mars shows more the sexual *energy*, the sexual *release*. But Venus is much more how she approaches the human relationship that leads into sexuality. Venus shows the quality of receptivity that precedes the Mars *activity*. Venus in most charts is more connected with romantic intrigue, which can be a kind of sexual turn-on also, but it's very much romantic *images*. You know some men want their wives to dress in a certain way because that turns them on, because it clicks with their own Venus. The woman's tastes may not be that at all, but she sometimes does it anyway because it makes him happy and makes him more sexually interested in her. And vice versa too—some women will push their men into acting or dressing in a certain way that will trip off their *Mars*, their *animus* that turns them on. And Mars in a woman's chart also shows what kind of man is physically attractive to her—the sign of Mars and its aspects, but especially the sign.

And then for men . . . I don't know if there's going to be time to go into all these variations, homosexuality and all that. If we don't get to it now, maybe in the next workshop or something. But for most heterosexual men, Venus has to do with their *ideals* about love and sex; it's very much his mental *images*, what is romantically right or gives him pleasure on the level of images and also feelings. But it's not specifically sexual. Mars is much more the symbol of sexual energy. In women's charts you really can't separate it that much because Venus is very much a sexual planet in a woman's chart.

Now I'll try to give you an idea of how important the elements are in relation to Venus and Mars. Venus and Mars in water signs first of all—since water of itself is formless (unless you've got earth—something to hold it), water is just dribbling and flowing all over the place. These people often don't *know* what they feel or what they want. With either Venus or Mars or both in water signs, they don't know what they want unless they experiment, unless their feelings are given form by some other person. In other words, they have to follow their feelings to some extent and *experiment* with them somewhat in order to do certain kinds of "reality testing," to test out their feelings by experimenting with them. And sometimes that means a lot of sexual things, too, before they really know what they're doing, before they really know what they want or what is motivating them. Also, all the water signs are naturally sort of passive signs. They like it if somebody else gives form to their feelings. They like it if somebody else receives their feelings and reinforces them, provides some channel for them. They also like to be *wanted*, whether it's men or women, if Venus and/or Mars are in water signs, but particularly with Venus which is the more passive of the two. If Venus is in a water sign, that person particularly wants to be *wanted*. They want the other person to come on with the initiative.

Venus and Mars in water signs are extremely sensitive. Water is always a sensitive element, and anybody with Venus or Mars in water signs can experience sensual or sexual pleasure with very subtle stimuli. It's a very subtle communication as contrasted with Mars or Venus in earth or fire, which tend to be grosser, more definite and overt sorts of signs. Also, sex is strongly tied in with emotional security, if you have Venus or Mars in water signs. Sex is never *solely* an instinctual thing for these people. It's more like you tune in on deep security feelings through sexuality. And, being fairly sensitive, you find people who are sensitive to *other* people's feelings too—especially with Venus in the water signs. You find people who can tune into other people's feelings, sexual and emotional needs—very intuitive to other peoples' feelings. Remember Venus is the social planet, and if you put it in the water signs, very sensitive signs, you've got a very keen intuition about where other people are at. This can make good lovers too, with Mars or Venus in water. They know what the other person feels.

The one other thing about water that's worth mentioning—water signs and the water houses are connected with purging and purifying. When you have Venus or Mars in a water sign, there's a kind of purification process that takes place through intimate interchange with someone you really like and really feel close to, a kind of purging and cleansing of psychic and emotional tension. That may be somewhat true for everybody, but with the water signs it's an absolute need or else they can get emotionally ill, or they get psychically tense. And yet, because water is so unconscious, they often don't know what's bothering them.

Q: Do you mean that sexual energy would be purging or just the relationship in general?

A: Closeness. Some kind of emotional closeness. That can include sex or not include sex, but it's got to be a *sharing of feeling*. I would even say a sharing of pain and needs. The water signs, when they're in touch with their feelings, are also very in touch with pain. They're so sensitive, very much in touch with the fact that they are weak and that they have needs. Whereas, take fire as an element or earth, they don't admit their weaknesses. They have them, but they're not in touch with them so immediately as the water signs. Which is one reason why you find Venus in the water signs, especially in Cancer or Pisces, being very sympathetic people; because they are so sensitive themselves and so in touch with pain and just how living in the material world can hurt, that they can identify with other people's suffering also. It's not lacking with Venus in Scorpio, but it's not so obvious. They aren't very tearfully sympathetic, in a mothering way, although their work often involves that same kind of emotional involvement with other people.

Venus and Mars in the earth signs indicate a very basic and down to earth attitude toward love and sex. Sex for them is tied in with basic needs and instincts and also with duties. With Venus and/or Mars in the earth signs, you often find people who are very *efficient* lovers. They're not necessarily very emotional, but they're very efficient. It *can* get to the point where they're very mechanical. They're very duty conscious. So say someone with that in the chart is married and feels it as his or her duty to take care of the other person's instinctual needs, it can become a very mechanical thing, which isn't bad if the other person doesn't mind a little mechanical sex.

Q: (Somewhat inaudible) . . . sounds like all this research into sex. . . .

A: Yes. Like Masters & Johnson and such people who have all these people screwing around in their laboratory. I would think that they had Mars in either earth, or maybe air, to take an intellectual interest in sex. I doubt that they get many volunteers with Venus or

Mars in water, because water is very private and very sensitive and could not stand the idea of being watched in a laboratory. Because sex is not primarily a physical act for people with Venus or Mars in water. It's primarily an emotional act.

Q: So it seems such researchers are getting only half the story, if most of the volunteers are. . . .

A: I personally think they are getting far less than half. But there *are* people who can benefit from those kinds of therapies. (Interruption from audience—inaudible.) Yes. That's their problem to begin with, that they have this attitude toward sex that it's a mechanical sort of thing.

One other thing to mention about Venus and Mars in the earth signs—like I said before, they are very capable and very much interested in efficiently and practically taking care of the other person's basic physical needs; they're very much in touch with physical needs, especially Taurus. Taurus so understands sex, it's just ridiculous. They may not understand all the emotional sides of it, but they at least understand other people's instinctual needs. But if they don't have any water, they could be kind of impersonal and cold. And another thing about the earth signs is that Virgo is a very sensual sign. A lot of books will talk about Virgo being so puritanical, and there is or can be a puritanical streak in them; but it's an *earth* sign. The puritanism and pickiness is a *mental* quality resulting from constant analysis of everything in relation to their idea of perfection. But their sensuality is part of their body and instincts, not mental. The earth element relates to the *physical* body, *physical* instincts, the *physical* senses. If you put Venus (which shows your tastes and your emotional sensitivity) in *any* earth sign, you've got somebody who is very sensual but also very controlled. All the earth signs are very controlled. I learned a good thing about the earth signs this summer: the earth itself has a crust to it, and the earth signs have a sort of crust; Capricorn very serious, Taurus very self-contained (they stick their jaw out and don't let on at all), Virgo always tied up in knots, always keeping everything in. All the earth signs keep everything in. But you put Venus in an earth sign and you've got a very sensual being, although you'll have to get through their blockages and defenses before they let down their crusty guard.

Then Venus and Mars in air signs. Here you have people who are not particularly sensual; they aren't really "touchy" type people for the most part. Now you have to remember these are generalizations and something else in the chart can compensate, like if you have Taurus rising or Cancer rising or something that could give you much more of a desire to touch. But specifically Venus and Mars in air signs are not very sensual. They don't particularly need a great deal of physical closeness or intensity. But what *do* they need with love and sex?— *communication.* They need a sense of being a mental peer of the person they're sharing with. Sex particularly can be a kind of dialogue, a very definite kind of communication; and the air signs are very light and playful too. Venus and Mars in air signs can be playful, and they can be very cold too. They can be very detached, very cold and unemotional. Specifically, since I mentioned before that Mars has to do with the attunement of the sexual energy, Mars in the air signs is not a particularly strong sexual energy, if you talk about it just in terms of *quantity*—how much and how often can they have sex. There you find that Mars in Taurus, Mars in Leo, Mars in Capricorn, or Mars in Scorpio are much more energetic than Mars in air signs. The air signs are much more mental.

There are two good friends of mine, guys whose Mars are in Aquarius. And neither one of them seems very interested in sex, and I could never understand that until I got into astrology. It seems they are very happy just in talking. One said he was very interested in taking some woman to dinner and talking, but the physical interaction is something he's come to dread because most women are more passionate than he is. So these people are, in fact, often kind of wary of sex. They just aren't particularly horny people. They can get a lot of energy flowing through talking, through communication. So sex is tied in with communication and sexual feelings are stimulated by mental dialogue if you have Venus or Mars in the air signs.

And then Venus and Mars in fire signs. I just learned an interesting thing about this last week sometime. This woman with Mars in Sagittarius told me that she's much more interested in sex and much more seductible if she's been having a good time and laughing a lot. "Laughter" was the key. When she laughs a lot when she's with somebody, she automatically gets more open toward sex. And what are the fire signs noted for?—spirited, animated behavior, spontaneity, having a good time, releasing energy randomly. So with Venus and Mars in the fire signs, the sexual relationship is somewhat impersonal, which won't bother you if you're somewhat attuned to fire. If you're a watery person, though, you might not like it. You might feel that the person is *too* impersonal, too much into their own thing. Just like Sun in fire signs, they're very self-centered; they're very much into their own trip. That's not a criticism, but that's just how they function. Likewise, people with Venus and Mars in fire signs are very direct in their sexual and emotional expression, often rather blunt in fact. But the rest of the chart could somewhat compensate for that.

Of the three fire signs, the strongest in terms of *steady* sexual drive is Leo. Venus or Mars in Leo in women and specifically Mars in men. With Sagittarius, the sexual energy is very strong once it's flowing, but it's a mutable sign; it's kind of erratic. It's not a constant sort of drive that those people have. Aries is easily turned on, but you know how Aries is—they're good at starting things but don't always finish them too well. I learned a lot about Mars in the fire signs when I was younger, because a couple of girl friends I had had Mars in Leo and Mars in Sagittarius. And it always surprised me how immodest they were; they had no sense of modesty. The bluntness was what struck me particularly; Mars in fire signs is very blunt, very direct. The water signs like a more subtle kind of seduction routine. The earth signs can get into a more sensual kind of seduction. In the fire signs, the seduction happens by kind of entertaining each other. You know, take them out to dinner and have a "good time," the usual social things, going dancing and getting them laughing and joking and drinking.

Q: I'm wondering about having them in the same sign—maybe that would make it stronger regardless of the sign. . . .

A: Venus and Mars in the same sign is inevitably . . . inevitably there's a tremendous interest in the opposite sex. There's usually the ability to attract the opposite sex also. But there's not always a strong sexual drive. It depends on the sign they're in. A friend of mine with Venus and Mars conjunct in Gemini loves to flirt around with women, and women are flirting around with him all the time. He's kind of the cute Taurus type. Taureans are kind of boyishly cute sometimes, and then if you add some Gemini, they're just disgustingly cute. He's had a lot of experience to get to know himself (he's about 35 or 36) and he says he finds his basic need is to have sex once or twice a month. He is very satisfied in dealing with the opposite sex by talking to them. Talk, talk, talk, that's Gemini. He'll do their charts, transits, etc., and there is no sexual feeling. There's a kind of flirtation that gives him pleasure and the communication. . . . It does not have to be a physical thing to be satisfying. But with Venus and Mars in the same sign, there's always a strong need for interaction with the opposite sex in some way; it's not always sexual. It's also a very creative combination. Venus and Mars in the same sign (the closer they are to a conjunction, the more powerful it is) is often very capable in some art. It's not always art in the narrow sense of drawing or painting. It could be all kinds of things. One guy I know has Venus and Mars conjunct in Aries; his artistry is through stained glass and metal. You put Venus and Mars in Virgo and you sometimes get excellent craftsmanship; I've seen them making musical instruments by hand, sometimes other crafts, portrait painting—something that calls for a great attention to detail and concentration. So Venus-Mars combinations, especially the conjunction, are very artistic too, not just an emotional-sexual thing. As a matter of fact, there's a great deal of emotional and aesthetic satisfaction (Venus) that they get from doing actively (Mars) some kind of art.

I think we ought to go through Venus in the signs now. We'll mention a few general things about Venus in the signs, and then we'll get into male and female differences. The more I talk about these things and the more things change these days, the more difficult it is to make generalizations about "this is more for men" and "this is more for women," without having somebody get uptight. But at least I'll have to risk that. The main thing is to go with general *principles*; as with everything astrological, you have to apply them to individual situations. Venus in a woman's chart, remember, has a lot to do with how she expresses her affection, how she relates, how she gives of herself, as well as how she seeks to attract other people. Whereas Venus in a man's chart *also* shows how he expresses his feelings and how he senses he is cared for and appreciated, but also it has to do with that *anima* image, that image of the ideal mate.

VENUS IN ARIES

So Venus in Aries in general is someone who loves with their head instead of their heart. They're pretty impulsive; they tend to jump into things pretty quickly. And they're not known for subtlety; they tend to be quite direct. If they like you, they let you know it pretty directly. I've known men with Venus in Aries—when they like you, they smash you on the back. Very independent in love too. People with Venus in Aries tend to be independently motivated, into initiating things, and fairly impulsive and aggressive. But also, if you women want some guy who can appreciate *your* independence, find a guy with Venus in Aries; because that's the image of the kind of woman that he would be turned on by, that is, someone who's independent. Some males with Venus in Aries will even push for the woman to be more Arian or more independent. If she's that way naturally, then she'll dig it, she'll find it supportive; if not, she'll feel like she's being manipulated. Venus in Aries in a man's chart shows that he likes that kind of woman, an independent woman, and he'll allow that kind of freedom to her.

VENUS IN TAURUS

Venus in Taurus, for *anybody*, is very sensual; naturally, Taurus is a very physical, sensual sign. With Venus there, you've got a "double whammy," what is called a "dignified planet"—very conscious of appearance, physical comfort, physical beauty, often a love of luxury—sometimes tastes even get a bit gaudy. Women with Venus in Taurus are very attuned to their appearance and tend toward a bit of luxury; they don't like just simplicity in appearance, they want a little bit more than that—a little bit extra. It depends on their generation too; there are huge differences between some generations. Venus in Taurus people understand what makes people comfortable; and, particularly if it's a woman with Venus in Taurus, if she likes somebody she'll be particularly physical—very touching and very much looking after the person's comfort. A male with Venus in Taurus is another number. He's attuned to comfort and all that, but he's very much (in most cases) hung up on a Taurus-type image of woman. He doesn't want anybody who is too quick or too agile or too independent or even too intelligent. He wants more the archetypal earth mother; that's what will turn him on. Venus in a man's chart doesn't necessarily show what kind of woman you'll marry, or what kind you even prefer to live with. Likewise, Mars in a woman's chart does not show much more than the *physical* attraction; it's the ideal romantic *image*, not who you're probably going to live with. Venus in Taurus men like fairly shapely women, often really voluptuous types; and they usually insist on the usual culture role of passivity, which they regard as feminine.

VENUS IN GEMINI

Venus in Gemini—obviously very social, very talkative, and they feel the need to communicate with other people. There is often a certain versatility with words, whether it be in speech or printing or editing or publishing, or sales. You often find considerable aesthetic cleverness with Venus in Gemini. Women with Venus in Gemini don't usually tend to be too domestic. Venus shows where you get pleasure, what you like doing. Venus in Gemini tends to be more social, more interested in reading books than in cleaning a sink. They tend to be rather diplomatic and rather tactful, although anyone with Venus in Gemini is fickle, very fickle. You're never quite sure where they're at. Their feelings can change very rapidly. They can get sick of a relationship very quickly. Many people with Venus in Gemini can have two and three relationships going simultaneously.

Q: I have this friend who has several planets in Gemini, including Venus, but she has this need to have a long term relationship that is very deep. Yet she's always on the tennis court, running around doing all kinds of things, making it impossible to maintain the kind of relationship she says she wants.

A: Yes, really.

So what about a man then with Venus in Gemini in his chart? For one thing, he'd be attracted to some woman who fit the Gemini mold—versatile, curious, keeping him guessing; he'd like that, someone who is always changeable. Definitely he would crave intelligence, more than the physical appearance of the woman; she would need to be intelligent and fairly verbal, curious, anything that fits the Gemini mold to some extent.

VENUS IN CANCER

Venus in Cancer naturally is a very sensitive person, with Venus in the Moon's sign. This is somebody who is much more domestic. Men with Venus in Cancer often help out around the house somewhat spontaneously. Venus in Cancer people are very protective of anyone they're attached to, whether it be their children or anyone that they just like. Venus in Cancer also tends to be very old fashioned about love. Their images of love and marriage tend to be quite traditional and rather "clingy," not that that's a bad thing—it often keeps the family together. When it comes to passion (this is particularly true in women's charts), Venus in Cancer is not very passionate. In fact, they're more *compassionate* than passionate. If they like you, their love-making tends to be sort of motherly. They kind of take care of you, try to please you, be nice to you, make you feel comfortable, but not terribly passionate. (But as we'll see when we get to Mars in Cancer, Mars in Cancer is another thing entirely. Mars in Cancer is often super-passionate; no textbook will tell you that either.) Venus in Cancer is also very sensitive to the atmosphere and to other people's moods. You can sometimes have real hard-type businessmen who seem real gruff, but if they have Venus in Cancer and they see that you're not feeling too good, this whole motherly quality will come out. Sometimes they'll even give you money—and Venus in Cancer is not what you would call generous. You have to show them that their security is not only *not* threatened but even probably augmented by you. They don't want to just give it away. Men with Venus in Cancer like the Cancerian image in women. They want a good cook, a homemaker, the motherly type, someone that will take care of them. My parents are a good example here: my father's Venus in Cancer is conjunct my mother's Ascendant. So that's a nice combination. He has his Venus wish fulfilled, you might say. And his Moon in Aries is conjunct her Sun. So he gets both—he gets Venus and the Moon; both his needs are fulfilled. And that's fairly rare that that sort of thing happens. It's been interesting to watch my mother, in addition to the children, mother her husband. She picked out many of his clothes, packed his suitcase when he had to go out of town, and so on.

VENUS IN LEO

Venus in Leo—you have someone who invariably is proud in their close relationships, and their pride is easily hurt too, if they're rejected. They have to feel like they're respected. They tend to be fairly demonstrative and generous in relationships. And also loyalty—Leo tends to be a very loyal sign, and Venus in Leo is no exception. As with other things in Leo, if you get to the point with Leo where you insult them so badly by your behavior or words that they can no longer respect you, they can't have any affection for you either. They may have some lingering feelings, but *respect* is a big thing for fire signs.

From audience: (inaudible).

A: Well, you know Leo always likes to be first, not only first but also on top. In this consultation a while back, it really blew my mind, the lady had Venus in Leo. First she said, "I found out that my husband has been having an affair, and it has been going on for years. And just as soon as I found that out, I could never respect him again. I'm filing for a divorce because I can't respect anyone who would do that." And then I found out later that *she* was having an affair on the side too. Talk about double standards, that was pretty amazing! She has Scorpio rising and Scorpio Moon, Venus in Leo. But that hurt pride was Venus in Leo. So then with Venus in Leo (particularly for men), they're involved in a kind of ego-trip with what women they're seen with. They want a queen, not just any old woman. They want someone they can show off. They're often attracted to actresses or dancers or somebody who's out in the public or someone who behaves in a very dramatic way. They tremendously want admiration. Anybody of either sex with Venus in Leo really wants admiration. They want recognition; they want to be the greatest.

VENUS IN VIRGO

Anyone with Venus in Virgo tends to be a fairly disciplined, faithful sort of person, also a bit puritanical, often fussy, often quite critical. Of course, you have to remember that Venus in Virgo is traditionally known as the position of Venus' fall—and that's not to say that Venus in Virgo is bad. Venus in Virgo people should simply keep their mouth shut. If they want to express their affection for someone, they should cook a dinner for them, rub their back, or do something practical for them—not criticize. Venus in Virgo can be very critical.

Q: I've heard that women with Moon or Venus in Virgo never have dirty hands. . . .

A: They're very cleanliness oriented. Virgo is a very self-conscious sign. Look at Virgo rising people especially. They're always getting in their own way; they put themselves down all the time. With Venus in Virgo then, you find someone who in love is faithful, efficient, honest, methodical. They're great lovers if you like someone who is very efficient and reliable—and clean. If they like you, they also fuss over you. They like to serve you. And in private they're much more sensual than they ever publicly let on. They often seem like icy people, very controlled; but not all of them are like that. But that's always the way puritans have been—publicly you're one way and privately another.

Men with Venus in Virgo want a proper woman. They are attracted to women who fit the Virgo mold—intellectual, intelligent, neat, clean, disciplined, proper. Where I used to teach, I was always exhausted after a three-hour class; and I met this couple there—both Virgo Suns. Well I would be tired afterwards, too tired to drive back right away, and I would go to their house after class—they were in the class. I would just lie down on their couch; they would bring me food, herb teas, they were into health foods and everything. I would stay there for an hour and recuperate and be served and then I would drive home. It was fantastic.

VENUS IN LIBRA

Venus in Libra people, as are all the air signs, can be somewhat cold, not particularly passionate—very broadminded about other people though. They're capable of meeting people on their own level; justice and fairness are a big deal. Remember Venus is in its own sign now. Things have to be fair. What they would really like in a love experience or relationship is peace and harmony. They may not like passion at all. They may not care if it's passionate at all as long as it's peaceful and nice—everybody being nice to each other. Say you're trying to please someone with Venus in Libra. (In fact, this is something that everyone should know: if you're trying to please somebody, find out where their Venus is.) If you want to please someone with Venus in Libra, you be nice to them. That may mean ignoring them, it may mean being as superficial as hell to them—you be nice to them. Anything that is harmonious, pleasant, and relaxing.

Women with Venus in Libra tend to be feminine in appearance and yet surprisingly cold, aloof, very often intelligent but very distant, somewhat conventional in attitudes toward love and sex. One thing not brought out in books very much is that Libra is a very conventional sign in most ways. I would say it's second only to Capricorn in conventionality and being conscious of reputation and public appearance; everything has to be nice on the surface. Remember Saturn, the ruler of Capricorn, is exalted in Libra. There's a close resemblance between many Capricorn and Libra characteristics. Venus in Libra is not very emotional, but they tend to be sentimental. Say you have a woman with Venus in Libra and she may appear not to have an emotional bone in her body, but if you forget her birthday she'll cry. Usually very good looking too, Venus in Libra. Women with Venus in Libra, like that Venus de Milo statue, often have an archetypally symmetrical and shapely body.

Men with Venus in Libra (like the women) insist on harmony in relationships. They're very idealistic in love, as are the women. What kind of woman are they attracted to? Someone who's a lady, somebody who's not just a "gal," someone who's ladylike, sophisticated, but real, sincere, sort of hard to please; they very much like sincerity. It's funny about Libras, they're such contradictions. Because they crave sincerity and they hate phoniness in other people, and yet they are often accused of being phony because they try so hard to be nice and to keep things going smoothly.

VENUS IN SCORPIO

Anyone with Venus in Scorpio is invariably rather emotional, super sensitive, and very, very intense. All their feelings are intense, whether it's feelings about a person, money, their work. All their feelings come out with great intensity. They're explosively loaded with a certain passion. If the passion goes out of their life, they're like the dead; they're like walking corpses. They've got to feel passionate about whatever they're doing. In relationships it's that way too. There has to be an open channel for that passion if they're going to feel totally satisfied with a certain person; there has to be an open channel if there's going to be an intense interchange of emotion. And Venus in Scorpio is very, very sexually oriented. It's also very secretive and quite anti-social too. Venus in Scorpio people are often anti-social, highly unconventional although it's not always obvious. It's the Pluto sign, and Pluto in many ways has to do with anti-social behavior.

Also Venus in Scorpio can be very jealous, very possessive. If the person has a lot of Aquarius or something like that, they're not quite so jealous. But invariably there's a strong sense of survival that is tied in with their closest relationships. In other words, they're very conscious of being safe; and if it looks like the other person might take off after someone else, their whole survival is threatened—at least that's how they feel emotionally. Venus in Scorpio can be very loyal, in spite of all the books saying how nasty Scorpio is. Venus in Scorpio can be loyal, but the loyalty tends toward an *emotional constancy* rather than toward their overt behavior. Scorpio is a fixed sign and fixed signs don't like change too much.

With Venus in a man's chart in Scorpio, you have someone who likes very vital women, women with lots of spunk, you might say—lots of guts. Marsy type women, Aries or Scorpio types. They like powerful women. They don't like someone who's too wishy-washy or too passive. They get bored with them. They like intensity in relationships, and—in a man's chart with Venus in Scorpio—they like intensity in any woman they're interested in. There's also quite a bit of sexual pride in women who have Venus in Scorpio, pride in their sexual prowess or attractiveness. And that's likewise true of men with Mars in Scorpio because—remember—Mars shows the male ego. Women with Venus in Scorpio often have their female ego tied up closely with their sexuality.

VENUS IN SAGITTARIUS

With Venus in Sagittarius, you generally have very idealistic people in their relationships. They're often very hard to please; Sagittarius is an incredibly fickle sign. Most books don't tell you that either. They just say they're great philosophers and so honest. They can't stand dealing with reality in many cases; they hate living in the present and they don't always like facing the facts of life. And likewise when Venus is in Sagittarius, they have feelings of great idealism about the kind of relationship they want, and it's often something they'll talk about—all these wonderful ideals. It's very hard for them to settle down to one relationship and to deal with all the garbage as well as with all the good things. Pisces and Sagittarius, which in ancient astrology were both ruled by Jupiter, both have a lot in common in that often they are both escapists. They both tend toward wanting to escape from the immediate present.

Venus in Sagittarius people, once they are attached to somebody, tend to be quite generous with their affections. They like to play too—"horse around;" it's the sign of the centaur. They have a horsey sense of humor too. They also generally make a big deal about blunt honesty. They won't even put a thin veneer of tact on anything they say. And so if Venus in Sagittarius people like somebody, you can't expect flattery or praise from them; they will just tell you what they feel. They will tell you your faults, your weaknesses and everything else, but "even though you're like that, I still like you." They're real blunt, and yet broadminded. Now men with Venus in Sagittarius, what do they want in women? They want someone who's Sagittarian, someone who is reliable, a pal, someone they can horse around with, or someone who is philosophical, very idealistic. They want someone who is very honest and direct. So they probably wouldn't want anyone who's too sly and watery and kind of sneaky.

Q: How do you use that word reliable?

A: I meant reliable in the sense of very *upstanding*, mainly in the sense of honesty—so they can count on the person's willingness and intentions.

VENUS IN CAPRICORN

With Venus in Capricorn in anyone's chart you find someone who is very conscious of reputation and material security, very serious about love, very serious about relationships. Not too much humor in general, unless it's dry and often biting. Remember Venus shows what makes you happy, what is pleasant to you. I have known people with Venus in Capricorn who never laugh, they are that serious about everything, not just relationships—a very serious minded person generally. In relationships, it tends to be very cautious and very much wants a commitment before they let go of their feelings. You have that outer crust that you have to break through, the Saturnian wall that you have to break through before you know their real feelings or their real passions.

Venus in Capricorn women are usually very passionate critters, with a great deal of earthiness and sexual energy and endurance. They won't let you know where they're at sexually or emotionally until they feel safe; they have to feel there's some kind of commitment there. (And this is true for men with Venus in Capricorn also.) It has to be a big commitment—even marriage sometimes. But again, when you have these signs like Libra and Capricorn that are very conscious about conventional behavior, you have to be careful not to be fooled. Venus in Capricorn and Venus in Virgo, as I mentioned before, often look very straight and very proper and you can't really know where they're at and what their feelings are. They're rarely publicly demonstrative. With Venus in Capricorn, there's a great deal of self-control and self-containment. They don't want to be embarrassed or humiliated. In fact, their feelings are very hard to express. The person feels that the only way he or she can express his or her feelings is to be very practical and faithful, helpful to the person they like—give them a hand up the career ladder or do a lot of things for them. They often have trouble *verbalizing* their feelings.

Men with Venus in Capricorn—what do they want? They're attracted to a woman who has the Capricorn characteristics, someone who's fairly formal and aloof. Sometimes you find men with Venus in Capricorn marrying socially superior women, women who can give his career some kind of boost or perhaps a lot of money. Venus in Capricorn is not above marrying for money. I'm not saying that all of them do it, but you can bet many of them have at least thought about it quite seriously; and many of them stay married for money if they're in a bad marriage and there would be a financial uncertainty if they broke up; they'll often stick it out for 30 to 40 years of hell just for that material security. Venus in Capricorn especially needs a really *deep* love, and they're short-changing themselves if they hold onto somebody just for the security.

VENUS IN AQUARIUS

With Venus in Aquarius in anyone's chart, you have somebody whose attitudes toward love are naturally very open and unconventional and very free; they hate jealousy. It's quality is diametrically opposite that of Venus in Scorpio; and of course Venus in Aquarius is in square to Venus in Scorpio. They can't stand jealousy and they insist on having as many friends of either sex as they want. And also, in their attitude toward love and sex, they're quite detached, quite experimental even. It strikes me that Linda Lovelace the "porno queen" has Venus and Mars in Aquarius, and her whole public reputation has been based on her unconventionality and her willingness to publicly flaunt her unconventionality. Aquarius can be very detached, and you *know* that in order for her to make the kind of movies she makes she has to be pretty detached. You probably couldn't have Venus and Mars in water signs and make porno movies like that. You might want to go see it but you wouldn't want to act in it. (We might mention also that Hugh Hefner has Mars conjunct Jupiter in Aquarius.)

Venus in Aquarius in a man's chart then shows that he would be attracted to a woman who would be somewhat Aquarian—knowledgable, intelligent, unconventional, very active, experimental, someone with a very powerful independence, someone who would keep him guessing and someone who was not too intense. Someone with Venus in Aquarius won't feel too comfortable with emotional intensity; just like the sign Aquarius itself, it tends to be very liberal and a bit detached. And this detachment often causes problems in one-to-one relationships. It seems so impersonal to others, and men especially have difficulty understanding women who have Venus in Aquarius.

VENUS IN PISCES

With Venus in Pisces, you have feelings, feelings, feelings—supersensitive, can be very devoted, can be very healing too. A lot of people with Pisces in their charts have natural healing powers. Anybody with Venus in Pisces is kind of a romantic idealist—it's a Neptune sign and a mutable sign. It's undoubtedly a little bit fickle when it comes down to committing themselves, but not fickle in *general*. In fact, they're often not choosy enough. You remember Pisces is opposite Virgo and Venus in Virgo is especially discriminating in relationships, even too much so verging on over-criticizing. Venus in Pisces tends to be just the opposite, especially if they're drinking or taking drugs. They tend not to be able to discriminate too well. This is also true when Venus is in aspect to Neptune, especially by square, opposition, or conjunction. They get into this woozy state where they often don't know quite why they're doing what they're doing or whether they should do what they're doing. Very seductable people are those with Venus or Mars in Pisces or in stressful aspect to Neptune; because they're not quite sure what they're doing, they often get pulled into things.

Venus in Pisces tends to be very evasive in their emotions. You try to pin them down as to what they really feel and they evade you. You'll still know it if they like you, but it's hard for them to express it in words. It's kind of a mysterious, unfathomable thing. And at the very best, like the Pisces Sun, they can be very devoted to somebody. It's not always physical faithfulness, but there's a kind of inner devotion that you can count on if the relationship is very decent and solid. Very sympathetic and compassionate, Venus in Pisces is the position where Venus is "exalted" and where—at best—the individual feels a kind of generalized compassion for all human beings. The only trouble is that the person with Venus in Pisces sometimes feels so much compassion for all these suffering human beings of the opposite sex that they figure they're going to take care of all that suffering by themselves.

Venus in Pisces wavers between self-centeredness and selflessness. Sometimes they seem so incredibly giving, full of empathy, and other times they seem to be wallowing in their own emotional misery and isolation. Venus in a man's chart in Pisces would naturally be attracted to someone who was rather Piscean. He would want someone who was very emotional, very sensitive and devoted; and that mysterious or intriguing kind of behavior that is often shown in Pisces people would arouse his interest indefinitely.

MARS IN ARIES

Mars in Aries, for anybody, would have a certain degree of brashness—someone who is very direct and often competitive. In a woman's chart with Mars in Aries, she would not only have some of those aggressive qualities herself but she's also attracted to men who exemplify those qualities. Her Mars is activated or tripped off by someone with Aries qualities. So she would like someone who is adventurous, brave, daring. For some reason, a lot of women with Mars in Aries end up getting involved with men in uniform—soldiers, policemen, men like that. Mars in Aries in men's charts, according to everything I can learn, makes very dashing lovers who love the chase but sometimes they get more boring after they get married; but of course everyone gets more boring after they get married—routine sets in.

MARS IN TAURUS

Mars in Taurus in a man's chart shows someone who likes to show his regard tangibly. Remember Mars is the "male ego," and he tries to prove himself by how much he can buy or by what a good provider he is. I know lots of men with Mars in Taurus who put off marriage a long time mainly because they feel they have to have money to do it. They would never think of getting married if they didn't have a good income. Mars in Taurus men can be bull-ies, possessive, really jealous, and sometimes really cruel. They sometimes throw tantrums in childlike ways. Mars in Taurus in a woman's chart generally shows someone who wants to be dominated, a very strong willed person but yet someone who wants to be dominated by some male; and she also wants to be comfortable. Basically she is attracted to Taurus-type men who of course like the role of the dominant male. Mars in Taurus, in either sex, shows a strong sex drive and powerful sensual urges; but it's usually quite controlled.

MARS IN GEMINI

Mars in Gemini in a man's chart—if he likes you—will want to impress you by talking to you all the time. He'll tell you all these things and try to show you how smart he is, how clever he is, how funny and witty; and if you have Venus in Gemini or other air signs, you'll like him. And if you have your Venus or Mars in earth, you'll think he's an idiot. Mars in Gemini in a woman's chart will be attracted to a Gemini-type man—someone who is clever, mental, someone who is changeable and keeps them guessing. Mars in Gemini, in either sex, is not—by itself—particularly strong sexual energy.

MARS IN CANCER

Mars in Cancer, like I mentioned briefly, is a very strong sexual thing, strong sexual drive. Most books don't talk about Cancer being anything but motherly. Mars in Cancer people really crave being *wanted*. They really like being wanted and *needed* also. With Mars in Cancer in a man's chart, you'll find someone who is protective and who basically has a pretty good understanding of women—really sensitive. In another workshop similar to this one, a woman spoke up and said the best lover she ever had had Mars in Cancer, because he was so understanding, gentle, etc. Mars in Cancer in a woman's chart shows someone who responds to men who exemplify certain Cancerian characteristics—protectiveness, strong desire for security, and clinging to the home. Mars in Cancer is a pretty complex thing. Mars shows what you want, but Cancer by its nature is unconscious; so with Mars in Cancer, even more than Mars in Scorpio or Pisces, it seems the person is somewhat unconscious of what they're doing or what they want. There's a very strong sexual drive, very fast sexual responses in many cases, very much an archetypal female thing in relationship to men. Women with Mars in Cancer can tune in on men very well, emotionally and physically. They like to feel a deep security with anything sexual; it can't just be play or something light—it's got to be something emotional too.

MARS IN LEO

Mars in Leo is also a pretty strong sex drive, very steady. Mars in Leo in a man's chart is someone who would try to impress others with a certain generous or dramatic flair, sometimes overdoing it; sometimes rather luxurious—like giving jewelry and all kinds of expensive things. It depends on how much they want somebody. They tend to be very truthful and tend to expect a lot of honesty back also. Mars in Leo, however, is very hot tempered—at least as sharp a temper as Aries. Aries is sort of a harmless temper in many cases, just to blow off steam and then it's gone. When Mars in Leo explodes, they can get really angry. Mars in Leo in a woman's chart is the woman who likes to shine in the man's glory. She is also very proud about whatever man she is with. She is very attracted to someone who is demonstrative and warm and who has all the Leo characteristics, someone who is above pettiness. Say there's a woman with Mars in Leo and you come on like a Virgo, real petty and fussy, you're going to turn her off very fast. They can't stand any kind of humiliation.

MARS IN VIRGO

Anyone with Mars in Virgo is often every exceptional when it comes to detail, some specific detail work like crafts. Virgo has always been known for being an analytical sign. With Mars in Virgo in a woman's chart, does this mean that she would analyze men or analyze sex? At a workshop a lady with Mars in Virgo spoke up and said, "Yes, you know I have this little rating chart in my head from 1 to 10!" As she dealt with men, and she dealt with many, she would rate them on her scale. That's Mars in Virgo. They can be very very analytical and sometimes very critical. They will often evaluate your sexual performance, and sometimes verbally; they'll tell you how you did. Mars in Virgo in many people is not particularly a strong sexual drive. In fact, it's not generally known for a strong sexual drive at all. One guy I did a chart for has Mars conjunct Jupiter in Virgo. And his life was pretty liberated and I said, "OK, I would be interested to know if the Jupiter also in Virgo makes up for the somewhat moderate physical energy that Mars in Virgo is supposed to have." Apparently, even Mars conjunct Jupiter in Virgo didn't give him much sexual energy. His wife told me privately that he was secretly terrified that he might be homosexual because he had so little sexual energy. But that was a normal thing for him. There was nothing wrong with him at all. But the entire culture, and especially men, tend to emphasize all these things in terms of quantity. So he got caught up in that, and it was really screwing him up.

MARS IN LIBRA

Mars in Libra is not particularly passionate—communication, verbal things, a fairly refined attitude toward sex. You know there are all these sex books on the market wanting you to try all these different sex positions, but Mars in Libra often doesn't want to try anything but the old standard. I have that from a number of people who have Mars in Libra. The best example is one man. This guy has Sun conjunct the Ascendant in Scorpio—Scorpio rising, Scorpio Sun, and his Mars is in Libra. He lives in L.A., and he says he really has trouble. He says, "I'm attracted to all these women all the time, but they're into all these kinky things." He's really straight when it comes to sex. He's very refined and traditional. But all his Scorpio energy attracts all these Scorpionic, kinky people; but then his Mars is in Libra and he can't handle it. So people with a Libra Mars want sex to be personal, romantic, even a bit formal and polite.

MARS IN SCORPIO

With Mars in Scorpio for anybody, there's a strong sexual urge. It's not just physical; it's also a big emotional thing. It's a need for an emotional closeness and intensity with somebody else that is related to sex. Sex is kind of a channel for that happening. Mars in men's charts in Scorpio tends to be passionate and quite magnetic. Some people with Mars in Scorpio have a sort of charisma (and not just Mars, it can be anything in Scorpio). You have a particular energy field or magnetism.

The best example was Robert Kennedy whose Sun and Mars were in Scorpio. I saw him in person once, and his energy field was just incredible, just this tremendous aura. Scorpio in general, and Mars in Scorpio in particular, elicits strong responses from other people, because they're so strong. They either tend to turn people off quickly or tend to attract them immediately. Mars in Scorpio in a man's chart is what one woman calls "a self-satisfied soul," which I think is very accurate. They don't like to be changed and in fact they will *never* be changed by anybody. They may be tamed a bit, over time, or they may grow and change on their own; but they will not allow anybody to manipulate them, that is, if they know they're being manipulated. They're very impatient and can be very jealous too. Mars in Scorpio in a woman's chart would be attracted to someone who is pretty intense and in fact might even like a little jealousy, just to tell them that the person really cares about them. They are very intensely amorous and physical. They sometimes have the magnetism we spoke about, but they always exude strength of will. I don't know if it's true or not, but one author says that women with Mars in Scorpio don't really want too much independence. They want to feel needed a great deal. I suspect that's true for many people.

MARS IN SAGITTARIUS

Mars in men's charts in Sagittarius is someone who loves philosophically. If they want to impress you, they try to impress you with their honesty, their future aspirations, their idealism, or they take you out for fun and games. They can't stand lack of truthfulness. They'll always try to stimulate any new interest toward self-improvement in their lover. Anyone with Mars in Sagittarius, male or female, is very blunt, very matter of fact about sex. They'll think about it, and if they decide to do it, they get to it very directly. But of course it has to meet certain moral and ethical standards. All the fire signs tend to be quite moral or at least to have very definite moral beliefs, whereas the air signs are geniuses at rationalization. Sagittarius Mars in women's charts shows that she would be attracted to someone with Sagittarian qualities. She would demand high moral characteristics in a partner, or she couldn't respect him if she felt he didn't live up to her ideals of honesty and morality. She would also be attracted to someone who could teach her something and serve as a moral guide or spiritual teacher or anything like that, who could help her improve herself and develop.

MARS IN CAPRICORN

Mars in Capricorn is a very strong sexual nature, but so self-controlled that you'd never guess it unless you had intimate contact with those people. Capricorn makes a big deal about control, so you put Mars in Capricorn and you've got a big deal about controlling sexual energy. And they can do it, and they can do it in an amazing way. I've seen Mars in Capricorn people remain celibate for years and years. These very same people at another time in their lives have been extremely active sexually. Mars in Capricorn in a man's chart is someone who is very cautious about asserting himself. Mars—*assertion*, Capricorn—*caution*. And so he's not going to come on too strong or too sexually until he knows it's safe. He doesn't want to be rejected. He hates the idea of being ridiculed and definitely wants praise. And Mars in Capricorn will often try to sell themselves on what they can provide, in the material sense. It's very hard to express affection and to let the sexual energy flow. But once they get into it, it's rarely boring—very earthy, extremely earthy. In a woman's chart, again a strong sexual energy, a very strong person, usually a very determined and capable person. And it shows what kind of male she would be attracted to—someone Capricornian. She would be intrigued by someone who was serious, detached and inscrutable.

MARS IN AQUARIUS

Then you get Mars in Aquarius, and their attitude toward sex is often ultra-modern and experimental. They're usually very open, very unconventional, but in their *behavior* they don't have a particularly strong sexual drive. They're often more interested in it as a curiosity or as a study. Now men with Mars in Aquarius love intellectual activity. Say they're trying to impress some woman, they come on with a big intellectual rap, to prove their intelligence. They're also unpredictable; nothing Aquarian or Uranian can you totally predict. So with Mars there, the attitudes toward sexuality are unpredictable—usually, as a matter of fact, fairly experimental and especially intrigued by the unusual. Mars in a woman's chart would naturally be attracted to someone who was somewhat Aquarian. A woman with Mars in Aquarius is "faithful but not rigid," as one writer puts it. I think that's quite accurate.

MARS IN PISCES

With Mars in Pisces you often have someone who likes extra sensation. It's often hard to verbalize what they're yearning for. Sexually, they often like an aphrodisiac, like booze or pot or something. They definitely have a fondness for extra sensation, especially the sensual sort. There's a very strong drive, *Mars*, to escape, *Pisces;* and often love and sex provide a convenient channel for that energy. Of course that urge to escape can also manifest as spiritual aspirations. They're often attracted to a somewhat secret relationship or love affair, a somewhat hidden relationship. Venus in Pisces is very much into that too, as is Mars or Venus in the 12th house, the Pisces house. Mars in Pisces is a very imaginative person, not just in love but in everything—strong imagination, strong psychic sensitivity. You'll often find that men with Pisces Mars have a definite softness and sensitivity that they can express at the same time they're being energetic and assertive. In a woman's chart with Mars in Pisces, you'll find somebody who is attracted to men who exemplify some dominant Pisces quality—whether he is spiritually oriented, weak and in need of help, musical or artistic, or just a spaced-out, confused, dreamy visionary. People of either sex who have Mars in Pisces tend to be extremely romantic and involved in fantasy, sometimes to the point of living in a fantasy world and other times expressing an artistic or literary talent that springs from their imaginative activities.

II — Techniques of Chart Comparison

What I'd like to emphasize in comparisons is a two-fold thing: part one is to look at the aspects between the two charts (which is the traditional method), particularly all the *close* aspects. And by "close" I mean within 4 degrees if at least one of the planets involved is a personal planet (Sun, Moon, Mercury, Venus, or Mars) or if the Ascendant is involved.* Any such close aspect within 4 degrees or so between two planets in the two people's charts is always important, and the closer it is the stronger it is. Also underlying what you can find out by doing that is a more general thing which I would like to get into today and which is my second main emphasis: using the elements and getting a sense of the blend of energies with which the two people experience each other. (Hands out the outline reproduced in this book—see Part II of outline.)

First of all, what are you doing when you do a chart comparison? You've got maps of two human energy fields, you might say. And you're trying to analyze how these energies are going to affect each

---

* I mean to emphasize by this statement that the main aspects to be considered as especially important in a chart comparison are the close aspects involving at least one person's Ascendant or personal planets. The *close* aspects involving *only* the outer five planets are mainly important in themselves if such a planet is the ruler of a chart or otherwise personally significant in a marked way.

other. I think you have to be careful not to just do what many astrologers do, that is, just looking at the aspects alone. Even if you look mainly at the close aspects, you're still missing a lot if you don't look at the elements. Likewise, some people do it just the opposite way, which is also a very unreliable and incomplete method. Some people just say, "Oh, is your Sun compatible with my Sun?"—meaning air and fire are compatible and so also water and earth. "Is your Moon compatible with so and so's Moon, Mercury with Mercury, Venus with Venus, and so on?" That is an important step also, but if you just do that, you're really going to blow it in many cases because there's often aspects between any number of planets that make the whole relationship very difficult even if the Suns are in harmony, the Moons are in harmony, and so forth. Everything can be in compatible elements in terms of the personal planets when you just compare them with each other, but you have to look at *every possible aspect*, because just a couple of things can make a difference.

I've often used as an example of this two charts of people I know who were married; they have the same rising sign, their Suns are in sextile, their Moons are harmonious, their Mercurys are in the same sign, their Venuses are in the same sign, their Mars are in sextile. All their personal planets and their Ascendants are pretty compatible, and yet that marriage was a disaster. And when you do the close aspects in the comparison, you really see why. There's one Saturn-Venus square and one Saturn-Venus opposition. I'm not saying that every couple with a Saturn-Venus square is going to have problems that are going to manifest as a broken marriage, but these people have two of them and —as you'll find out later—that's what I call a "double whammy." When you have the very same thing showing twice, whether it's in a natal chart or in a chart comparison, that is a powerful, powerful theme in the person or in the relationship; and it invariably is pointing out something that you have to pay attention to. This couple also has one Uranus-Sun opposition and one Uranus-Sun square in the comparison (another "double whammy"), which is always an indication of an "up-in-the-air" kind of relationship. *One* of these aspects you can sometimes live with; with *two* of them, it would be doubtful if the people would stay together very long, because they can't count on each other at all. They tend to be very unreliable toward each other.

I always do a comparison *after* looking at the individual charts and, like I tried to point out at the last workshop, that's the first step because sometimes you just have to say, "Look, you'd have some difficulty relating to *anybody* in close relationships; the first thing you have to work on is yourself." In other words, are you able to relate to *anyone* well enough that, even if you met someone that you would be compatible with, you could take advantage of it? In many cases, the person can't.

Also, compatibility is very much a matter of judgment too. You really have to understand the individual's nature in the individual's chart to get a feel for what would be "compatible." All the old astrological books tend to emphasize tension as bad or any kind of differences as bad: "The squares are bad, the oppositions are bad." And in chart comparisons it's true that the squares and oppositions are often problematical, especially the squares; but if you don't have any of those things, the relationship will often be dull, really boring. So it's often really positive to have a couple of "stressful" aspects in a comparison. However, if you get to the point where you have 60–70% stressful aspects, it's highly doubtful if the relationship is going to be pleasurable at all to either party. So it is a matter of judgment. By that I mean some people like excitement; some people like fighting; some people like challenges. You put an Aries or a Scorpio in a relationship and they'll die of boredom if they can't fight once in a while, or at least yell at one another or do something a little bit energetic or intense. Likewise, a Sagittarius doesn't just want dry routine. But with the Venus signs, if you take a typical Taurus or Libra, stressful aspects will often indicate things that bug them more noticeably because they want things to be easy, harmonious, and comfortable. In other words, some people can handle more stress. Then also some people are more open-minded too. Put a Gemini in any relationship—Gemini is open-minded and can be curious about people who are extremely different from them. Some people are more compatible with people who are similar to them. Other people, especially Gemini I think and the other mutable signs too, like variety and are often quite compatible with people who are really different from them. It takes considerable insight into the meaning of mutable signs to be able to analyze relationships that they're into in a very accurate way.

Doing chart comparisons, like any other kind of astrology, is very dangerous because so easily you can give into a rigid way of thinking and a very rigid way of approaching it, not only in your own life but for other people too, and you start saying these things that in fact aren't true. However, out of all the comparisons I've done, which is many hundreds, I must say that I've seen very few cases where both people were really happy with each other; such relationships are rare in life. I'm talking now about a male-female relationship. You can use comparisons for any kind of relationship, however; one of its most valuable uses is between parents and children. Parents have sometimes asked me to do comparisons between them and their children, and that has been really revealing. Invariably you find at what level of depth the two people love each other. And what you can do about it, in most cases, is that the parent has to adapt while the child is still young.

I don't think I've seen any case where the people are at ease with the relationship and feeling good about the whole thing, where the majority of the aspects were very stressful. I've never seen that. However, something I should emphasize is that a few very stressful aspects shouldn't freak you out, because—just as a mathematical fact, a statistical probability—if you get ten planets and the Ascendant and you combine them, how many possible combinations do you have there? The odds of finding a couple of so-called "stressful" aspects is probably well over 90%. In fact, a little bit of stress, a little bit of challenge is to be welcomed or the relationship might become incredibly boring, almost deadly it's so boring. So I always say you've got to look at the closest aspects, but you've also got to look at the elements. Aspects alone won't tell you everything. You have to look at what's *there in the chart.* That's probably one of the best rules of astrological interpretation, whether doing individual charts or comparisons: *don't worry about what's NOT there.* Don't worry about empty houses, empty signs, and empty this and that. Look at what *is* there. Where are the planets in the signs, in the houses? And in the case of the elements, can each person relate to the other person on all four levels?

"FEEDING" YOUR ENERGY FIELD

My philosophy of comparisons is based on the fact that human beings are functioning energy fields; we're composites of many energy fields that are functioning simultaneously in an inter-related way. And all of you who have read *Born To Heal* by Ruth Montgomery have gotten some insight into the human energy field because that's one of the best books to introduce people to not only the fact that people are made up of this dynamic kind of energy which can be activated through various kinds of healing techniques, but also that it can be activated in relationships. This "Mr. A." mentioned in *Born To Heal* talks about how people *feed* each other. He talks very specifically in terms of having a starvation of the nervous system or a starvation of your energy field. Everyone has to feed themselves at the air, fire, earth, and water levels. And one way you try to feed yourself is through close relationships. If you just look at the basic structure of astrology, the first house, which is your self, *you* individually, is always opposite the 7th house, which is *you relating to another person,* having a dynamic interchange. So that kind of feeding is necessary for everybody, even people who seem very cold on the exterior. They get lonely too. Loneliness is probably one of the biggest problems of human beings in an urban civilization, surrounded by people but they don't relate to anybody.

So what does this feeding mean? If anybody here has read my book on the elements, you'll know quite a bit about the elements already. For example, you've got to feed your mind, *air*; especially if you're a very airy person, you've got to feed your intellectual nature. And therefore in relationships, if you have a lot of air in your chart, you've got to have an intellectual rapport, a communication flow going with the other person or else you'll get bored with them. Air signs are flighty; they get bored easily—all of them, even Libra; Aquarius and Gemini get bored *real* fast. They crave excitement and new things. And so, if you have a lot of air in your chart and you're relating to someone who doesn't, you're thinking, "Oh, gee are they slow!" Really, because they don't have that mental quickness that is interesting to you.

If you have lots of fire in your chart, what do you need from somebody else? You need them to give you lots of energy. You need them to be rather invigorating, rather energetic, to show some initiative and stamina. If you're a real fiery, dynamic person, the last thing you want is some lazy, sluggish person to be your partner, because they'll bring you down. They'll interfere with your way of life and self-expression. I'm not saying, though, that there's no place in relationships (or in comparisons) for compensation. Many, many people will be attracted to people who have what they lack, but that's always a questionable thing too. In some cases it seems to work out very well if both people are open-minded and if both people can tune in on the other. Say you don't have any water and you hook up with somebody who has lots of water, that will most likely work if what you do have is a lot of earth. In other words, there's a kind of merger at that level. If you don't have any water or earth and you hook up with someone who is *mainly* water or earth, it's probably not going to be a very compatible relationship. But these are just general principles and you have to run them down to specific charts; it's much more difficult and that's where caution is always required.

But from what I've seen, it seems that people are attracted to what they *lack* in one of two ways. Either they're fairly young and inexperienced in relationships and they're unconsciously drawn to people who exemplify what they aren't or what they don't have; but in that case, those relationships are just learning experiences and once you've learned what you're supposed to learn from the other person, the relationship is often dead. Or, the other way is when people are older and fairly experienced in relationships; they are often more objective. Hopefully, people do gain objectivity as they grow older, as old Saturn keeps clunking you every once in a while, getting you more detached. In that case, you can *appreciate* qualities in other people that you couldn't when you were younger because you weren't objective enough and you were probably too defensive. But there again, that doesn't define *compatibility*. Just because you can now admire somebody's qualities doesn't mean you could live with them or be that close with them. Again, you have to look at the individual chart most of all.

If you're a very practical person—say you have lots of earth and the outer form of life is important to you; in other words, the intimacy itself is not that important and it's mainly a question of convenience—then you can live with somebody with whom there isn't that much flow or intimacy and it could still be a fairly workable thing. But if you're someone who craves a very intense closeness (say you have lots of water in your chart), there's no substitutes; you've got to have that kind of closeness, and therefore your relationship has to be at a deep level, very compatible and very intimate for you to feel satisfied. Take any sign, say you have lots of Libra; invariably you've got to have a close relationship where there's a tremendous communication or else the person gets really bored. Aquarius is very detached, very cold in many cases. Aquarius is often—somewhat like Capricorn—able to live in a certain relationship or marriage or business relationship that isn't really that compatible, where the people don't even communicate that well, but they can often handle it. They can rise above it; they can be detached from it.

Anyways, if you have lots of water, what do you need in terms of feeding yourself, feeding your energy field so you don't have a kind of starvation of your emotions? First of all, you need emotional feeding.

You need intense emotional experience and involvement in your life, and then in your relationships you also need it. And therefore it's a question of: Can the other person handle your emotions? I saw an interesting case this last summer—one person had lots of water and he felt a great deal of compatibility with someone with lots of earth. And the person with lots of earth had *no* water and was kind of a cold person, not very sensitive, and certainly not a gushing emotional type at all. The earthy person had a Capricorn Sun and a Taurus Moon; that's getting pretty earthy. And earth is a receptacle for water; so this watery person found that he could just dump all his emotion into this woman, and she was very stabilizing for him. She would just accept all of his feelings. She wouldn't react like water signs do, very sympathetic with "oh you poor dear" and all that. But she *accepted* it all and understood it, and there was some kind of rapport. It was a good lesson for me because she has *no water at all*. And he has lots of water, but he has no earth. Each person has what the other lacks, but since they're compatible elements, they are able to merge on a level that's compatible. I don't know how it would be in the long term though. We'll see; they're just living together now. You see, earth is a receptacle for water. Without earth (that is, some kind of tangible form), water has no form at all; it just drips all over the place. It's like being a cosmic Pisces-type, splashing all over. Earth gives it form.

But now what do earth signs look for in relationships? This is a good question, and I don't know if I can answer it. They would probably like a little bit of everything. But invariably, one thing that is motivating them is *security*. They want some kind of security, some kind of stability. One thing that isn't mentioned in any astrological book I've ever seen is that, of the four elements, the three "dynamic" elements are air, fire, and water. Earth by itself is not that dynamic an element. And therefore, when you do the chart of someone who has lots of earth (especially an earth Sun sign), you have to look at the whole rest of the chart even more than usual, to see what other energies are activating their behavior. Earth is the most sluggish kind of energy. If you do healing work in polarity therapy, you can see the airy, fiery, and watery energies working very dynamically. But earth energy—you can't observe it or feel it except as a kind of *grounding*. One time I had a Polarity Therapy treatment by this guy with a Capricorn Sun, a body-work energy treatment. As soon as I got off the table after the treatment, there was this rush of energy down my legs and into the ground. That was a neat experience because I don't have any earth and I'd never felt it before. Unfortunately, I've never felt it since. That's the problem with many kinds of therapies: they're good for about an hour or two, but then you go back to your karma (you might say), to your natal attunement and have to live with your limitations again. So it's the energy flow in terms of the elements that sets up the tone of the relationship; that's how I conceive of it. What are the dominant elements in the two people's charts? Is there lots of air, lots of fire, lots of water? Where are those two people really tuning in on each other?

Q: You talked about how the energies of earth and water merged. Can you also discuss how other elements tend to blend together?

A: Air and fire I can tell you about. Fire and air need each other desperately, because air without fire is an intellectual dilettante. They're filled with ideas but they never do anything. Fire without air, though, can be a kind of person who's very lost. They're busy, busy, busy, but they don't really know what they're doing. They don't have any perspective on their activities. They don't have any real understanding of the implications of their actions either. So fire and air need each other in the sense that air signs live in their heads; so when they come in contact with a fire person (if it's a very compatible thing), their air is *ignited*! Fire needs oxygen, so fire also needs air to burn; also the air signs are just full of gas, hot air unless it is ignited by some spirited action such as fire can provide. So air and fire do need each other, but this is all on a theoretical archetypal level. In terms of actually getting along with each other, fire and air sometimes irritate each other. Air signs have a very delicate nervous system, and fire signs don't. Fire signs tend to be quite gross in the way they express themselves, and often they overwhelm and irritate the air signs. I've talked to a lot of air sign people who have had Aries mothers, by the way. Of course Aries mothers probably have the ability to irritate all their children, no matter what their signs. You know how pushy Aries is. The air signs like to sit back and think things over; and if they've had any kind of stressful experience that day, they like to sit back and relax and maybe read a magazine or something—to retreat from the world of activity and just live in their minds for awhile because indulging in intellectual activities recharges their batteries. But if you live with an Aries, it's hard to relax because they're always rushing around and saying "Get moving!" And so, on the theoretical level, air signs really need that push, that impetus that the fire signs can give them; but actually with day-to-day living, they sometimes get bugged by the fire signs. And likewise fire signs sometimes feel that the air signs are impractical dreamers and extremely frustrating for action-oriented people to tolerate.

Q: How about fire and water?

A: Didn't you read my book? It's all in my book. . . . You can really figure out the elements by envisioning them and their physical nature, and then envisioning what happens when the two meet each other, and what kind of reaction takes place. It's amazing. I used to live with a Cancer once. Cancer Sun sign, and I'm quite airy. At least my Sun and Moon are in air. And of course Cancer is square to my Sun in Libra. But I never knew how much I was drowning. You know, it's air and water. You can keep air under water, and you'll start gasping. It's like, "All this yucky emotion all the time! I've got to get above this water." And to the Cancer person it became apparent that she thought I was just up in the clouds somewhere. "Gee, he's always doing these stupid things with all these ideas; I've no use for that." So when she finally moved out, it was such a relief! It was like this big ocean was sitting on my head and now it was all gone. And all of a sudden I was *breathing* much differently. My energy doubled in three or four days. My energy was just fantastic. I realized that I had been depleted by all that water.

THE SUN & THE MOON

Which brings us to one of the main considerations in comparisons, the Sun and the Moon. The Sun and the Moon have to be considered as a pair. They are a polarity, the positive and the negative poles of your whole nature, your whole personality, especially useful in assessing compatibility of two people where you really want a close intimacy. But there are different kinds of compatibility too. If you're doing a business comparison, you don't really need such wide-ranging compatibility as ideally you would like to find in a marriage or in a living together arrangement. If it's a business comparison, what you mainly need to look at are Saturn and Jupiter aspects, and Mercury; look at the communication—can they communicate with each other; Jupiter aspects often show whether you would be of benefit to each other financially, as well as whether you really trust each other. Problematical Neptune aspects should also be examined because those can show all kinds of misunderstandings, deception, and what not. For business purposes, you should *still* analyze the complete comparison; but sexual compatibility, for example, with your business partner would be unnecessary in most cases. You don't need the Sun and Moon things to be quite so compatible either, although it can certainly help the relationship.

Since most people are interested in doing the kind of comparisons that are appropriate for the most complete kinds of relationships (which are always a merger of male and female, because you've got the two kinds of cosmic polarities interchanging and living with each other day to day), then you've got to look at the Sun and Moon. My experience is that having compatible Sun signs is really nice. It's just what all those little basic textbooks say, and I'd say that's a good thing but it's not *necessary* for a good relationship. Ideally, at least one, either the Sun or Moon, should be in harmony with the other person's Sun. In other words (speaking in terms of an ideal), there has got to be at least one harmonious interchange between one person's Sun and the other person's Sun or Moon. There has to be something like that. It doesn't have to be an exact aspect. It could just be compatible elements. Say one person's Sun in Gemini and the other person's Moon is in Aquarius; right there you've got a flow of communication, a rapport with each other. What we experience with compatible Sun-Moon aspects or Sun-Sun aspects is a *mutual identity*. You *identify* with the other person and their nature.

The lunar aspects (especially the Moon-Moon aspects, such as Moon square Moon, Moon sextile Moon, or just how compatible one person's Moon is with the other person's Moon according to the elements, even if *no* close aspects are present) are especially important for living-together situations. I've seen quite often people who had very, very compatible chart comparisons in most areas—say 80% of the aspects were harmonious—but who had Moon square Moon or even Moon quincunx Moon, and they had a hard time living with each other. Sometimes they're super best friends or great lovers and they have everything going for them, but they can't live with each other. So often they just move apart and then they keep seeing each other for years and years and years. And then it even happens with people who are married who have those stressful Moon aspects, and they find they can't live with each other—mainly because the Moon shows your everyday moods, your everyday way of *reacting* to many things. And if you and your partner react in totally different or conflicting ways, you get to bugging each other—little tiny annoyances that tend to build up and up and up until there's a lot of emotional tension. In these cases, you can't quite be *comfortable* with that person. I've seen cases with people who are married and it looks by the comparison that they should be really good friends, and yet they move into separate quarters; sometimes they get divorced and sometimes not. Often for the rest of their lives they're in touch with each other in a compatible way, in a harmonious way.

ASPECTS IN COMPARISONS

Now one of the reasons that the close aspects are really important is that this is what has been called "shared experience." If you have a real close aspect—say within two degrees—between one of your planets and one of the other person's planets, you'll then often have what is sometimes called "shared experience." This is particularly true of the close conjunctions and oppositions. In other words, all this means is that transits will simultaneously activate both of your planets, and therefore whatever that close aspect indicates in the relationship will be activated. Uranus is now in early Scorpio. Say person A's Sun is in 6° Scorpio and person B's Venus is in 7° Scorpio. One is going to have Uranus hitting Venus and the other will have it hitting their Sun; and, since they will be hitting at the same time, they will have in many cases this "shared experience." In other words, what they will be going through will have such an impact on the other one that it's pretty safe to assume that there will be some change in the relationship too. It's not just each person doing an individual thing, but the relationship as a whole will go through some kind of transformation, some kind of awakening, hopefully, with a Uranus aspect.

You know Uranus is the "awakening" planet and when you have a real strong Uranian thing happening to you, it's very hard to sleep. It speeds you up so much; it speeds up your nervous system so much that it's really hard to get enough sleep. Your nervous system is being overwhelmed with Uranus energy so intensely that you really need sleep to recuperate, and yet it's just vibrating you so much that you can't get it. The only thing I find that gets me to sleep when Uranus is real strong is eating a whole lot. If I eat a huge bowl of granola or something I can crash into bed and get to sleep real fast. It's not a very healthy thing to do but none of the herbs or anything have worked. You know the so-called "tranquilizing" herbs often have no effect at times like this.

Anyways, these close aspects not only indicate a tremendously dynamic interchange between the two people but also show the potential for the shared experience. Sometimes it will seem, "Oh, my husband is changing, so I'm going through this." But if you look at the transits, you'll find that there are activated planets in both their charts.

JUPITER ASPECTS

I don't believe I've ever seen any marriage or real long-term close relationship where there wasn't at least one or two close conjunctions. And the longest and happiest relationships I've seen have involved at least one Jupiter conjunction. It isn't surprising, because Jupiter makes you tolerant and gives you positive energy. Neptune can also make you tolerant, somewhat compassionately and sometimes pityingly. From the relationships I've seen, it seems the Jupiter conjunction to the other person's Sun, Ascendant, Mercury, Venus, Mars—it's a really nice aspect to have. For one thing, the Jupiter person brings out the best in the other person's nature. I know just before my first book got written, I met someone whose Jupiter was conjunct my Mercury; and she thought my writings were just wonderful and I had never before had all this feedback. I had had positive feedback about my writing, but I'd never had anyone *push* me to write more. And that encouragement helped me become more determined to put energy into the writing that I really wanted to do anyway, but I lacked some motivation or confidence to really work at it until this person convinced me that I *had* to! With a lot of the stressful aspects, some people are *so* different that you wonder what in the hell is going on—how can they *stand* each other. And then you'll see that one has Jupiter conjunct the other person's Ascendant. They just *like* each other! If you get some of that positive Jupiter stuff going, especially Jupiter-Ascendant aspects or Jupiter-Sun or Jupiter-Moon, the people just *like* each other. They make each other feel good. They make each other feel expansive. They give each other energy too. So you see these Jupiter aspects can do a lot to ameliorate various difficult or stressful factors in the relationship.

STIMULATING ASPECTS

During this workshop, I'll occasionally mention three different types of aspects in comparisons—*stabilizing*, *exciting*, and *over-exciting*. Different types of aspects emphasize different qualities in a relationship, and the planets involved in any given aspect must be taken into consideration (as well as the aspect itself) if you're trying to classify a specific aspect in one of these categories. And also, it's somewhat a question of judgment because what would be an over-exciting aspect for a real mellow Taurean might not necessarily be over-exciting for an Aquarian. But these are useful categories when one is attempting to sum-up the general impression and tone of a given comparison. Basically, the *over-exciting* aspects tend to be some of the oppositions, and to some extent certain conjunctions. *Exciting* aspects can be any number of combinations between planets whose merged energies result in vitalization, increased energy flow, and intensified mutual interest and activity. *Stabilizing* aspects are often those involving Saturn, even some of the squares and conjunctions; but this category also includes many of the trines and sextiles which contribute to long-lasting and steady mutual commitment or appreciation. Some aspects may start out being exciting aspects and wind up being stabilizing aspects years later. The oppositions we'll now discuss can be either "exciting" or "over-exciting", but you can safely regard all oppositions as *stimulating* interchanges, whether or not they turn out to be *too* stimulating for the people to live with.

Of all the books on comparisons, Sargent's book* is extremely accurate and is my favorite. Basically it's an analysis of individual aspects. That's why I don't feel it's necessary in this workshop to go through details on every little aspect. Sargent has already done that better than I could anyway. But when you get familiar with the various kinds of aspects, you'll find that sometimes there are things that are really interesting, that are indicative of a very exciting rapport of energy, or exchange of energy, between the two people. It can be over-exciting, over-stimulating. The opposition, particularly in chart comparisons, should be regarded as an aspect of stimulation. It's not a "negative" aspect. It's not necessarily an indication of conflict as are squares and some of the stressful conjunctions. The squares, in general, are the most problematical of all aspects in natal charts, as well as in comparisons. Especially in comparisons, oppositions are very much *stimulating* aspects. It's a question of how much stimulation you can take and what is involved in that opposition.

SUN-MOON & MOON-MOON OPPOSITIONS

One of the best oppositions, in terms of a real rapport with the other person, is the Sun-Moon opposition or the Moon-Moon opposition, especially in relationships with the opposite sex. Often the people

---

* Lois H. Sargent's *How to Handle Your Human Relations*, published by AFA, Inc., and available from the publisher of this book.

just really like each other and really get a lot of energy from each other. I've seen so many cases where, say, someone with a Taurus Sun and Leo Moon will come in and say, "How come I'm always attracted to Aquarians?" Because the Aquarius Sun is opposite that Leo Moon. And they'll say, "All these books tell me that Taurus and Aquarius are really *incompatible.*" And on a level of basic energy flow that's true, but you have to look at the whole chart. Moon in Leo and an Aquarian Sun is often a very compatible thing. *Generally* you can say that Sun-Moon and Moon-Moon oppositions are some of the "best" oppositions in comparisons, in the sense that the two people complement each other and stimulate each other.

Q: Would that be true for oppositions by sign, or would it have to be by degrees?

A: I'd say by sign even, although the closer an aspect, the more intense the energy exchange.

SUN-SUN OPPOSITIONS

And then you could look at the opposition of the Suns too. It's not an uncommon relationship, but they tend to be better as friends than as marriage partners in most cases. (Again, there *are* many, many factors that could make it work fine as a marriage or as a long-lasting relationship.) But with Sun opposite Sun there's some kind of stimulation and complementary energy flow. I learned quite a bit about that when I was in college; I had a friend who had Sun and Moon in Aries. We could get more work done together in a shorter time than any two people I had ever seen. He had that Aries and I had the Libra Sun, and I could point out to him the order in which to do things; I would sort of plan it. We would both do the actual work, but somehow our energies blended so that we could accomplish so much it was just amazing. We rented this old fraternity house that was totally destroyed because the fraternity had been told by the landlord that the house was going to be demolished, and so they all had a big beer bust and decided that they would help demolish it. And so all the doors were smashed in and it was just a wreck. And within two weeks we had that place looking like a new house. It was just incredible. There's something about oppositions in comparisons that can be really nice, really stimulating, a unique kind of complementary energy flow.

However, if you live with someone whose Sun is opposite your Sun, there's often a pulling apart also. There's an attraction because you're complementary to each other, and yet you're also pulling in opposite directions! Some of the oppositions are much harder to live with than others. Oppositions between the fixed sign Suns are the hardest because they're the *stubbornest*. I've rarely seen a marriage between a Taurus Sun and a Scorpio Sun. Leo-Aquarius, I've seen only once. It's better for those fixed signs not to be with other fixed signs. But a Scorpio-Scorpio marriage is so common that it's just ridiculous. And often it's long-lasting too. Just the other day, for the first time I saw a Sun Scorpio-Sun Scorpio marriage actually breaking up. Those Scorpios are tenacious. So this is a definite exception to the idea of fixed signs being better off with non-fixed signs.

VENUS-VENUS & MARS-MARS OPPOSITIONS

There are other kinds of oppositions to examine too, but most oppositions are stimulating in comparisons. I use the word "stimulating" literally. It doesn't always mean "pleasant." Take Venus-Venus oppositions; you often find a mixture of attraction and repulsion. First of all there's attraction because your Venuses tune in and are kind of complementary. But often there's a certain repulsion too. Say your Venus is in Cancer, opposite someone's Venus in Capricorn. You can see that the attraction might be a stimulation *emotionally*, but also the Cancer sensitivity might be a little bit wary of the Capricorn aloofness. Capricorn Venus people are capable of great coldness and detachment. A Venus-Venus opposition is found occasionally in close relationships, although it's more common in short-term flirtations.

A Mars-Mars opposition is another one—very stimulating, very activating. Both people often feel a certain excitement from the relationship—very complementary to your whole Mars nature. But can you live with the other person? That puts it in a whole other light. If you're just going to work with them, if they'll just be a friend that you see now and then, then the Mars-Mars opposition is nothing to be particularly wary of at all. But if you're going to live with someone and try to harness your energies (Mars and Mars) toward a common goal, that's where you get into trouble. Most Mars conjunctions, Mars sextiles, or Mars trines in comparisons are excellent for harnessing your mutual energies—taking two people and saying, "We're going to accomplish this by harnessing our energies toward the same goal." And they can do it and they can work together very efficiently. Mars, among other things, shows your specific *methods of getting things done*. Mars says, "I want this; I want to accomplish this." It shows how you seek to assert your desires, how you seek to get things done. Mars opposition Mars and Mars square Mars show a problematical thing in terms of getting things done.

I once had this girlfriend whose Mars was square my Mars. I was constantly just kind of thrown back by her. I would be very intensely involved in doing something or saying something, and she would just bolt up and split, walk out the door. It would kind of jolt me. Mars square Mars was almost exact in the comparison. Naturally, that relationship didn't last long. And that was fortunate. That's one way to learn chart comparisons—have lots of relationships with different people. Also, if you do astrological counseling, it's incredible for learning chart comparisons. After the person leaves, look at the comparison. If you look at it beforehand, you might be too prejudiced. It is really hard to know in advance how things are going to work out; but once they've already been there, then look at the comparison and you'll learn quite a bit.

MERCURY ASPECTS

Look in Sargent's book about Mercury squares and Mercury oppositions, which traditionally are the most problematical. Personally, I think that that is true, but also having Mercury in incompatible elements is just as problematical. In other words, say one person's Mercury is in Cancer and the other person's is in Leo; there's no major stressful aspect between them, but right there it shows that the two people think in different ways, they perceive things in different ways, they express their ideas in different ways, and therefore they may have some difficulty in coming to an agreement on their common goals or plans.

Q: Would you say something about someone with Mercury at 0 degrees and some odd minutes of Libra, right at the cusp? When you're doing a chart comparison, how would you look at that? Is it more Libra or Virgo?

A: Well, if it's mathematically in Libra, I would put the emphasis on Libra; but when it's right on the cusp there's always the possibility that the other sign's tone is still there.

Q: Well, if you were doing a chart comparison and that was the problem . . .

A: What was the problem? Communication or something?

Q: Say we're doing a marriage comparison. In the wife's chart, Mercury was 0 degrees and 28 minutes of Libra. How would you read that?

A: I'd have to compare it to the other chart. I would probably treat it as Libra, especially because Libra is a more outgoing sign than Virgo. The outgoing signs tend to dominate the inward signs in obvious expressions of energy, except in the case of Scorpio which is the exception to everything. But with that kind of question, you've got to look at the individual case. My father was born August 23rd and his Sun is technically 0 degrees and about 20 minutes of Virgo; but he's a Leo, Leo, Leo! People that just read Sun sign columns also know he's a super Leo. And his Sun is not even mathematically in Leo, but Leo predominates because it's so close to the cusp and Leo is so much more of an obvious dominating influence (especially much more so than Virgo, which is more inner and humble, you might say). The main thing is to relate it to something specific, because then you can see how it's working out. Say you're doing a comparison, you could still do the aspects with—for example—Mercury, which would tell you quite a bit; but also you could *inquire about the communication as the person experiences it!*

There's a book out by Lois Rodden called *The Mercury Method of Chart Comparison,* * and all it does is analyze Mercury—Mercury aspects to every other planet. It doesn't supercede the kind of thing that Sargent has done, but it's quite an interesting book. I find it to be accurate in many ways. For instance, what she says about Mercury square Mercury I've found to be very true. It's something like: "With Mercury square Mercury you'll often find that people initially will be somewhat wary of each other." Mercury, like Gemini, is spontaneously friendly. Mercury makes connections, Mercury makes quick connections with people. But if Mercury is square someone else's Mercury, there may be some reticence to involve yourself with them too quickly. As she says here, with Mercury square Mercury, "There is an initial obstacle or incompatibility that stands between you. That difference may be an attitude or circumstances. Change in understanding is needed for the breakthrough to communication. However, once that breakthrough is made, a bond is built that is mutually stimulating. However, unless

---

* Rodden's book is published in hardcover and is available from the publisher of this book.

both the people make that effort, they will regard each other with a degree of wary formality." I thought that was very accurate because, with Mercury square Mercury, you don't have that quick, friendly "Oh hi, how are you?" and start talking. There's this sense that you're interested in each other; but the Mercuries don't hook up perfectly, so you've got to somehow work your way into the relationship. Mercury-square-Mercury relationships can be some of the finest relationships you can have, people who have a deep bond of enduring friendship. The relationship can include problems, but the give and take leads to growth of understanding.

The main thing that I find with Mercury square Mercury is that the people do think entirely differently; they express their thoughts totally differently. It's mainly when it's a real close square that I would expect it to be at least a little problematical in the two people coming to an agreement on anything. If it's a real close square, you'll often find that they will interrupt each other. It's a stimulating aspect, but it's Mercury stimulating Mercury to *talk*. So when one is talking, it's stimulating the other to talk. And then that Mercury starts talking and it stimulates the other one to start talking. They cut each other off repeatedly.

Q: I think that may be a language problem in that they don't hear what the other person is saying . . . seems like they would need an interpreter.

A: In the worst cases it's like that, yes. Again, it depends on how aware the people are and how detached they are from their Mercury, you might say. If in your natal chart Mercury is conjunct your Sun quite closely, then a Mercury-Mercury square in a chart comparison would be much more problematical than if your Mercury was separate from your Sun. If your Mercury was separated from your Sun by quite a few degrees, you, consciously, (the Sun) would be detached from the Mercury-Mercury problems. So you could just kind of laugh at them. Two of my best friends have Mercury square my Mercury. And I cannot say that the communication has always been perfect with either of them, but it's always been real interesting, and "enduring friendship" describes these relationships accurately. They do have a very. different approach to things.

Also, it's how patient you can be. If you have Mercury in Aries, for example, and have an impatient tongue and an impatient mind, chances are when someone's Mercury squares your Mercury you're not going to like it too much because you won't be able to wait. I know one person whose Mercury squares my Mercury and the few times I've ever talked with her we both just started going crazy with talking. We start cutting each other off repeatedly until finally I just sit back and give up. And she blabs and blabs and blabs. It's not always *communication*, though; that's the thing. Two people often think they're communicating because there's lots of talking. This is also true of the opposition of Mercury to Mercury. They think, "Gee, it's always so much fun to talk to you," but they're not always communicating. They're just getting a kick out of that stimulation, but wait until they have some problems and have to iron out their problems by being logical and by *really* communicating and listening. That's where the Mercury-Mercury squares and oppositions get much more problematical. As a matter of fact, that Cancer woman that I was with once had her Mercury in Cancer square my Libra Mercury. And the communication there was just hopeless. But of course I think too that's the difference between Cancer and Libra, not just the square aspect. It's such a different mentality than Libra. Whereas all the good friends I have whose Mercury squares my Mercury have Mercury in Capricorn. And Capricorn and Libra are quite similar in many ways. Saturn is exalted in Libra; they're both very practical; they both want to keep things organized and to keep things clear.

Q: You're talking about the square?

A: Yes. I'm saying the square between the Mercuries in those two signs (Libra and Capricorn) I haven't noticed as very problematical. But the square between a Cancer Mercury and a Libra Mercury I've always seen as a severe communication difficulty. So I suppose this just brings out one more factor in a comparison; just like in a natal chart, you've got to look at the whole thing right down to what signs are involved. Astrology is really impossible, isn't it? It's so incredibly complex. I'm glad it's also so absolutely simple, once you begin to perceive the fundamental principles. In most cases, though, regardless of the signs, just doing the closest aspects, you'll find so much information that you'll have plenty to work with. In my experience, in at least 90% of the cases, the people whose charts are being used can identify with the meaning of the closest aspects. Just pick up Sargent's book and start reading out of that; you'll identify with it.

INTERACTION OF ENERGY FIELDS

On this outline here I have the word *interaspects*. Under *2a*—"how the two energy fields of the two people interact. Look first at all close interaspects." *Interaspects* are simply inter-chart aspects. *Interaspects* is a term that Kenneth Negus started using. He's done a lot of work in synastry and chart comparisons. So interaspects are inter-chart aspects within 4 degrees of exact. And then look too at how the two people *feed* each other—look at the elements. Is one person lacking some element? If so, does the other person balance that out? There's something else to look at too. You pay attention not just to *lacks*, but does one person have problems with planets in a certain element? Say you had two or three planets in Sagittarius but they were in square to everything else in your chart, and say that's all you had in fire in your chart, all this Sagittarius. You may be more attracted to an Aries or a Leo than to a Sagittarius because a Sun Sagittarius person would activate all of your squares. They would activate this tension that you already have. But you may be attracted to people with lots of Aries or Leo because that would create trines to your Sagittarian energy, so you could start to *express* that energy that is all blocked up within yourself. Say someone has Scorpio planets squaring an Aquarius planet and he or she may be very attracted to people with planets in Pisces or Cancer, because what is problematical for the person (shown by the squares) and difficult to express and to fulfill could be shared with these watery people. That is, the person's Scorpio energy could easily blend with another person's Cancer or Pisces energy. It wouldn't even have to be the Sun or Moon; it could be Venus or Mars or Mercury that is involved and that is ordinarily hard to express. So that's something that you find also.

In looking at the elements, it's not just a question of "do you lack a certain element and, if so, does the other person have it?" it's also "do you have some difficulty expressing a certain element, a particular energy?" Do you have some difficulty in *feeding your needs* in a certain dimension of life, and—if so—would this relationship with this other person help to satisfy those needs? A trine is often a mutually *feeding* aspect; it can thus be mutually nourishing. If you lack a certain element, that doesn't *necessarily* mean that you want to be with someone who has that element attunement because it may be hard for you. You may be *attracted* to people with that element, but you may also get really tired of it because you're not naturally attuned to it. They might just really bring you down.

Say you are an earthy type and you lack fire and you try to get a relationship going with someone who's real fiery. It may be very stimulating for a while, but it may also be very upsetting to you because in your nature you have no fire; you don't have that spiritedness. Or say you lack air and you're trying to get a relationship going with someone who's real airy; there may be a short-term curiosity for you, but eventually it's possible that you'll find them rather infuriating. Because if you lack air, that means your energies are into your emotions (water), your practical considerations (earth), and your actions (fire). And the last thing that really matters to you is intellectual speculation and gathering of data.

Perhaps the most valuable thing about astrology is that it shows that everyone has a niche in the creation. So the most important thing is giving people *confidence*. All children should be given lots of support to express whatever they are, because then they'll be confident and they'll be inwardly happy. Confidence is an important thing that anyone needs. There's no need to be down on Aries, Taurus, Capricorn, whatever, because they're all universal principles that have definite value. And yet, because of a certain conditioning, karma or whatever, almost all people are down on themselves in some way, in conflict about certain of their qualities, various parts of their nature. I think understanding the "overexciting aspects" will help to explain that.

It's particularly true of *oppositions* that they can be a little *overstimulating*. Discussing "overexciting aspects," you can also bring in Uranus aspects because Uranus by its nature is *excitement*. And if you get *Mars-Uranus* conjunctions, squares, or oppositions in a comparison, that is an overexciting aspect in most cases. I've seen two couples where they had *two* of them. They had a "double whammy" with Mars and Uranus. They had Mars conjunct Uranus and Mars square Uranus in the comparison, and they were always fighting. They were always at each other's throats, always disagreeing. That's an aspect of considerable insistence on your own way of doing things without any restraint and generally shows that you don't want to cooperate with the other person, or simply that you're unable to.

Basically the "stabilizing" aspects are the harmonious aspects. The stabilizing aspects *specifically* are the harmonious aspects with Saturn. In other words, *some* of the conjunctions of Saturn and the sextiles and trines of Saturn are very stabilizing. In a way, you can even say that the squares and oppositions of Saturn *in a comparison chart* are stabilizing and that's true, but they can be *overly stabilizing*. Saturn is always the structuring principle, and Saturn naturally can also get rigid. We'll get to Saturn more later in terms of karma, etc., but my experience has been that in marriages (that is, *legal bond marriages*: that's coming under the domain of Saturn), 8 out of 10 have a very strong Saturn conjunction, square, or opposition. And those *are* stabilizing aspects, but they can be over stabilizing too. By "over stabilizing" I mean there could be so much emphasis on security in the relationship that it could become a stultifying experience; it could become a deadening sort of experience, since Saturn is always able to squeeze the life out of anything if you go too far in terms of discipline or trying to achieve "security." Everything is a question of balance, says Libra. It's obviously a cosmic truth though. If you do without Saturn, then you have no order, no form, and you have chaos. So you start using the formative or discipline principle of Saturn and you have a nice little organization. Then if you use too much discipline, you start squeezing the life out of everything and everybody. And so this is what I mean by overly stabilizing.

If you have too much emphasis on Saturn aspects in a comparison (especially the stressful Saturn aspects), you'll have too much of an inclination on the part of one or both people to have security, to derive security from the relationship. And in order to ensure or try to ensure that security, they will often try to stop the other person from growing, to stop the other person from changing. It's often the Saturn person that will do that. That is the worst manifestation of it. I'm not saying that with one Saturn aspect you should start freaking out or creating problems for yourself, because, like I say, most marriages have at least one very powerful Saturn aspect involved—one person's Saturn and the other person's Ascendant or personal planet; and very often it's a conjunction, although squares and oppositions are not uncommon. I'll talk more about that later when we get to the subject of karma because I think you've often got a real definite karmic payoff when you have such Saturn aspects in a comparison. And obviously, any marriage could be considered a karmic payoff. Why would anyone want to live with just one other person? ... unless they owed them something or were very deeply attached.

Exciting aspects are primarily the more harmonious aspects with Uranus and with Jupiter. You could also throw in some others ... a Sun-Moon trine, or a Sun-Moon opposition, is also exciting because it's not just excitement; it's more of a kind of positive energy that you get from it. But exciting aspects (particularly enthusiastic aspects) tend to be the harmonious aspects of Uranus and of Jupiter. Uranus trine somebody's Venus, or Jupiter conjunct somebody's Mars, and similar interchanges—those are aspects of energy, enthusiasm, and excitement.

PUTTING IT ALL TOGETHER

At the end of a comparison it's often good to review your overall impression after you go through all this data and all these details. Is the overall emphasis on excitement, is it on stability, is it maybe *too much* on excitement and stimulation, or is the emphasis too much on security? Again, it's a matter of judgment. There's one thing that's valuable that at least a few of you have already seen. I just thought I would show you how I keep track of things in a chart comparison. (Puts example on board—see Illustration No. 1). Does everybody know that in a chart comparison you not only look at the aspects and the interchange of energy shown by the aspects and by the elements, but you also use the houses? There's an article I wrote a few years ago on how to use the houses in a comparison. (See Section III of this book.) What you do is to take the planets out of one person's chart and put them in the same zodiacal degrees in the other person's chart. (Shows an example on board and explains.) You use the *aspects* of all the planets, and you pay most attention to the *house positions* of all the planets but Uranus, Neptune and Pluto, unless one of those three planets conjuncts an angle of the other person's chart—that's important!

I do comparisons between any *two* people, because a relationship by definition is a one-to-one thing; although you can study families as a group and see in some cases tremendously obvious astrological themes. Another thing about aspects in comparisons—it's just like in the natal chart—the most important aspects are those that involve the *personal planets or the Ascendant*. For example, in a comparison, say someone's Saturn squares your Uranus; that is not so important as those configurations or aspects which involve a personal planet. With Saturn square Uranus, you'd probably feel it as, "Oh, that person gets in the way of my freedom" or something similar; and it may also be that that person makes me express my creativity in a more practical way. Squares can be very positive things. But if you have, for example, the *Moon* conjunct Uranus in your natal chart and then someone's Saturn *squares that conjunction,* that's a real doozy. It's much more important because a personal planet—the Moon—is involved. It's where the *personal planets* are that you have that *immediate experience.*

Illustration No. 1

Sample *Chart Comparison Data Sheet*

A. *"Ned"*		B. *"Norrie"*
Natal planets of person requesting comparison or who is experiencing the most problems.	A's planet falls in this house in B's chart.	Planets in B's chart that are importantly related to A's planet in far-left column.
(1) ♄	6th	□ ☽ ♃ ♅ ; ☌ ♀ ; ☌ ♂ ; w. △ Asc ; ⚹ ♆
(2) ♂	8th	☍ ♄ ; ⚹ Asc. ; □ ♀ ; incomp. ♂
(3) ♀	9th	☌ ♃ ; w. △ ♄ ; incomp. ♀ ; w. □ ♂
(4) ☿	10th	□ ♄ incomp. ♀ ; □ ♆ ; □ ☽ ♃ ♅ ; ☍ ♃
(5) Asc.	3rd	comp. Asc. ; △ ☉ ; w. □ ☽ ♃ ♅ ; ⚹ ♃ ; △ ♀

Explanatory Notes on Use of Data Sheet

1) This is just an example of how to write out the information used in a comparison in astrological shorthand, structured and organized so it's quickly accessible during a consultation. The data above are not from real charts but are only used for illustrative purposes. (See Illus. No. 3 for a complete Data Sheet.) In a complete comparison, *every* planet and the MC and Ascendant will be listed in the left-hand column. After one draws out the above Data Sheet, Norrie's planets are then put into Ned's natal houses, but all aspects will remain the same.

2) EXPLANATION OF ABOVE CODES & ABBREVIATIONS:

   a) One underline means this aspect is either fairly close to exact (i.e., within 4° or so) or especially important within the context of the entire comparison.

   b) Two underlines indicates that this aspect is either exact (or within 1° of exactitude) or that it is of outstanding importance in some other way.

   c) "w." before an aspect indicates that it is *wide* (i.e., 7° or more from exactitude) and so of dubious importance except in a general way as it fits into the entire pattern; and it may be ineffective.

   d) When an aspect has none of the above three codes, it is probably close enough to be effective, but it's certainly not particularly strong. This is used either for aspects that are within 7° of exact but not within 4° of exact *or* sometimes for aspects involving no personal planet, which are less important.

   e) "comp." and "incomp." show the compatibility of the two planets by element placement only and are used only with personal planets being related to other personal planets (or the Ascendant). This indicates an overall blend but not specific intensity.

3) Ordinarily, the planets in the left-hand column that rule that person's Sun, Moon, Ascendant, and MC *signs* are so designated so that one pays special attention to them during the consultation. (See Illus. No. 3 for example.)

4) "DOUBLE WHAMMIES": In the example, two aspects are circled and connected by a line. Ordinarily, I do each such "double whammy" (or repeated interchange of identical planets) in a different colored ink so that they stand out quickly at a glance. In this example, Ned's Saturn is *exactly* opposite Norrie's Mercury, and her Saturn is square his Mercury. Hence, you have two interchanges of the same planets in the comparison, which is always important, even if one aspect is wide. The fact that one aspect here is *exact* makes it all the more significant.

Illustration No. 1

Explanation of Each Line in Data Sheet

The following are "translations" of each horizontal line in the preceding Data Sheet, so that the reader can understand this method of organizing the data needed in a comparison and hopefully design his or her own data sheets for regular use. Note that once you're familiar with the structure of this type of Data Sheet, the headings at the top of each column are not necessary. They're used here only to clarify what goes in which column.

Line 1—Ned's Saturn, when placed in the same degree of the zodiac in Norrie's chart, falls in her natal 6th house. His Saturn is square her Moon & Uranus, *exactly* opposite her Mercury, conjunct her Mars, *widely* trine her Ascendant, and in a fairly close sextile to her Jupiter.

Line 2—Ned's Mars, when placed in Norrie's chart, falls in her natal 8th house. His Mars is opposite her Saturn, fairly closely sextile her Ascendant, square her Venus, and is incompatible by element with her Mars.

Note that, since his Mars is in a major aspect (a square) with her Venus but not with her Mars, you only note the general compatibility or incompatibility between his Mars and her Mars. The relationship between his Mars and her Venus speaks for itself—defined by the square between them. But in all cases, each person's Venus *and* Mars are related (either by major aspect or just generally by element) to both Venus and Mars of the other person.

Line 3—Ned's Venus falls in Norrie's 9th house and is *exactly* conjunct her Jupiter, *widely* trine her Saturn, incompatible by element placement with her Venus, and *widely* square her Mars.

Line 4—Ned's Mercury falls in Norrie's 10th house and is square her Saturn, incompatible by element placement with her Mercury, square her Neptune, square her Moon & Uranus, and is in a fairly close opposition to her Jupiter.

Note that Mercury is *always* compared to the other person's Mercury, either by major aspect relationship or by compatibility of elements. Likewise, each person's Sun and Moon are *always* related to the other person's Sun and Moon. This procedure is unique to the personal planets and the Ascendant, for the outer five planets' relationships with other planets are noted down specifically *only* if a major aspect is formed.

Line 5—Ned's Ascendant falls in Norrie's 3rd house and is compatible by element with her Ascendant, in a fairly close trine to her Sun, *widely* square her Moon & Uranus, sextile her Jupiter, and *exactly* trine her Venus.

Note that the Ascendant's house position and close aspects are always crucial and show something essential in the relationship. And therefore, the two Ascendants are always related to each other, at least by element compatibility, since such an interchange reveals much about their ability to express themselves spontaneously when together and *especially when in public.*

ADDITIONAL COMMENTS: a) Note that a quick scan of lines 2, 4, and 5 reveal immediately that Ned's Mars and Mercury may be quite frustrated with Norrie since his Mars and Mercury energies do not flow smoothly with her, but that his Ascendant is not blocked or inhibited with her whatsoever—which may be equally or more important. Gaining such quick information from the Data Sheet is one of its values, since one can often pinpoint precisely where a problem lies or what is motivating frustrated or discontented behavior.

b) Another important use of this kind of data sheet is that, by going down the middle column, you can see what houses are activated and also what *types* of houses (e.g., fire houses or angular houses) are especially energized in the comparison. For example, Ned's Saturn, Venus, and Ascendant all fall in Norrie's cadent houses, and his Saturn and Mercury both fall in her earth houses.

The person who requested the comparison or—if both request it—the person who's experiencing the most problems in the relationship—that person's planets should be put in the left-hand column (see Illustration No. 1) because, once you have all this data written down in columns, you can look at any one factor in that person's chart and see how that energy, how that urge, is expressed *with the other person* and how the needs shown by that planet are fulfilled. For example, say Ned comes in and says, "You know, this relationship is really great except I'm always horny—this lady really frustrates me sexually." All you've got to do, then, is go down the left-hand column to his Mars and read across what the aspects are to his Mars from the other person's chart—in other words, what kind of energy flow is happening between his Mars and the other person's planets. Without the person saying anything, very often all you've got to do is scan one of these lines horizontally, and if *any one planet* is in primarily "stressful" or challenging aspects to all sorts of different things in the other person's chart (see Mars in Illustration No. 1), you know that you're onto something that you should bring up in the consultation—because you know then that this energy is somewhat frustrated or irritated in this particular relationship.

In fact, when you systematically write these things out in columns, it's always a good idea to look at how Mars and Mars, Venus and Venus, Mercury and Mercury line up, even if there's no aspect between them. That means write down the compatibility or lack of it *just by element placement*, even if Mars is in no close aspect with the other person's Mars. In fact, with Mars and Venus, I always relate them by element to each other too. If, however, Mars is in a close aspect to Venus, you don't necessarily have to relate Mars to Venus by element, because you've already got something to work with right there.

So just by scanning these lines, you can often find big things. Like very often you'll find all kinds of really nice aspects, harmonious things, and the people have a good sex life and everything, and then you get to, say, Mercury; and Mercury will be square or opposite everything in sight (see Mercury in Illustration No. 1), and so immediately, rather than doing what psychologists and marriage counselors and psychiatrists do—mainly waste hours and hours and many dollars—you can immediately know that one of the major problems in the relationship is communication, particularly that this person undoubtedly feels that his ideas are not understood, are not accepted, not listened to by the other person. Because everything else in her chart seems to be resisting his Mercury, shown by all the squares, oppositions, etc.

ASPECTS WITH THE ASCENDANT

Lois Sargeant points out, and this seems to be true also from what I've gathered, that "Most important in judging attraction is the aspect between the Ascendant in one chart and the planets of the other." And that's why, when you do a comparison, all the major aspects to the Ascendant should be included and, I personally feel, even the quincunx and semi-sextile. Now, naturally there's no point in doing it if the Ascendant concerned is not accurate, if you don't know the birth time very accurately. But if you do, then it's definitely worth doing.

Q: If she feels it's so important, why didn't she put the aspects with the Ascendant in her book?

A: I'd like to know that too.

Q: Yeah, that's really—she totally neglects them. It's like she forgot it.

A: It would have been nice to put it in. But basically, it's easy to interpret aspects with the Ascendant in comparisons. All you've got to know is: if it's your Ascendant, any planet in close major aspect to your Ascendant *tones*, or puts a kind of vibration on, how you're trying to express your *whole self*. In other words, if somebody's Saturn conjuncts your Ascendant, you're going to be *disciplined* by that person. There may be great loyalty, but they're gonna also put some heavy things on you—not necessarily bad; you may learn great things from it, but they might stomp on you a bit too, while you're being "formed" and tested (and perhaps ultimately strengthened) by them. You might find that your physical vitality, even, is lessened by that person, at least for a while, until you can meet the test with strength of character. But say somebody's Jupiter aspects your Ascendant (this could be by almost any major aspect), you'll feel it—optimism, positive energy, expansion—the same with the Sun, particularly if somebody's Sun conjuncts or trines your Ascendant, which gives it the same element as your Ascendant.

If Saturn is *trining* your Ascendant—you're kind of slowed down by that person, but it will probably be a constructive influence, too. But definitely they would temper your mode of self-expression, but in a way that wouldn't be stifling. But if Saturn's *conjunct* your Ascendant, there's the tendency for it to be stifling, at least until you "get your *Self* together" and define who you are. The relationship tends to be something that is really important for a long time with all Saturn-Ascendant aspects. In other words, if Saturn is opposite the Ascendant, it's going to be conjunct the Descendant, so there's something very *important* about that relationship. And most likely, if the people get into a relationship, it'll last for a while, because there's something important there to be worked out, or paid off, or whatever.

Say Mars is conjunct your Ascendant, or in any close aspect, then there's an energizing type of thing that goes on, *especially* if it's a conjunction or trine. The other person then will naturally push you to express yourself more dynamically. This friend I had once, many years ago, had Mars trine my Ascendant; and he really pushed me to assert myself, to express myself more. I got a lot of confidence from him.

To finish Sargent's quote: "Most important in judging attraction is the aspect between the Ascendant in one chart and the planets in the other. This is true not only for marriage, but for all comparisons. Unless the Ascendant or Descendant of one horoscope combines with the planets of the other by sign—not necessarily by a close aspect, but by sign—it is doubtful that the attraction would result in marriage." In other words, by sign or by actual conjunction, there's got to be some link between the Ascendant or the Descendant of one chart—or the rulers of the Ascendant or Descendant—and your own chart. And I would say such aspects are almost always there not just for marriage, but for it to wind up as any long-lasting partnership, whether it's marriage, a long-term business thing, or even a long-term living-together thing (that would depend on how long it was, and your *attitude* towards it).

Living-together relationships are basically fifth house things in most cases—the emphasis being on *pleasure*. And a lot of people say, "Oh, I don't see any difference between living together and being married." But people I know who are into astrology, and who have lived with a number of people and have also been married, tell a different story. Listen to them sometime. You'll hear a really different number. The seventh house is so different from the fifth. One friend of mine, for example, he's got a bunch of Gemini planets in his seventh house, okay? You think he can stand being with one partner? Of course not. Especially with Venus and Mars in Gemini in the seventh. So, he tried getting married once. He has four planets in his fifth house. He likes to have little flirtations and love affairs. But when it comes to marriage, he just gets real nervous and jumpy. And the only time he was married, he married somebody whom he had been living with for about four years. They were getting along just great, and they were real happy with each other. And as soon as he got married, the relationship started to go down the tubes. And in no time he got a divorce, in less than a year. And he said—he knows quite a bit of astrology—with his chart he's much better off just living with people and not messing with the seventh house anymore than he has to.

For other people—you get people who have a packed seventh house, and particularly if the Sun is there or the Moon or some other major thing, generally they have to sign on the dotted line, so to speak, to make some kind of legal contract in order to really deal with their karma in that area. It's funny to me that the fifth and seventh houses are basically in harmony—planets in those two houses should be in sextile, theoretically, but it's interesting that in many cases, you'll find squares between the fifth and seventh house planets. This is assuming you're not using the equal house system. And that makes a lot more sense to me, in many people's lives, because oftentimes they have big hassles between marriage, living together, and love affairs. Love affairs are much more "fun;" they're a fifth house thing. Marriage is work, seventh house. See, the Libra-seventh house principle, among other things, always deals with work, with a *working partnership*. Saturn is exalted in Libra, you know.

Okay. (Referring to *2c* on printed outline.) "Note that any aspect involving at least one personal planet or the Ascendant or Descendant is most important." That was pretty much discussed already. (Continuing to read *2d* on outline.) "Every *conjunction*, of either person's Ascendant, Descendant, or the ruler of the Ascendant or Descendant to another person's planet will be important in indicating the overall tone of the relationship." That's basically what Lois Sargent has written.

USING THE HOUSES IN COMPARISONS

Okay, then we get to the houses .... Everybody knows how to take the planets out of one chart, then, and put them into the same degrees of another person's chart, right? Is there anybody who doesn't understand that? That article (Section III of this book) explains that in detail, anyway. Okay, in this case, take Ned's planets and put them into Norrie's chart. That shows what impact Ned's energies have on Norrie's life. It also shows, according to what houses they fall in, what areas of her life are energized or activated by him, and by his influence on her. However, you don't usually have to worry about the house position of Uranus, Neptune, and Pluto, unless it makes a close conjunction to a planet or angle. Say you take Ned's Uranus and it falls in her sixth house—as long as it doesn't make a close conjunction, you don't want to waste time interpreting that one isolated factor . . . *unless the people are of quite different ages.* See, if you're doing a comparison of a couple that are within three or four years of age of each other, Uranus, Neptune, and Pluto's *comparison* house positions just don't matter that much because they're always going to be identical with the natal chart position. In other words, if Norrie has Uranus in her natal sixth house and Ned is only one year older, in almost all cases his natal Uranus—by zodiacal degree—also falls in her sixth house; so there's no point in spending a lot of time on things that are not going to give you important information. I'm not saying they're totally meaningless, but what you've got to look for are the things that are really different and that signify major individual differences.

However, Jupiter and Saturn's house placements you always look at in comparisons. The houses of the other person's chart that they fall in are very important, and, in addition to Jupiter and Saturn, as it says here, (*2e* of outline) "the houses where the other person's Sun, Moon, or ruler of the Sun sign or rising sign fall are especially important." In other words, if you look at your chart and you're doing comparisons between you and other people, it's the houses of your chart where other people's Suns, Moons, or the rulers of the Ascendant or the Sun sign fall that indicate a lot of activation and energy from those other people. Say somebody has Taurus rising and therefore Venus is the "ruler of the chart" or ruler of the Ascendant, then the house in your chart where their Venus falls would be very much emphasized; that area of your life would be activated by dealing with that other person. Likewise, say somebody's Sun falls in your fourth house—your whole fourth house *lights up,* your whole fourth house is energized, which you may like or you may hate. The person may make you just want to stay home all the time, and you might not always like that. But if you have natal Venus in your natal fourth house, the other person's Sun might conjunct your Venus and you may just love staying home with that person.

PREDOMINANCE OF SPECIFIC ASPECTS

"Any inter-aspects that are repeated twice are always indicative of a major type of energy exchange between the two people. (See *2f* on outline.) This is called a 'double whammy' by some clever souls." This means *any* interchange of two basic principles that is repeated twice in the comparison. The identical aspect doesn't have to be repeated. This kind of double clue to an essential quality of the relationship is more common than you might think, and it's always important. An example of this would be if my Venus was conjunct your Jupiter while your Venus was trine (or even square or quincunx) my Jupiter. Another example would be if my Moon was trine your Mercury and then your Moon was conjunct my Mercury. Again you'd have a strong indication of a dominant theme in the relationship, as well as a pointed symbol of specifically active energy flow between the two people. And quite often you even find instances where the exact same aspect is repeated twice—say your Uranus is trine my Sun and my Uranus is also trine your Sun. When you have this kind of "double whammy," you'd have to be blind not to see it and foolish not to emphasize it in your evaluation of the relationship.

Okay, another thing is *2g* in the outline. "Likewise, if there is a great predominance of a certain type of aspect *with one particular planet*, for example, many harmonious aspects with Jupiter (or many stressful aspects with Saturn or many trines with Uranus or whatever), this tone of energy exchange colors the entire relationship." I don't know how else to express that, except how it is there. But basically, say you have—in comparison between your chart and somebody else's— many harmonious aspects with Jupiter; right there, that will go a long way toward making that relationship enjoyable and liveable, and I would give it a lot of weight in terms of any kind of judgment or evaluation of whether those two people were compatible—even if they also have lots of stressful aspects. A lot of harmonious aspects with Jupiter (including the conjunction) can give the whole relationship a tone of growth and positiveness and optimism, and the people will often be tolerant of each other's negative or incompatible qualities. For another example, if you have a lot of Uranus emphasis in the comparison, by way of trines and sextiles, the whole relationship has a tone of excitement, openness, experimentation, and the people tend to find each other constantly *interesting*, no matter how erratic or frustrating they may be to each other in various ways. If a comparison is dominated by many Uranus squares and oppositions (and some of the conjunctions), that tone of erraticism and exasperation and undependability will be powerful.

Now, as the outline says in paragraph *2h*, what kind of impression predominates after you've examined all the major factors? A good balance in most ways? Too much emphasis on excitement and stimulation? Too much emphasis on security? Does either person provide what the other lacks, especially in terms of the elements? If so, are the people *too* different? Can they handle each other's differences? You know, sometimes you find people who are just too different. They're attracted to each other because they *are* so different, and in some ways, therefore, they can *complement* each other; but if they're too different—after some time—as both people grow and individualize even more, they may find themselves just growing more apart all the time, especially if they started pretty far apart to begin with.

One other thing to mention, too, is the levels of attraction between people; I suppose that's pretty obvious to everybody, at least everybody here. . . . It's amazing how unobvious it is to a lot of people in the world. Because so many people get involved with other people and get married to other people where the level of attraction is really basically just physical. Sometimes you'll have it basically physical and emotional, like all Venus and Mars stuff—there'll be all kinds of Venus and Mars aspects, but the Suns and Moons won't have anything in common. It's like there are these two souls, whose bodies are always resonating with each other, but their higher selves, and their minds and egos have nothing in common. And that kind of relationship gets rather dull, rather quickly . . . unless, of course, the people are just really into a heavy number with emotional and sexual stuff. And of course you also often find relationships, especially in marriage, where the two people may have found each other powerfully intriguing because of a mutual sense of identity (shown mainly by Sun & Moon links between them) or because of especially interesting communication (Mercury aspects), but where the emotional and sexual energies just don't mix. This can also be a real problem that tests both people.

CHART COMPARISONS & KARMA

In comparisons, you can find many things that relate to karma, assuming of course that reincarnation is true, which I believe in. I don't know if everyone here believes in that, but it seems to me that many relationships make a lot more sense when you view them from that consideration. In terms of karma, you can go on forever if you believe that karma is indeed a cosmic law and therefore that everything is due to cause and effect and that everything we experience, including all aspects of life and all aspects of relationships, is intertwined with this karmic give and take and cause and effect. Then you can view everything in the chart that way, and so it becomes almost an absurdity.

However, there are some things that seem to be especially and obviously related to past life things, situations wherein the people can usually feel, or identify with the idea that "I kind of owe somebody something," or "that person really has something over me," or "that person has power over me."

So the first thing to look at is Saturn, naturally. First of all, whatever house someone's Saturn falls in—in your own chart—always indicates an area of life where they can teach you some lessons. But those lessons can be extremely positive; you don't have to look at Saturn as a negative thing—like, "Oh, George's Saturn falls in my second house, and that's why we've always been poor, ever since we got married." There may be some truth to that, but what's behind that? What can you learn from that experience? Many friends of mine have had Saturn falling in my fifth house, but there have been some really good lessons there too; and in fact, one person whose Saturn fell in my fifth house really taught me how to enjoy myself more, even though Saturn supposedly is restriction. On the contrary, he didn't really restrict that at all. He was a Sun-Moon Taurus, and Sun and Moon in Taurus know how to enjoy themselves. And they know how to relax.

But anyway, just take Saturn aspects. If somebody's Saturn hits your personal planets or the Ascendant—especially, though, the Ascendant, Sun, Moon, or Venus—there's usually a strong attachment there. And by attachment, I just mean that literally. It's not good or bad, necessarily; it's just an attachment. There's some kind of security thing that you have with that person. How it's often experienced is: that person whose Saturn hits your Sun, Moon, Ascendant, and so forth, has something *over* you. In some cases they have you under their thumb. Saturn is authority, right? They have authority over you. Then generally, at least at the beginning of the relationship in this lifetime, you automatically feel that you owe them something—they have authority over you. You either owe them something, or you respect them, or you look up to them, or in some way—because of this feeling you have for them—you feel more secure around that person. The Saturn person is always the one that does the *structuring*. "Look, we'll do this and then we'll do this"—they do the structuring, the planning, they're in charge, they're in the position of authority.

Now this Cancer friend of mine—Cancer Sun *and* Cancer rising—who's into astrology; he's a bachelor with Venus in Gemini and he's always playing around. And he once told me, "You know, I just met this lady, and it's amazing because my Saturn is conjunct her Venus and we spent the night together last night, and there was no sex at all; but we just hugged each other all night. Just this tremendous feeling of security." And you know, when a Cancer's emotions are flowing, you know how they can really get into just expressing themselves—so he was just expressing how there was this tremendous feeling of security with his Saturn conjunct her Venus. It's physical and emotional comfort, but it's also tied in with security—a security that comes, if you view it from a karma perspective, from the fact that you're already familiar with that person. You know that person already; that's one reason why it's so secure—because you've been involved before. Maybe he'd spent many nights with her in past lives, or at least he was glad to see her again.

Q: So you said his Saturn was conjunct her Venus and this was in Cancer?

A: No, in Leo.

Q: Well, what I'm asking—whether the sign and house have a bearing?

A: Well, yeah, but the aspect is the major thing I'm talking about now. Actually, whatever house is activated, there could be an impact there too, because wherever Saturn falls in a house in a comparison, that's often where you've got things to learn—where you'll be tested and challenged to define your approach to life in that area. Primarily, I'm just talking about the aspects now.

You see, when I first started doing chart comparisons—in fact, I started doing chart comparisons just intuitively, without having ever read any book on it, many years ago. In fact, I wrote that article on using the houses in chart comparisons before I had ever read any book on chart comparison. And that was just things I had discovered. I didn't even know that some people were already doing that, using the houses and so forth. But, one thing that really struck me was how many marriages had these Saturn aspects. Saturn-Venus, or Saturn-Sun were the most common. And then Saturn and the Moon were second in quantity. And that they had very long-lasting relationships—a lot of long-lasting relationships had, in their comparison, what supposedly were "hard" Saturn aspects. And yet, these marriages often lasted twenty years, thirty years, forty years.

Q: What would it be, in a case where Saturn was conjunct someone's Ascendant, but then that person's Saturn was square your Ascendant? In other words, the partner's Saturn was conjunct the female's

Ascendant, but the female had her Saturn square her Ascendant and then it would also be square his too.

A: Oh, I see what you mean. It's something that kind of amplifies what's already in your natal chart. I suppose you could say that that relationship, at least partly, would have the impact, then, of forcing you to work on what you really had to work on anyway. That would kind of bring it to a focus. But especially if it's related to marriage. With so many people, their lives are kind of disordered until they get married. And then all of a sudden, in a very short time, they start realizing what they've got to do. Saturn comes into their life very markedly. Marriage is a kind of Saturnian institution; it's very much structuring your whole life.

Q: That situation you just mentioned exists between my husband and myself. His Saturn is conjunct his Ascendant, and my Saturn is square his Ascendant. That's what you just said?

A: Similar. But, person A's Saturn squaring person B's Ascendant is not nearly so powerful as the conjunction. The conjunction of Saturn to the Ascendant is very common in marriage comparisons. It's a funny thing, though, because attachment is mutual and goes both ways. Often the Saturn person will act like he or she is not attached. That person is the boss; that person has something *over* the other person. And the "underdog" in the situation will often feel like: "Oh, I've got to work real hard to please this authority figure." But wait until there's some kind of crisis, or till the "underdog" decides that he or she is sick of working so hard under the thumb of the Saturn person and then even threatens to leave. Then the Saturn person starts freaking out, because it's the person whose Saturn is involved in this aspect, in a comparison, whose security is tied up in the relationship, even more than the other person. You know, it's their *security*, because Saturn is the structure of a person's security. It's a very complex aspect.

Say somebody's Sun or Ascendant conjuncts your Saturn. Now, first of all, they get you where you're most defensive because Saturn always shows where you have built certain defensive patterns of behavior, walls around yourself; and it's an area of your life—shown by your Saturn's house and sign—where things don't flow that easily for you, where you've got a lot of caution or fear or anxiety. So if you marry someone, or live very closely for a long time with somebody, who has planets conjunct that point where your Saturn is, they're activating what in you is most insecure; so they're constantly challenging you—without consciously trying to—but they're still constantly, by their way of being, forcing you to deal with your own insecurities and with your own anxieties and fears.

And Saturn, of course, being the Capricorn planet, is always trying to manage and control things. If somebody's planets hit your Saturn, you'll always try to be controlling them, partly because they may make you feel inadequate, they may make you feel that anxiety that's shown by Saturn. And there's often the feeling, almost always unconscious in the Saturn person, that "If I can somehow control this situation with this person, I'll be real secure." But then usually the other person, the "underdog" whose Sun or Ascendant or Moon or whatever is aspecting your Saturn, will get tired of being controlled and inhibited. And then some real interesting things happen when the underdog starts rebelling, saying, "Look, I'm not going to have you dumping on me all the time and always ordering me around." The Saturn person at first (it depends on the person's level of awareness, naturally) often reacts with even more authority, and they'll say, "Oh, you've *got* to do this, it's important, it's your duty," and so forth.

But if the other person says, "No, I've done my duty to you now," then something's got to give! And this is often how you feel during the Saturn return or during a Saturn transiting square to natal Saturn— these seven year Saturn things—you'll often have the end of an old pattern of duty, an old obligation will have been paid off. And particularly with the Saturn return, there's often the feeling that an old debt has been paid, and you no longer owe what you used to owe to a certain person. At that time, you no longer *have to*—there's some kind of "have tos" or some kind of "shoulds" in your life, or duties or obligations that are no longer real; they're gone. You've done it; you've paid it off. And so, a lot of relationships naturally change when Saturn transits are happening. Because it feels like the end of a karmic cycle.

Remember, Saturn also has to do with getting more detached, more objective, or more aloof, and sometimes even cold and kind of calculating. So likewise, when people have these Saturn transits—and there could be any number of them that could manifest like this, Saturn hitting natal Saturn, or Saturn aspecting the Sun, Venus, or the Moon—the person who's having those cycles will often feel strangely detached from somebody, say a partner, whom they used to be real attached to. And so they may announce to their partner, "Well, I no longer really care about this relationship as it is; and so, if it's going to continue, it's got to be changed, and we'll have to do certain things."

And then it's all up to the people, you know, how they want to work it out, *if* they want to start forging a new pattern of relationship at that time, based on new considerations.

But, you know, that is the biggest thing that is missing in most astrological books—an understanding of how people potentially can grow and change, how they can get a different perspective on their lives if they're really open to learning. For example, Saturn transits are much different for young people than for older people, because the first time around *is the first time around*; and there's this unformed youth being "Saturnized," you know: "Oh, God, these Saturn aspects are heavy, all this limitation, how boring." But after the Saturn return, if people have accomodated themselves to the basic necessities of material survival, the basic duties, the Saturn aspects are often experienced as much less troublesome when the person's older, *if* they've learned the lesson the first time around. Many people, needless to say, don't.

But anyway, one way of working with a stressful aspect in a comparison—which is especially appropriate for rigid, uptight, self-critical people—is to be easier on yourself and thus to be easier on the other person by learning how to relax and let things flow. Another way of dealing with such aspects is just to kind of *step back*, and instead of saying "no" to the other person, say "no" to your own behavior patterns. Say, "Instead of trying to discipline so and so, I'm going to discipline myself here." Say you have Saturn aspecting the other person's Sun or Ascendant and they're getting tired of your telling them what to do and trying to structure their lives for them, it might be beneficial to look at your own life and see how you might try to structure your own life. Because if you concentrate on developing a certain kind of deep security within yourself through your own efforts, you won't need that security feeling from your partner so much, so there won't be that motivation to manipulate the other person in order to insure your own stability or security. But I don't know any way of working with Saturn aspects except for the Saturn person, on one hand, to step back and get more detached about their behavior and their fears—it's necessary for them to face their own fears, instead of trying to project their fears or insecurities onto the other person.

And then, the other person can learn what kinds of behavior, what kinds of things they do, make the Saturn person react very anxiously. Say, the husband's Saturn is hitting the wife's Sun or Moon, and she's always spending a little extra money, or at least she's spending money on things that make him feel real anxious, make him feel like, "Gee, we're going to be in the poorhouse in two weeks if you keep buying this stuff." She can probably alter her behavior somewhat, without infringing on her own integrity, in a way that will make it easier. She could either buy things in secret, she could buy things a little less often maybe, or buy not quite the same things, you know; it often doesn't take a whole lot of adjustment to make the other person feel like: "Oh yes, things are under control." That is, the Saturn person has to feel like, "Well, things are under control now, I can relax." But if another person's planets hit my Saturn, it's going to make me feel kind of threatened—like, "Something's getting out of control; I'm getting anxious."

So often though, I've seen long-term relationships where you'd think, "Gee, how could they ever stay married that long?" And indeed, if you talk to them, see how they feel, they often feel, "Yech! I don't know why I did. Twenty, thirty years with this clod that I now have come to hate." Or "God knows why I've stayed with this person who never gets off her butt and never even cleans the house." One couple I remember, the husband's Saturn squared the wife's Sun and the wife's Saturn squared the husband's Sun. They were miserable for years and years and years. She finally got the courage to leave him, after incredible pain for over twenty years. Now, one Saturn aspect doesn't have to make you miserable. It depends on the rest of the comparison *and* on how you deal with it. But if you have a "double whammy" such as this with Saturn aspecting the Sun—well, I've never seen a happy relationship with that combination.

Some other things that seem to be related to karma in comparisons are Neptune and the twelfth house. If you have somebody else's planets, especially the Sun, Saturn, or the personal planets, falling in your natal twelfth house, or even the Ascendant falling in your twelfth house, your twelfth house is activated then; so you'll often feel like you owe them something. The twelfth house and Neptune have many meanings, but one of them is *experienced* as a sense of obligation, a sense of owing something to the other person. You get a similar feeling with Saturn too, although Neptune's not so *heavy*. So if you have planets activating your twelfth house, you often feel like you owe that person something. And you may want to run away from it, because Neptune— and the twelfth house also—is the principle of *escape*, wanting to avoid the whole thing. The urge to escape, or to avoid. But if somebody else's planets fall in your twelfth house, circumstances will often compel you to give a lot to that other person, to give of yourself to that other person in ways that you might not have ever expected or ever wanted.

I remember one guy, who's a really good friend of mine now—his Sun and some other planets fall in my twelfth house. And I didn't feel very comfortable with him for a long time, but because we both were doing a lot of the same activities, we had to deal with each other a whole lot. And so we slowly got to know each other and develop some trust. It's kind of like: once you let somebody in who has planets falling in your twelfth or strong Neptune contacts with you, once you finally let them into your life, there can be a tremendous, *very subtle* and even telepathic kind of rapport. In fact, one of the reasons that people often feel anxious or awkward in their attitudes toward other people whose planets are in their twelfth house is that the twelfth house is your house of secrets; you know, it's your subconscious, your hidden motivations, and so forth. And if somebody's Sun falls in your twelfth house, that person will often have the ability to telepathically "read" you. They'll often be able to understand you "inside out," understand your motives, your feelings, and all kinds of things which you would often like to keep secret.

And then with Neptune too, especially if Neptune is conjunct Venus in a comparison, or conjunct the other person's Sun or Moon— there's often this sense of mutual identity. It's a kind of mystical identity with the other person, and there's usually a very strong sense of compassion. In some cases, even a sense of pity. But invariably a sense of compassion—which often manifests, then, as generosity of feelings, of money, of sympathy toward the other person. And it can go either way. If, say, the Sun hits your Neptune, or Neptune hits your Sun, there can be that link-up. And I don't know any way of telling who's going to be giving to who; usually it's a kind of simultaneous compassion that both people feel. It's a sense of oneness that both people feel. So if there is a true sense of oneness, naturally, how can I withold something from somebody who is the same as me? And if I give them something, it's not really giving it to them, because they're *me* anyway. You know what I mean, there's often a kind of mystical identity and thus a spontaneous sharing and rapport.

Q: Would that hold true for the planet Neptune in your chart falling on some other planet in the other's chart, even if it wasn't in the twelfth house?

A: Oh yeah! This is a totally separate thing from the twelfth house, now. I mean, there are a lot of similarities between a twelfth house emphasis in a comparison and a Neptune contact in a comparison, a lot of similar things; but in my experience the twelfth house emphasis seems to manifest as a little more anxiety or a little more guilt, often not quite such a whole-hearted sense of oneness as you find with Neptune contacts, even though that can be developed with time. I'm not saying that, for example, *all* Neptune conjunctions with somebody's Sun or Moon or Venus are going to be ultimately compassionate; but usually there's a strong trend toward compassion or pity or something like that that comes from the people's sense of identity with each other, their sense of oneness.

Q: This compassion would be felt by the person who's Neptune . . .?

A: Either way. That's what I was trying to explain before, that it can be felt by both. Sometimes it's only felt by one, but I don't know how to distinguish who's feeling what from the charts alone. Lots of times it's just a kind of mystic merger, and it doesn't matter if the two people are male and female; it's a totally asexual thing; it's just two human beings who feel like they're somehow one. It's hard to explain Neptune. It's a mystical, mystical planet. You can only perceive Neptune through intuition, the higher mind.

THE WATER & FIRE HOUSES

One other thing about using the houses in comparisons that is worth looking at—in relation to karma—the water houses: 4th, 12th, and 8th. If somebody has a lot of planets falling in your water houses, you're very vulnerable to them; you're very open to them. Even if you don't want to be, you're open to them. Like I mentioned, with planets falling in your twelfth, that person can read you, they can tune in on your subconscious. To some extent this is also true for the fourth and the eighth houses too. Because then their planets, so to speak, are penetrating into your secret houses, the houses of your inner life, and therefore in those areas you're particularly open to them. You can't defend yourself. So there are only two things you can do: try to run away from the relationship or open yourself up to the person and try to work with that level of intimacy in a positive way.

Another thing that I've noticed, and maybe somebody here can tell me if you've seen similar things—if there's a major emphasis in a comparison on the fire houses, 1st, 5th, and 9th (in other words, a lot of somebody's planets, or at least the Sun or Moon, fall in your fire houses), they'll often make you feel really alive. Really, really, *dynamic!* They give you energy. And they give you confidence, too. Can anybody here identify with that?

Q: The houses, now, not the signs?

A: Right, the houses. In other words, if somebody's planets fall in your first, or fifth, or ninth houses—planets falling in those houses in *your* chart. . . . Well, maybe you can study that. One thing I'd like to find out too, and this is related, because actually the Ascendant is inseparable from the first house—oftentimes with somebody whose Sun sign, Venus sign, or Moon sign hits your Ascendant (or are the same sign as your rising sign), there's an immediate identity, there's an immediate energizing experience with that person; and you often feel much more confident, much more assertive, much more like you can be yourself around that person whose planets hit your Ascendant. Now, what I'd like to see is if anybody can relate to that. This is kind of simplifying it somewhat, since the first house often has two signs in it; but just take your rising sign, and see if anybody has noticed whether they are particularly attracted to people whose Sun or Moon or other major planets are in that sign. Can anybody identify with that?

Q: Yeah, Em-mm. I can. Unh-huh. (Many people nodding and agreeing.)

A: There's a lot of yeses.

Q: And opposite the rising sign too.

A: Yeah, because that'd be your seventh house, sure.

Q: I know my son's—all his planets fall in my first, fifth, and ninth, you know. . . .

A: One of your sons?

Q: Yes, you did his chart.

A: Have you gotten a big kick out of him?—his growing up?

Q: One way or another (laughter).

A: Did you kind of identify with him?

Q: He's always energizing me, let me put it like that.

A: But I mean, can you *identify* with him?

Q: Yeah. I have really. His Moon falls in my first house, you know, by my Ascendant.

A: It's especially the first house contact, more than the fifth or ninth, where there's a tremendous sense of identity with the other person.

Q: And his Sun and Jupiter and Venus are all up there in my ninth with my Saturn. He's made me work, too. But I have always somehow related to him so closely, I mean, instinctively, and he's been a lot of fun, you know. . . .

A: The fire houses are the *fun* houses, because that's where you get that spirited behavior; it's not thinking, it's not just emotions, and it's not practical considerations—it's just pure release of life energy. I've just been tuning in a lot on the Ascendant lately, because the Ascendant is probably the most ineffable, undefinable thing in the whole chart. And that's sort of nice too, because it's a kind of mystery; as you live and grow and develop, more and more the Ascendant symbolizes something so crucial about the way you have to express yourself and your whole way of being—your whole approach to life. I don't really have very good words for it, but if people can express what the Ascendant symbolizes, what their rising sign symbolizes, if they can express *that*, then in most cases they feel much better. They feel like they're *being themselves*; they feel liberated. It's a liberating kind of experience.

But of course, in so many charts, there are planets in square to the Ascendant, or there's a planet in opposition to the Ascendant, so that there is a kind of inner struggle: "Should I express this or that?" Oh well, I don't have any answer about those things; but in such cases, one has to *work* (and sometimes *sacrifice*) in order to attain that fully free and spontaneous kind of self-expression.

EVALUATING THE *PEOPLE* INVOLVED— NOT JUST THE CHARTS

Also, one thing that's occurred to me lately (all these things are obvious when you really realize them)—say you do a chart comparison and, as in most chart comparisons, you'll come up with quite a few problematical things, because people who are super happy will rarely ask you for a comparison. You see, you have to be careful, too, because you can often get a very unbalanced attitude toward chart comparisons and how to interpret chart comparison factors, just by the fact that most comparisons you do will most likely be for people who aren't very happy with each other. So pretty soon it's easy to start thinking, "Oh, that aspect is negative because all the people I've seen with that aspect have experienced such-and-such." So, it's useful to find relationships where they're not even asking you to do their charts because you know they're a happy couple, if you happen to ever meet one. If you can get their birth data and study their comparison, it might be very illuminating.

But anyway, what has really hit me lately is that (assuming both people *want* the relationship, but they're having some big crisis and they're thinking about getting divorced or something like that) there is no point in doing *anything* unless both people want to work on it. That should be obvious, but so often in astrology work, you forget the counseling side of it, and you just say, "Well, this will work, and this is incompatible, and this is compatible, and here's how it is." Then, the question is—is it possible for the two people, assuming both of them want to make their relationship a fairly healthy thing, is it possible to make it a fairly healthy thing? Sometimes it isn't. That's my feeling. Sometimes the relationship is so bad, and the aspects indicate it with so many stresses, so many places where the people pull in opposite directions or are undermining each other and going at cross purposes . . . sometimes it's just hopeless.

But in many cases it'll be a kind of borderline case. You can see a lot of really good things in the relationship—really good energy flow, really good harmony on certain levels, then problems in other areas. If through the astrology you can help them to get some kind of awareness of what's going on and why they're doing it and maybe hint to them that they shouldn't be looking to their partner for everything, well, sometimes there is a little hope. I'm getting cynical in my old age, but nowadays, it seems people have the leisure to cause themselves a lot of problems. You know, like thirty or forty years ago, or during wartime or during the depression, a marriage had to be pretty hideous to think of ending it. Because the people were so obviously *mutually dependent*, and their survival was tied in with each other. And also, they didn't have time to think about "Am I compatible with so and so?" because they were working all the time. Larger families were common, too.

Q: You've said it all, Stephen, you've said it all. It's true.

A: But, you know, so many times I've done a comparison for somebody, and then when I really finally peel off all the layers of their game-playing and realize where they're really at, I see that one or often both have just had a Uranus or Pluto transit or something similar and they both want out of the darn thing. They don't *want* to work at it at all; they've had it. In most cases, they've *already* worked at it, and if they feel kind of negative anyhow, the chances are that working at it more isn't going to help that much. They have to accept it and accept each other as they are, or reject it completely. And especially now, it is socially acceptable to get divorced. In the old days, when everybody was living in small towns and belonging to a church, there was all this gossip and everything; *nobody* wanted to get divorced. Plus there's always the economic uncertainty of it. But nowadays it's kind of a fad, you know: "Hey, look at that! George and Mary just got divorced, and Thelma and Rudolph too," and pretty soon they think, "Hey, I ought to try that." And then, just as you're thinking that way, you get a nice little Uranus transit or something, and you go: "This is it! I'm going to be free," and the ego gets really bloated out of proportion. Uranus, by the way, is a very dangerous planet because it's extremely egotistical; you know, "I, I, I, me, me, me—I'm going to be free, I'm going to do my thing; regardless of what anybody says—spouse, culture, church or whatever—I'm doing my thing." Very, very self-centered. Not that that is bad, everybody's got to express that at times, but during Uranus transits, you often feel more like that. Which actually brings me to Mars and Venus aspects.

MARS & VENUS NATAL ASPECTS WITH
THE OUTER PLANETS
URANUS WITH VENUS OR MARS

If you combine Uranus with Mars or Venus in any major aspect, you've got a certain self-centeredness. You've got a certain need for excitement, in some cases even a craving for excitement. It's a need for *constant* excitement. If it's Mars aspecting Uranus, it has to do with *action,* a need for constant excitement through action, through going places actively, or race car driving, or sexual variety—some kind of extremely active and changeable activity. Also, when you get Mars and Uranus interchanges, there is almost invariably a remarkable sexual drive, an almost insatiable need for sexual *excitement.*

Q: Venus-Uranus?

A: To some extent. Mars-Uranus tends to be like that for everybody. Venus-Uranus would manifest as the sexual excitement thing especially with women, or if Venus is located in a particularly sexual or erotic sign. But right now, I'll just center on Mars and Uranus. Generally, there is this need for excitement, and there's this tremendous capacity to get bored quickly. Any type of activity, whether it be sexual activity or whether it be the kind of work the person does, you name it, there's just this need for freedom and excitement. The sign placement of Mars is the crucial thing for symbolizing the specifics.

Say you have Mars-Uranus conjunct in Gemini, a lot of that need for excitement will manifest as an essentially mental curiosity about "wild" or unorthodox things. Whereas if it's, say, in Aries, you'll want to act on it, you'll want to *do* it, you won't just want to think about it.

There are very often sexual "problems" with Mars-Uranus. They're not always felt as problems by the person, but almost invariably, even if intellectually they say "Oh, it's not a problem," so much of their energy goes into trying to satisfy their need for action and sexuality that it's a big thing in the person's life. The most famous example of this is Henry Miller, the writer who has now been married, I think, six times, and has had about seven-thousand other sexual experiences. He has Mars, Uranus, and the Moon conjunct in Scorpio in the seventh house.

Q: Ye gods. Oh, no. (Laughing and other comments from audience.)

A: So he changes partners very often. He just got divorced again, I think, in the last year or so.

Q: Doesn't Mars and Uranus sometimes indicate violence, too?

A: Yes, there's always that possibility, but not everybody with Mars and Uranus combinations expresses it as violence. These interchanges also give great drive, courage, and originality. In fact, the majority of people (even with the squares) do not act out their violence in public or *criminal* ways. But they'll often act it out in more private, personal ways. For example, one woman I've seen was married to a guy who has Uranus-Mars closely conjunct in Aries, both square Saturn—and in that case, Saturn would just increase the pressure of that tension; she got married to him and ran away from him about a month later and filed for divorce because he was quite insatiable as far as her taste goes. Of course, she's not too sexual, either; her Mars and Venus are both in Mercury signs, Virgo and Gemini, so they weren't too good a match. What she really resented was his "violence" being manifested, not as physical violence like beating, but he wanted sex five or six times a day, every day, and it didn't matter what she was doing. She could be sitting there watching the television, he would come up and physically pick her up and carry her off to the bedroom. And she felt that that showed a lack of respect for her. You know, he would just come up and turn the television off, not ask her or anything. . . .

Q: With the kind of thing you just described, though, would he have been turned on by her rejection of it?

A: I don't know. I don't think he was turned on by her disinterest in him. In fact, that made him more frustrated, made him more violent, you might say. So the violent thing does often come out—sometimes homosexuality or bi-sexuality comes out too. Don't get the idea that every person with a little Mars-Uranus aspect is going to be gay, or bi-sexual, because that's not true. But, invariably, they have such an eletrical and sudden kind of sexual responsiveness, that they can *feel* sexual attraction with any human being that is attractive to them, regardless of sex. Whether or not they act out the thing, as a homosexual type of activity, is totally another thing, which you cannot guess just from the chart in any way that I can know. You can maybe *suspect* it; if you meet the person and pick up certain vibes and there are certain indications in the chart, then you'll often be on the right track. (But not all gay people have Mars-Uranus aspects motivating them. There are other factors, too.) There's just that need for excitement, and sometimes if the person doesn't get the excitement they want with their own sex, they'll try the other sex and see how that goes. You shouldn't underestimate the incredible power of a Mars-Uranus interchange.

Q: Would that thing—you know, one person's Uranus in the comparison on the other person's Mars, would that be that compulsion for sexual attraction?

A: It's definitely a sexually exciting aspect, yeah. Mainly the conjunction, and to some extent the opposition. But those aspects, and also the square between Uranus and Mars in a comparison, can also arouse rebellion in each other and *toward* each other. But the conjunction, particularly, is a highly sexual combination in most comparisons. But you also have to look and see what other aspects are hitting those planets to see whether that is something that the people can *integrate* into the relationship, or whether it's eventually going to turn out to be open warfare. Because lust and passion are very similar to violence, you know, there is a very . . .

Q: thin line?

A: Yes, or no line at all.

Now, take Venus and Uranus. Now, this deals more with both "romantic" cravings and with the *social* realm, a need for—you might say—social and emotional excitement and variety. And, especially in women's charts, it's very important in regard to sexual relationships, because Venus does have a strong impact on deeply emotional relationships and sexuality and particularly so in women's charts—we could spend one whole workshop just on this. Remember that Venus has the social, romantic, and emotional impact on anyone of either sex, but it becomes specifically a sexual indicator in women's charts—having a direct impact on their physical sexuality.

First of all, people with Venus-Uranus squares and Venus-Uranus oppositions are often quite afraid of rejection, quite afraid of being hurt, and they often act a little like Venus in Aquarius people—somewhat detached, somewhat aloof. They're very experimental when it comes to love, emotional things, sexual things, but they tend to be very self-centered. This self-centeredness applies to Venus-Uranus conjunctions, squares, *and oppositions particularly*, much more so than the trines or sextiles, and much more.so than Venus in Aquarius. It's mainly the "tense" aspects of Venus and Uranus that tend to be *extremely* self-centered and in a negative kind of way, like refusing to adapt themselves or to cooperate in a way that would make things with other people flow easier.

There's often a certain coldness, too—you know, Uranus is always somewhat impersonal, and *that*, hitting Venus, gives a kind of impersonal tinge to their attitude toward emotional and sexual behavior. You're apt to find this manifestation of this interchange quite often, especially in women who go through lots of partners or who have gotten into homosexuality, although, again, the vast majority with Venus-Uranus aspects are not practicing homosexuals. However, you can know that there's a *craving* in anyone with that aspect for emotional or social excitement or rebelliousness. You see, some people want it just from a close relationship; but other people can, to at least some extent, satisfy those needs for excitement simply by having lots of friends and going out and doing all kinds of things. You have to look at the sign placement of Venus to tune in on what gives the person real pleasure.

But almost always, people with these aspects don't realize how they give themselves problems, how they create relationship problems for themselves. You know, in a lot of books you can look up Venus square Uranus or Venus opposite Uranus, and you'll see "this is the divorce aspect" and so forth. A lot of people with that aspect don't realize why they wind up getting divorced or why they wind up having relationship problems. And they almost always bring it on themselves through being "too cold" or "too impersonal." And by being "too cold" I don't mean lacking in passion, but rather being too impersonal, so that the other person you may be involved with might feel unappreciated as an individual and quite replaceable—your attitude toward him or her is "Oh well, these people are a dime a dozen." In some cases, especially with the opposition, you'll find people who foul up a lot of their close relationships through egocentric behavior and through acting out impulses that they sometimes regret later.

I remember one woman with a Venus-Uranus opposition; she went to Europe with a girlfriend of hers and they met these two guys. They rented a house in France and started living with these guys, and the girl with the Venus-Uranus opposition didn't have enough activity just having the one guy; she wanted a part of the other one too, who was sort of paired off with her best friend. (You have to remember that Uranus exhibits a rather perverse tendency and is often especially excited by breaking the social rules.) So she started making it with the other guy, and this naturally brought about a severe rupture in their friendship, which lasted about a year before they got on speaking terms again.

Another person—this one really awakened me to the extremes of behavior that this aspect can produce—this lady, I had a consultation with her, and after she left she stopped payment on the check she gave me. I don't remember all the details now, because I've tried not to; but essentially, she was a very unhappy, very lonely, very miserable person. She never had any decent relationships with men and she was about 35, and that was the main reason she wanted a consultation, so that she could see "how come every man I meet runs away from me so quickly?" And she gave herself a good example of "why" by cancelling my check—totally self-centered behavior with no rhyme or reason to it, totally unwilling to give an inch or to cooperate or to *sacrifice* her own personal freedom or impulses in any way, or to restrain her impulses in any way.

NEPTUNE WITH VENUS OR MARS

If you have a Neptune aspect to Mars or Venus, you get some really interesting combinations here, too. Both of which are commonly found, incidentally, in spiritual seekers—Mars-Neptune or Venus-Neptune. In fact, just about every person I've ever seen who was a very sincere seeker, really wanting some kind of spiritual liberation, has Venus-Neptune, Mars-Neptune or Sun or Moon in a close aspect with Neptune, or Neptune in the first house. Always a strong Neptune. And usually the Neptune aspects, in those kind of people, are the so-called "stressful" aspects; because it's the so-called stressful aspects that make you want to act on something, that make you want to do something about it. So really, squares, oppositions, and conjunctions with Neptune are the best aspects you can have for spiritual aspirations. With trines, you may have a curiosity about spiritual things, but you may not *do* anything about it. In fact, I've seen that in many cases, too. People with a lot of Neptune trines, especially Neptune trine the Sun—they'll read books about Zen and liberation and all this, but they often just sit on their butts and smoke pot and don't do anything about, for example, meditation or any kind of spiritual practice.

If you have Mars-Neptune or Venus-Neptune, there is almost always a tremendous capacity for self-delusion about relationships (in the case of Venus) or confusion about what they really want (in the case of Mars). And with both combinations, that includes confusion about what they want sexually, too. There can be a great deal of sexual fantasy, also, especially with Mars-Neptune combinations, as well as a particularly strange openness, a kind of openness to all kinds of things— you might say it's a sort of seductable aspect, making the person seem, and indeed *be*, able to be led into things, even though they consciously might not have wanted it. There is a strong self-delusion tendency in Neptune generally, but especially in Mars-Neptune or Venus-Neptune aspects when it comes to emotional and sexual relationships.

A lot of men with a Mars-Neptune conjunction, square, or opposition have problems when it comes to their "male ego." If you remember, those who were in the last workshop I did, I was talking about how Mars has to do with the male ego and how masculine the man feels. And lots of men with the conjunction, square, or opposition of Neptune to Mars are a little confused about their masculinity. In some cases, it will manifest as their actually getting into homosexual behavior. In other cases, it will manifest as a tremendous hatred of homosexuals and as their emphasizing *machismo* types of activity. They'll be big hunters and fishermen and killers, you know, super dynamic "Marsy" types—that's what they'll try to cultivate.

Women with Mars-Neptune "stressful" aspects—(I'm mainly emphasizing the "stressful" aspects because they're the *obviously* problematical ones—they come into manifestation very readily and obviously; the trines and sextiles very rarely give that many apparent problems). Anyway, women with Mars-Neptune "stressful" or "challenging" aspects usually have some difficulty in dealing with men, because there is this "openness" to being led or being seduced into things. And one can play on their sympathies—remember how Neptune is so sympathetic, so compassionate; so for people in general, and women in particular, with the Mars-Neptune combination, people can play on their sympathies. And people who might want to manipulate them pick up that they *can* play on their sympathies, since the person is open to being led or being manipulated in that way because there is a confusion about Mars—what they really want. They aren't quite sure what they really want or what they really want to do. Thus, they're easily led into all kinds of things, sexual involvements as well as other things—maybe a lousy business deal or something else. They're easily fooled.

Now with the Venus-Neptune *natal* aspects, people with almost any combination of Venus and Neptune, especially in a close aspect, have this yearning for an ideal (Neptune) love (Venus), that is, some experience of ideal love—a very "romantic" person, a very romantic combination. Especially if they don't have some kind of spiritual direction, they're very often looking for a new partner all the time, or fantasizing romance, or reading romantic novels, or watching soap operas. There is this great yearning to escape into this world of "perfect romance," perfect love. (Or sometimes a striving for perfect art or beauty.)

Now, I've got in my files an amazing number of cases of women with Venus-Neptune conjunctions or squares who have been married seven and eight times. (That's the maximum. A few with this combination were only married four or five or six times.) Now, for *most* people with that aspect, it's not necessarily going to work out in that way; many of these people I've mentioned have it in their seventh house—either the conjunction is in their seventh (or within a few degrees of the seventh cusp on the sixth house side) or the Venus or the Neptune in the square is in their seventh house. So if you've got that kind of combination and one of the planets or the whole conjunction is in the seventh house (or possibly even if you have such an aspect and Venus or Neptune *rules* your seventh), then you've really got a tremendously strong tendency toward what we might mildly call *poor discrimination in relationships.*

In many cases, the person will actually be defrauded. See, Neptunian people believe what they want to believe, you know, they don't want facts, they simply want to believe what they want to believe. That's why you find the occult and metaphysical studies and sciences jam-packed with Neptune people who are very open and very intuitive and very spiritually-oriented, but often they can't discriminate between what is true and what isn't and what is useful and what isn't—because if anything sounds good they'll believe it. So they believe what they want to believe. And this can be a beautiful, inspirational "leap of faith," or it can merely be self-delusion. I know one lady with this Venus-Neptune combination; she's only about 35 and she's on her fifth marriage. She had to take two of these husbands to court for fraud, because they were both guys who married her trying to get her house and money and car and so forth, and they didn't care about her at all. But see, she couldn't see that. You know, "love is blind"—that's Venus-Neptune. Sometimes it's a sense of "Oh, I must be in love because I'm blind or can't see straight."

Q: They don't have to have both planets in the seventh house; if one of them is in there aspecting another, that . . . ?

A: Right.

Q: . . . that's a lack of discrimination?

A: Yes, in most cases. I mean, these general statements will pertain to the aspect no matter where it is in the chart, but I'm just saying that the people who seem to go through the most marriages with this aspect either have the conjunction of Venus and Neptune in the seventh or, if it's a square, they've got one of the planets in the seventh. And a few other Venus-Neptune interchanges which are tied in with the seventh house can also manifest like this.

In other cases, people who have the Venus-Neptune combinations are so romantic that they have a hard time facing the harsh realities of relationships. In other words, what does a relationship really require? And if it requires getting down into the dirt of everyday life, they often don't feel like doing it. You know: "Gee, I thought this was all going to be peaches and cream, just like on our honeymoon in Hawaii," and pretty soon they're scrubbing floors and washing dishes and all that; and they also have a tendency to totally turn-off sexually if their every-day life gets too mundane. Like one lady with Venus-Neptune conjunct who was on her fifth marriage at the age of 31, she told me that she had totally ceased to respond sexually to her current husband unless she set up a very Neptunian, romantic atmosphere. She had to turn down the lights, and light candles, and put on certain music—she had to transform the experience into something rather unreal, rather romantic, in order to feel any kind of turn-on to him. And her husband, by the way, has

Mars-Uranus conjunct in Aries (this is a different one than I mentioned before), so he wanted sex a lot, and she has Venus conjunct Neptune in Virgo and she didn't want it very often at all. So she had to do this programming of herself with all these romantic images, candles and what not, to be able to stand the whole thing—because Mars-Uranus in Aries is pretty blunt, not romantic at all—on the contrary!

In other cases, too, where you have Venus-Neptune aspects, the person will *elude* commitment; sometimes the people jump into the thing so fast it's ridiculous, often being infatuated with things that are illusory, and in other cases they'll elude commitment in relationships forever and ever and ever. I know some really good-looking women in their forties and fifties who've never been married, or otherwise permanently committed to someone, who have this aspect. That doesn't say that they've never messed around. They've messed around a lot, and they've often had numerous "love" relationships. But they have never felt that they could commit themselves in any definite way in "love." Because, you know, Venus (love) is combined with Neptune (spaced-out); Neptune doesn't want to be defined. Neptune doesn't want to have a *commitment*, because then you're accepting limitations; Neptune wants to remain without boundaries and unlimited.

PLUTO WITH VENUS OR MARS

And when you bring Pluto in, combined with Venus and Mars, then you've got some real interesting things too. One of the particularly intriguing things that you might find is—this is more of a curiosity for the astrologer than something that you should necessarily *tell* clients—sometimes when Venus is conjunct or opposite Pluto, the person has a lover or fiancé die . . . .

Q: Yes, that's true of me. (Interrupting from audience.)

A: What aspect do you have?

Q: Pluto and Venus within a degree.

A: Conjunct?

Q: Yes, in the twelfth.

A: Yes, I've seen that repeatedly. I've also seen many cases where it doesn't seem to be true, too. So, you know if somebody has a Venus-Pluto conjunction, you shouldn't say, "Oh, you'll probably have a lover die sometime." There's obviously no point in that. One case really blew my mind: The guy—it was a guy with Venus conjunct Pluto—was engaged four times, and his fiancée died all four times, shortly before the wedding. Needless to say, he doesn't get engaged anymore. One woman with a Venus-Pluto opposition was involved with all these different people over the years; two of them died, one of them mysteriously left the country, and the other one had to move suddenly to Washington, D.C.—she was always being somehow frustrated.

Now, not in all cases do you have such obvious separations and deaths and all that, which is why you should be careful of what you say in a consultation. But invariably when Pluto is involved in anything there is a tremendous depth. And there is often a tremendously profound mystery, also, so deep that you can't really fathom it—in fact, "unfathomable" is about the best word for Pluto, tremendously deep. This tremendously deep energy and these tremendously deep experiences in relationships correspond with the Venus-Pluto aspects. Now, you might say that the best way to look at Venus-Pluto aspects is that the reason for going through this kind of emotional suffering, or emotional frustration, or being separated from somebody they love, or however it manifests, is that their approach to relationships and love (Venus) and their approach to giving and receiving intimately with other people has to be totally transformed. And if they're not going to totally transform it and work at it consciously, then a drastic change of attitude and transformation of their approach and values in this area of life is often forced on them by circumstances. *Why* this transformation is necessary is anybody's guess . . . you could no doubt think up many psychological, spiritual, or "karmic" reasons for it; but the individual can assign it the reasons and the value that feels comfortable and right for his or her particular philosophy of life. The chart just gives the facts, symbolizes the quality of experience encountered—it doesn't show the *why* in any precise and regular way.

Another thing you often find with Venus-Pluto natal aspects is that there's a tendency toward being emotionally insatiable. You never quite get enough attention, O.K.? Does that make any sense? (Venus in Scorpio is somewhat similar—it's another Venus-Pluto interchange.) There's this 5 year-old kid I know who has a Venus-Pluto opposition, and he's absolutely insatiable for attention. His mother spoils him rotten and he still wants more attention. He's the greediest little boy I've ever seen.

Q: Does this hold true for the square also? Say Venus in Scorpio squares Pluto?

A: Oh yes. If you have Venus in Scorpio *and* it's aspecting Pluto, that would be *especially* true. That would be a "double whammy"—the two Plutonian factors coloring or giving a tone to Venus simultaneously. In most cases where you have Pluto-Venus "stressful" aspects (the conjunctions, squares, or oppositions), you'll have someone who's at least *subtly* demanding in some way—subtly demanding of attention, subtly demanding of affection, or in some cases they'll have big power trips with sexuality or power trips with flirtation; at its worst, there's some kind of ruthlessness which is—if not cruel—very impersonal in attitudes toward other people.

Pluto can be very underhanded, very demanding. Pluto is the only planet whose energy simultaneously goes out and in; it's like Scorpio—the energy flow is tremendously dynamic outwardly but it also is sucking you in. Scorpio and Pluto are the only factors in astrology like that. So people with Venus in Scorpio or with Pluto-Venus close aspects (especially the stressful ones) are often subtly demanding. They put out this energy toward you to try to draw you in.

I remember one lady in my class many years ago (this was one of the first things that clued me in to Pluto-Venus aspects and how demanding they can be). I was selling books at my classes as usual and this lady was not reliable at all; she came to about one out of every three classes and I never knew if she was ever going to come back. She picked out about 4 or 5 books, and she walked up to the table holding her books and started to do this little number about she was going to take these books now and pay me for them some time later. Well, everybody else was paying on the spot because I required that, and I didn't have much money at all in those days and I needed every penny I could get. She had this pile of books and said, "I'm going to take these home now and I'll pay you for them the next time I come to class." And then she put on this almost hideous smile; it was as if she was demanding of me through this smile, she was demanding that she take these books. In fact, she was *ordering* me to let her take them, even though she didn't come to class regularly. And I actually let her, because back in those days I was a Libra. (Note that Pluto-Venus can affect how you deal with money *and* people.) But I had to write her sixteen letters; it took months to get any money out of her. But I learned a lot about Venus-Pluto aspects. That's the neat thing about astrology—no matter what you go through, you can learn something from it.

There are sometimes sexual problems with Venus-Pluto combinations too. I don't mean some big huge hassle necessarily, but an area where there's some kind of block or where you've got some kind of tension in your life that needs a lot of attention. One lady I saw had Pluto conjunct the Ascendant, which is a lot like having Scorpio rising— Pluto conjunct the Ascendant in Leo. So she had Leo rising, Pluto on the Ascendant. Then that Pluto was square Venus, and Venus was in Taurus incidentally. She had a big earth-mother kind of body, but she was only 21 years old. She wanted to do something big—Pluto on the Ascendant has big ambitions in many cases. Her ambition was that she wanted to become a big industrialist, to become one of the most powerful women in the world through gaining presidency of a big industry. Her father was a big industrialist, and this was part of the image. So she had all these plans for starting all these international projects. She was just a senior in college but she was super precocious. For her age she was really practical and really worldly, and she was tremendously ambitious with very specific ambitions. She knew a great deal about international economics that she had picked up from her father.

So, remember I said with Pluto-Venus you'll often *use* your personal magnetism and sometimes use it ruthlessly and sometimes impersonally, or you may use your attractiveness through flirtations or whatever to gain your objectives. She set up this meeting with five or six big businessmen in southern California hoping to get some capital from them for this big project she wanted to do. She was 21 years old and doing this thing! So with each one of them she turned on her electrical juices to get her way; I don't know to what lengths she went, but undoubtedly there was a very obvious flirtatiousness in her anyhow. After the meeting, then, it was decided that all these men would think it over and decide whether they wanted to have any part of her project. And everyone of them later told her individually that they wouldn't have anything to do with her because they couldn't trust her. They felt that she was too ruthless. So each one of them picked up on this. Now Venus-Pluto aspects and Venus in Scorpio are not always so ruthless, but they can be. They can be very willful and impersonal. It depends on the individual's whole nature, values, and level of self-knowledge. And so she was wondering why none of these men wanted to join forces with her—obviously, I told her, they can't trust you; they told you so in so many words. So you should *listen* to them!

Pluto-Mars aspects are quite a bit like Mars in Scorpio—you've got a compulsive drive for power, to *experience* power. And often it will be directed sexually or, in many other cases, it will be directed toward a tremendous ambition or toward a tremendous dedication toward some *mission* (whether this ambition or "mission" is positive or negative). A mission can be an inner transformation mission as well as an outer "I'm going to reform the world" type mission. Invariably there's a tremendously compulsive power drive, although it is often more *obviously* expressed in men and takes a longer period to come to the surface in women. Scorpio likes power; it likes to feel the intensity of power. So whenever you have Venus or Mars strongly aspecting Pluto or in Scorpio, invariably there's a power number that you have to deal with. How are you using your power? How are you using your will-power, and your mind power, and your magnetism? And so whenever you have Venus or Mars in "stressful" aspect to Pluto, there's always that to deal with—how are you using your energies? And in most cases where you have those aspects, there is some need to *transform* the mode of expression of the Venus or Mars energy.

A CHART COMPARISON EXAMPLE

[The following chart comparison deals with a couple whom I'd seen in a consultation. I had also seen the woman numerous times over the years and had watched her go through some very frustrating relationships. In the workshop, the natal charts were on the blackboard, so I could refer to specific factors easily. Since in the workshop I could point out any particular combination visually and thus go through things very rapidly, the transcribed text is at times hard to follow without the visual aids. So, I have edited slightly some of the following material for increased clarity, but the reader should still refer to the charts and accompanying material in Illustrations No. 2 & 3 to follow more closely what is being said.]

An Aries Ascendant here and this one has 16 degrees of Scorpio rising. The curious thing about this comparison to me is that the lady (whom we'll call Jean) actually seems to be extremely happy and compatible with this guy (whom we'll call David), although she and I had pretty much felt that she'd never be *happily* married. This lady is only 35 now; this is her third husband already. Now you may say look at her 7th house, and she has an active 7th house. And if you remember at the last workshop, we talked about when Uranus aspects the Sun in a woman's natal chart. She has an exact conjunction of Sun and Uranus.

Any person that has that is very independent—often quite a rebellious person. Women that have a Uranus-Sun aspect, especially the conjunction, square, or opposition, very often have a hard time handling a traditional marriage role because they're so rebellious and independent. So anyway, she got pregnant and married at 15 or 16. Then that guy ran off before her kid was even born. Then she married another guy who was a beach bum. She stayed married to him for another 3 or 4 years and that was a mess, but she had another kid by him. So then she swore to me, "I'm never going to get married again." And I thought from looking at her chart that maybe she shouldn't get married; maybe this type of thing would keep happening.

But there was only one thing I could tell her about the whole business and that is—look what a strong-willed person she is! Uranus conjunct the Sun, first of all: "I'm going to do my thing when I want to and I'm not going to be restrained." Mars and Pluto conjunct in Leo, quite elevated too—a strong will. Scorpio rising! A *very* strong willed person. Therefore, the only kind of person who could handle her would be someone who had a lot of inner strength—someone who wasn't going to battle her, have a battle of wills with her, because she would always win and then his ego couldn't handle it and he'd want out of the whole thing. But the only kind of person who could handle her would be someone who was *equally* independent and could handle her willfulness, and her strength and her power. So it's really curious; the guy she's married to now is an Aquarius. Remember she has Uranus (in the seventh house) conjunct her Sun exactly, and often the planet closely aspecting the Sun in a woman's chart (or a planet in the seventh house) will characterize the kind of man that she might marry.

Also, she was born with a very close Moon-Sun square, and the Moon square Uranus also. And I probably mentioned this in the last workshop also: Sun-Moon squares, particularly, incline the person to have some difficulty adjusting themselves to the culturally accepted role of male or female, active or passive. And she definitely has had that problem. All these planets here (pointing to the chart) are in the 9th house. A long time ago, before she even met this guy, I thought, "Look at this 9th house; I wonder what this means." It could traditionally be all sorts of foreign travel. It turns out her husband is from a foreign country, and through him she is getting into the importing business. He is a craftsman in antique furniture restoration, which is an art that hardly anyone in this country knows. His Mars-Saturn conjunction is exact in Cancer. Cancer so much lives in the past or is

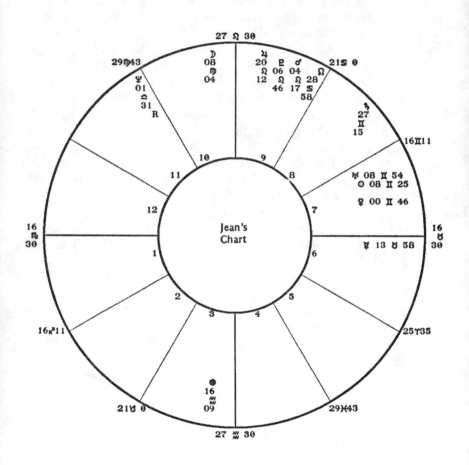

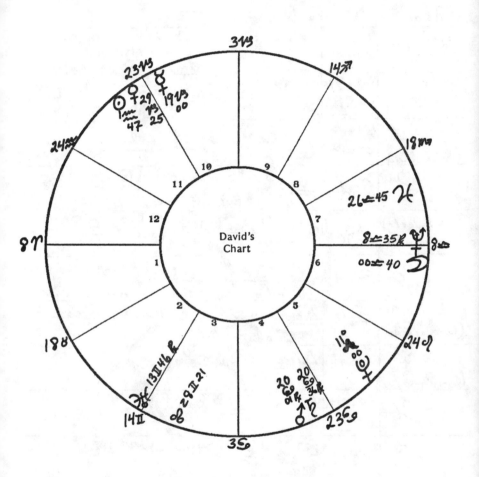

David's Chart

A. Jean	A's planet falls in this house in B's chart.	B. David
Natal planets of person requesting comparison or who is experiencing the most problems.		Planets in B's chart that are importantly related to A's planet in far-left column.
		(Note: ♃ = Sunsign Ruler ♀ = Moon sign Ruler ♂ = Ascendant's Ruler)
Asc.	late 7th or 8th	△♂♅♄ ; ⊼♃ ; incomp. Asc.; ⚹☿ ; □♀ (but both are ♂ signs)
☿ (Ruler of ☉+☽)	late 1st or 2nd	⚺♃ w. ⚹♂♇♄ ; □♇ ; △☿
♀	2nd	△☽ ; w. △♆ ; incomp. ♂ ; △☉ ; ⊼ M.C. ; △♀ (but different elements)
M.C. Ruler ☉ & ♃	2nd	♂♃ ⚹ Asc. ; ⚹♀ ; △♆ ; w. △☉♌☽
♄	3rd	♂♌ ; △♃ ; ⊼♀ ; ⊼☉ (comp. elements); □☽ (but compatible elements)
♂ (Co-ruler of Asc.)	5th	△Asc. ; w. ♂♀ ; ⚹☽♌♇ ♂♂☉ ; ⊼ M.C. ; incomp. with ♀&♂
♇ (Co-ruler of Asc.)	5th	△Asc. ; ♂♂☉ ; ⚹♆ ; ⚹☽
♃	late 5th or 6th	w. ⚹ ♃ ; ⚺♂♌♄ ; ⚹♃ , ⊼♀
☽	6th	□♃ ; ⚺♆ ; ⊼Asc. ; △M.C. ; comp. ♀ ; incomp. ☉&☽
♆	late 6th or 7th	♂☽ ; △☉ ; △♀ ; □M.C.
M.C.	6th	⚹♃ ; ⊼♀
♌	5th	⚹☽ ; ♂♀ (i.e., A's ♌ is ♂ B's ♀)

A. David	A's planet falls in this house in B's chart.	B. Jean
Natal planets of person requesting comparison or who is experiencing the most problems.		Planets in B's chart that are importantly related to A's planet in far-left column.
Asc.	5th	*Part II of this comparison.*
♅	late 7th or <u>8th</u>	
♂ & ♄	9th	
♀	9th	
☽	11th	
♇	11th	
♃	12th	
☿	late 2nd or <u>3rd</u>	
♀	3rd	
☉	3rd	
MC.	2nd	
♌	8th	

All Aspects remain the same and are written out on the previous page. One could repeat the process again, however, on this sheet if one wants to focus specifically on David's natal planets and his specific kinds of energy flow with Jean.

attached to things from the past, and his whole thing is hard work and ambition (Mars-Saturn) going into restoring antique furniture (Cancer)! With Aries rising, he's a very self-motivating type. He's also extremely self-assured—Aries rising, Aquarius Sun. They make a really interesting couple, actually. I though nobody could ever handle her, but they're doing fine.

Q: What about their Moons? They're not real compatible are they?

A: They're not (although both Libra and Virgo are extremely mental), and yet so far the whole thing is working for six years now. Both are so independent—Uranus conjunct the Sun here, and Aquarius Sun in the other chart. Seemingly, the two of them don't care about home life that much. At least she doesn't. She doesn't have anything in her 4th house or in Cancer. She has only one planet beneath the horizon. She is very much an outer directed person, very much involved in the world at large. His Mars and Saturn show that he has more of a need for a home base. The main thing, as I said before, is to look at what *is* there rather than what isn't. His Moon—his domestic needs, you might say his "wife needs"—is trine his Sun and exactly trine *her* Venus. So right there, there's a lot of emotional harmony; and for him, you might say his Moon is taken care of. Her Moon, fairly early in Virgo, is compatible by element with *his* Venus and with his Mercury, which helps good communication even though that's a very wide orb to call it a trine. His Uranus at 13° Gemini squares her Moon; but she was also born with that aspect anyway, so that's no big change. But if you look at some of the other aspects involving both people's Moons, you start to see some other less obvious dimensions of their relationship. First of all, Virgo is the most mental of all non-air signs, and so her capacity for analysis might fit in well with (and even complement) his air-sign Sun and Moon. Also, a thorough examination of this comparison shows many links between them that reflect their common enthusiasm for their shared work, and her Moon trines his Midheaven. I also think it's important that one of the "double whammys" in the comparison involves the Moon and Neptune. His Moon closely conjuncts her Neptune and her Moon is in almost an exact semi-sextile with his Neptune! You've got mutual sympathy there!

His Ascendant, 8° Aries, falls in her 5th house, so first of all you've got the Ascendant activating her 5th house: having a good time, love affairs, enjoying each other—children too, because now he's playing father to her two children. His ruling planet is Mars, right? At 20° Cancer. And his Saturn is also at 20° Cancer; and if you put them both in her chart, they trine her Ascendant. Another Ascendant contact that's very harmonious here is that the two co-rulers of her chart, Mars and Pluto (co-ruling her Scorpio Ascendant), are conjunct in her chart and trine *his* Ascendant. So this, combined with the fact that his Ascendant ruler Mars trines her Ascendant, makes this an extremely powerful "double whammy"—it's *especially* important since both people's Ascendant and ruler are involved. And if you really study the comparison closely (see Illustration No. 3), you then notice many other contacts involving the Ascendants. (Remember that the aspects involving one or both people's Ascendants or the rulers of the Ascendants are *always* especially important; and, to a slightly lesser extent, this also goes for the Descendants and their ruling planets.)

So, let's just run through the most important of these kinds of aspects—that is, those involving Ascendants, Descendants, or their rulers. Her Ascendant is in a fairly close quincunx (which I consider, along with the sextile, a pretty major aspect*) to his Uranus, which is the ruling planet of his Sun sign Aquarius. In addition, her Ascendant is also sextile his Mercury, which adds to the dynamic communication we mentioned before and which we'll also refer to next in relation to other chart factors. His Ascendant is exactly sextile her Sun-Uranus conjunction, and it might be noted that the Sun rules her Midheaven. (I did say before that their shared work and careers are one of the brightest spots in their relationship.) His Ascendant is also closely quincunx her Moon, and it's even in a wide trine to her North Node—in case anybody wants to take a swing at interpreting that. And you might notice that, although her co-rulers, Pluto and Mars (conjunct in Leo), are opposite his Sun, they are also sextile his Neptune and his Moon simultaneously! So don't isolate one aspect or one configuration and get all worried about it; see how any planet of one person merges with or combines with *all* the energies of the other person!

With the Descendants and their rulers, you also find some interesting contacts. Both of their Descendant rulers are Venus, first of all, and their Venuses are in quite a close trine, even though they are not in compatible elements. The closeness of the trine, I feel, makes it an

---

* You will note that, although I consider the quincunx to be a "major" aspect, I have not labeled the quincunx a "good" or "bad," "harmonious" or "stressful" interchange. With both individual charts and comparisons, the crucial thing is to see how a particular planet merges its energies with all the others; and especially in comparisons, isolating a single interaspect and artifically labeling it with a judgmental evaluation is misleading and narrowly limiting. With comparisons, the *overall* interchange of energy is what one is trying to perceive.

indication of considerable emotional compatibility, even without the accompanying harmony of the elements. Her Venus is closely trine *both his Sun and Moon*; and the fact that—as I mentioned earlier—his Venus is in a compatible element with her Moon gives them a mild Venus-Moon "double whammy." And if you look closely, you'll also see that they have a Venus-Neptune "double whammy," comprised of two Venus-Neptune trines. This almost always indicates a great deal of mutual sympathy, tolerance, soft feelings, and almost mystical love and closeness. And the emphasis on the shared work in their relationship is also shown by another "double whammy"—both people's Venuses closely quincunx the other person's Midheaven.

All this should point out to you that you shouldn't be thrown off by a few so-called "bad" or troublesome aspects; you've got to dig deep and really spend time at a comparison to do it right and to avoid misleading your clients. How can you possibly assimilate the meaning of thousands of possible combinations and interchanges if you only spend an hour or so looking at the charts? You can't; it's impossible. I always tell people to draw up the data in columns like I've shown you (see Illustration Nos. 1 & 3) and to analyze all the information in great detail *before* the consultation. In fact, I've found it useful to take colored pens and draw connecting circles around various factors to give me a visual reminder of "double whammies" and other important things when I'm referring to these columns during a consultation. Without the Data Sheet, I'd be lost.

And, while mentioning "double whammies," I might as well point out a few others in this comparison. (You'd never find so many important indicators repeated twice if you didn't spend a lot of time studying the data before the appointment.) Perhaps the most important which I haven't already mentioned, is that each person's Sun is *closely* trine the other person's Neptune! This can give an almost telepathic form of mutual identity and merging of their characters and creative energies. And when you combine this with the fact that they also have the Venus-Neptune double whammies that I mentioned earlier, you can see that it would take a lot to get these two people sufficiently hostile toward each other that they wouldn't forgive and forget. They *need* each other, and I'm sure they are quite aware of that mutual need. And the depth of the relationship is also shown by another double whammy: her Sun is sextile his Pluto, and his Sun is widely opposite her Pluto. So again, you have a double interchange involving the Suns and an outer planet.

His Sun at 2° Aquarius falls in her third house, which is a good place for it to be in a Gemini's chart because a Gemini needs communication. So that "lights up" or activates her house of communication. All of her other boyfriends or husbands were real dullards. None of them were up to her level intellectually; she has a very fast mind with Sun and Uranus conjunct in Gemini—new ideas and very good with her hands (especially crafts) with all the Mercury and Gemini emphasis. Take his Sun; not only is it trine *his* Moon at 1° degree Libra, but his Sun and Moon are both trine her Venus! So he's got that natal Sun-Moon trine, which in so many cases shows that you have no doubts about what sex you are. You don't get uptight. You can relate to the opposite sex without being threatened. If your wife is real aggressive or real strong, you don't care; that's just her trip—it doesn't have anything to do with you. And he's like that. There's this strong flow of energy through him, and a strong wife doesn't threaten him in the least. His Sun and Moon are also both widely trine her Sun, and they're both trine her Uranus, which shows exciting new changeable things and a great deal of independence in relationships. This relationship has just enough conflict that I think it's going to work out pretty well.

His Sun at 2° Aquarius is opposite her Pluto and Mars—the rulers of her Scorpio Ascendant. And indeed there could be a battle of wills at times, and she does push him now and then, but he doesn't need too much pushing and besides he can handle pushing because he has Aries rising. He even *likes* a little pushing. Aries likes to push around. If he had, say, Cancer rising and no Aries, then she could push him around and he might not like it.

Q: How about the Neptune relation with Pluto?

A: Well, what about it?

Q: Is that a precise sextile? (Referring to his Neptune being almost exactly sextile her Pluto.) Wouldn't that help manage some of her power drive?

A: Well, I don't interpret aspects like that as too important in themselves, because everyone born for many many months would have Neptune or Pluto in the same place. So, by itself it doesn't emphasize an important *individual* characteristic. How they merge with the personal planets, though, is important.

Q: What I'm getting at is: it seems she could charm him out of some things, and he could also charm her out of some of the power drive because of the tie of the Sun and Pluto and the Neptune.

A: You're talking about how his Sun links into a number of things at once then.

Q: Well, I tuned in on the Pluto thing first, and then it seemed to me that there were a whole bunch of things that would decrease the pressure that could be caused by the Pluto-Mars thing in her chart—like ameliorate it.

A: Yes. Just the sextile by itself (his Neptune and her Pluto) is not too important; but when you get all those other things in there, that's more important. And it gives individual meaning to the Neptune-Pluto sextile.

Something that's real important, especially for air signs, is some kind of harmonious or positive Mercury aspects. Their Mercurys are in trine also. They've started a joint business that seems to be going quite well, and so we should also look at Jupiter and Saturn aspects. What they have here is: his Jupiter at 27° Libra, first of all, is widely sextile her Jupiter—which is good for humor and mutual trust—and then his Jupiter is also closely sextile her Midheaven (a Saturn house). But this is only one Jupiter-Saturn interchange, because her Jupiter is almost exactly semi-sextile his Saturn; his Jupiter is trine her Saturn almost exactly. These Jupiter-Saturn combinations are excellent for business management, for managing your time, energy, and money. It's a nice blend of conservative and expansive, but of course you couldn't necessarily say that if they were in a square or opposition.

O.K., they've got a nice little Saturn-Moon square here. His Moon at 1° Libra is square her Saturn; however it's more than 4 degrees off from the exact square, and they're in the same element anyway. I'm not saying that that necessarily makes a big difference, but I think it's nice that they have a Saturn square here because they need something to stabilize them; and her Saturn loosely squaring his Moon and also closely quincunxing his Venus can provide some stability, in addition to his Saturn trining her Ascendant.

There are some things to look at in terms of houses too. His Moon falls in her 11th house, almost conjunct the 11th cusp—so it's an especially strong 11th house emphasis. The Moon or any personal planet falling in your 11th can be really nice because the 11th house shows where you look for a *friendly* kind of feedback. In other words, she would see him as a *friend* with his Moon falling in her 11th house, and not just as a mate and co-worker and so on, but as a friend too—someone to whom she could go for advice or help or relaxing companionship. And when you take her planets and put them in his chart, her Mars, Pluto, and Jupiter (this huge, strong-will, assertive Leo combination) all fall in his fifth house. He loves it! The 5th house shows what you really like, what you enjoy, what you get a kick out of, unless perhaps you have Saturn there—then you don't like anything. (laughter) Her Moon in Virgo falls in his 6th house, which seems to be manifesting as her activating his house of work through support and interest. She's helping him in his work. She handles some of the miscellaneous bookkeeping and bureaucracy and some of the customers so that he can be in the back shop doing the physical work. Otherwise he would be interrupted all the time.

A few other house placements might be mentioned briefly, since we're already running overtime. Her Saturn falls in his 3rd house, while his Mercury conjuncts her 3rd cusp—just another indication of learning from each other, probably rather intense communication, and an interest in each other's ideas. The fact that his Mars-Saturn conjunction is conjunct her 9th cusp also indicates a learning experience of some importance; in this case, she is encouraged to learn and expand her horizons through his influence on her. And, in fact, she has learned a great deal about antiques, their value, their market, and so on; and she's enjoyed learning all that. His Midheaven (career indicator) falls in her 2nd house, showing that she may well appreciate his knowledge and experience. Anything falling in your natal 2nd house can show that you *appreciate* that aspect of the other person's nature, that you value it a lot and indeed may even want to possess or control that part of the other person. But keep in mind that the 2nd house is a *Venus house;* and her Mercury (the Sun's ruler), Venus (ruler of her Descendant), and her Sun-Uranus conjunction all fall in *his* 2nd house, so he can also appreciate and highly value many of her qualities and abilities. Her Mercury falls in his late first house, according to traditionalists, but I feel it is close enough to the 2nd house cusp to be considered a 2nd house placement. And one final thing: his Uranus (the ruler of his Sun sign) falls either in her late seventh house or conjunct her eighth cusp, while her Ascendant has a similar placement in his chart. Whether the 7th or 8th house meaning will dominate would take some pointed questioning and investigation; it could be both.

Q: Pretty soon she'll have Uranus crossing her Ascendant, what will that do?

A: I don't know. That's usually an awakening to a new way of life. In some cases there are dramatic outer changes. In other cases everything on the surface stays the same, but the person starts having radically new attitudes towards all kind of things. Last year in my classes, I mentioned Uranus going across the Ascendant and that most people who have had it in recent months or years should be able to identify with it and remember what was going on then as a very important new development. Two people said, "I have such and such Scorpio rising, and I don't see what important thing happened then." So we looked up exactly when Uranus crossed their Ascendants for the first time, and it turns out that both of them got into astrology then, which revolutionized their attitude toward everything. So your whole life is revolutionized when Uranus hits the ascendant, either in a subtle way or an obvious way or often both. (Workshop is running overtime, so everyone gets ready to leave.) Does anyone have questions, comments, threats? [Chaos then ensues as people struggle to carry their coats, notepads, tape recorders, and books toward the door, some trying to leave as soon as possible while others are shouting questions through the crowd toward the speaker. Since it is impossible to discriminate one question from another through the din, the speaker attempts to disappear by hiding under the table. Nevertheless, a few determined people still manage to spot him and crawl under the table, gesticulating toward their own charts with frenzied eyes and frantic gestures as they demand immediate chart comparisons as the sole remaining hope in their desperate struggle to save their current relationships. Needless to say, none of this is distinctly audible on the tape recording.]

III — The Use of the Houses in Chart Comparison

It is intriguing how many factors in astrological interpretation (even those that are difficult to understand when interpreting an individual natal chart) are clarified when one begins to study chart comparisons (i.e., "Synastry"). The reason for this is, I think, that interpreting an individual chart demands that the astrologer concentrate on innate potentialities and tendencies *in the abstract*. These factors remain abstract in most cases as long as the astrologer has nothing to relate them to; he thus has no way of knowing what the *concrete* expression of the potentialities will be. It is only when a person comes into relationship with another person, event, or experience that his latent response-tendencies *come into being* clearly, i.e., become manifested *in the world*.

I feel that the use of chart comparisons in astrological research can clarify many subjects that are now the source of so much debate and confusion among astrologers. For example, the question of which

---

*The following, in its original form, first appeared in *Aquarian Astrology* magazine, published by Popular Library. It was then reprinted in an anthology, *Synastry: An Astrological Study of Relationships*, published in 1973 by the British Astrological Association. Hundreds of photocopies of the original article have also been circulated privately. However, this version represents a revised and edited improvement upon the original article.

house system is superior can be (and desperately *needs* to be) more thoroughly researched by using this method. I have experimented with the Placidus, Campanus, Equal House, and Koch House systems in chart comparisons. And, although the first three all have qualities to recommend them (especially the Equal House System), I regularly use the Koch system in both natal chart work and comparisons.

In comparing horoscopes, if I want to know how someone *experiences* me, I place all my planets and my ascendant in his chart. If I want to see how *my* experience of another is symbolized astrologically, I place his planets and ascendant in my chart. The planets and the ascendant are placed in the same degree of the zodiac in the other's chart where they are located in one's natal chart. I cannot emphasize enough that synastry provides a way of understanding how a person *experiences* the *wholeness* of another person. There are many kinds of associations between people, and all of them are complex because of the very nature of human complexity.

Therefore, when many planets fall in my angular houses, for example, there is an *emphasis* on this *type* of association. But this one factor by no means *defines* the relationship. In doing chart comparisons, we must at all times remain conscious of the wholeness of the two people involved and therefore aware also of the wholeness and subtlety of the relationship itself. Like the individuals involved, the relationship is itself a living entity. The emphasis will vary according to which planets fall in which houses, and according to how the planets from another's chart aspect one's own natal planets. Although the other's planets in my chart will reveal an emphasis on *some* kind of association, I feel it necessary to point out that it may be hard for the astrologer to know exactly what type of association the two people themselves are *consciously* attempting to create with each other. For example, if I am contemplating marriage, the other person's Moon falling in my natal seventh house will be more evident to me and more important (at least at this time) than, for example, her Saturn in my natal sixth house. What I am emphasizing here is the need for the astrologer to exemplify what psychologist Carl Rogers calls "unconditional regard" for the client. It is better to say nothing than to say something based upon personal bias or on an incomplete experience of the relationship at hand.

THE EFFECT OF THE PLANETS
OR THE ASCENDANT

A planet will stimulate or affect the area of life and field of experience indicated by the house in which it falls in the other person's chart. There are always numerous possible meanings; however, either the positive or the negative will tend to predominate during a given time period, depending upon how the planet is aspected with the natal planets and upon the priorities, values, and level of understanding of the people involved. Over time, it should be noted, the meaning of a particular planet's placement may change—for better or worse.

The brief meanings of the planets that follow are particularly applicable for use in chart comparison. They are only guidelines and by no means are considered exhaustive or complete.

The **Sun** gives life, energy, and vitality to that area of life indicated by the house in which it falls; it stimulates self-expression and creativity in that area; its position reveals a *dynamic* point of contact with the other, wherein a great deal of life force is expressed openly and, at best, with great encouragement.

The **Moon** can have many meanings. It can reveal flux and constant change in the relationship in that area indicated; it can mean an emotional contact, either emotionally supportive and receptive or emotionally unstable; it can indicate how the other person's "personality" affects me; it can reveal feelings of domestic comfort; and it can indicate marked responsiveness that we feel from the person in that area of life experience.

Mercury stimulates communication in the area indicated: a great deal of thought and analysis as well as the potential to synthesize and share diverse ideas; it can mean adaptability and versatility in a positive sense, or too much change, emotional coldness, and superficiality.

Mars stimulates whatever area of life it touches, giving a push, an impetus, courage, initiative; e.g., Mars falling in my fifth house can powerfully stimulate my self-expression and/or strong romantic attachments; it can cause disruption, destruction, or flare-ups of temper; it always indicates the release of some kind of power, and its aspects provide insight as to how harmoniously this energy will be expressed in a given relationship.

Venus, if "well-aspected," shows harmony, ease, comfort, pleasure and a general "beneficent" influence in the area indicated; it can also mean love, appreciation, and attraction; it can indicate possessiveness, jealousy, and a feeling of aesthetic revulsion in some cases where the aspects with it are the traditional stressful ones.

Saturn can indicate limitation, frustration, obstacles, fear, guilt, and suspiciousness; it can stimulate self-consciousness, feelings of inferiority, awkwardness, and a sense of inadequacy in the area indicated. It usually signifies a point of both difficulty (or pressure) and depth of learning in any relationship; and most often, it is experienced (*at least at first*) as rather "heavy." However, it can have the following good effects: helping one to define one's attitudes in a given area and awakening a sense of duty, ambition, and economy. Another's Saturn falling in one of my natal houses can indicate that the other's influence on me will cause me to be more self-reliant, to have more of a responsible, inwardly-serious attitude toward the area indicated. Also, another's Saturn falling in my chart can help me to tone down my innate negative tendencies or undisciplined energies and habits.

Jupiter can indicate growth, preservation, prosperity, broadened learning, expansion, enthusiasm, feelings of strength and well being, generosity, and the development of a more universal approach in the area indicated. It can also indicate wasteful extravagance or encouragement to over-expand one's plans or activities.

Uranus usually indicates some sort of upheaval, friction, sudden change, or radical departure from social norms. It can also symbolize the unexpected, eccentric, and erratic. It is often experienced as troublesome and disturbing at first, especially to those not open to free-wheeling experimentation and new ideas. But it can lead to original ideas, new kinds of personal growth, inner transformation, or a new birth of personal freedom and independence. The position of Uranus often shows excitement and, simultaneously, often instability.

Neptune indicates a point of contact with the profound depths (or heights) of human experience. It can indicate deception, deceit, confusion, illusion, or dissolution in the area indicated. But even the dissolution can lead to a rebirth of one's approach to the area of life symbolized. It can also signify mystical feelings of oneness or grace, inspiration, intuition, imagination, or spiritual awakening. It is usually experienced as *at least somewhat* confusing at first, or at least as curiously intriguing.

Pluto falling in a particular house of my natal chart can indicate that my attitude toward that area of life must be totally destroyed and then rebuilt in a new way. My orientation toward this entire field of experience may undergo total change and regeneration. Pluto's influence is often experienced as profoundly disturbing, unstable, and often agonizingly painful. But here again, as in the cases of the other trans-Saturnian planets, we find an opportunity for personal rebirth.

Note: the **house** positions of Uranus, Neptune, and Pluto are not nearly as important as the aspects when comparing charts of people the same age.

Where the **Ascendant** of another person falls in my chart indicates how that person will *essentially* affect me. It also often signifies how he will most pronouncedly enter my life and what sort of first impression he makes upon me.

ANGULAR, SUCCEDENT & CADENT HOUSES

The planets and the ascendant will fall in angular, succedent, or cadent houses of the other person's chart. If the Sun, Moon, Ascendant, or two or more planets fall in a particular type of house, that sort of association is emphasized.

Angular Houses (1st, 4th, 7th and 10th): An emphasis on my angular houses indicates an active, dynamic, intense relationship, an association based on common intention, direction, or goal. The relationship is focused upon a specific activity; and the two people will *do* things together. A great amount of emphasis on my angular houses indicates that the other person *acutely* affects my own identity. If the specific activities retain our interest and continue to stimulate us, the relationship can be long-lasting.

Succedent Houses (2nd, 5th, 8th and 11th): An emphasis on my succedent houses indicates potential stability in the relationship. Major planets or the ascendant falling in my succedent houses can indicate an enduring, long-lasting association, founded on unchanging orientations and attitudes. This sort of relationship is not necessarily exciting, but it has the advantage of reliability. There is often an emphasis on money, possessiveness, or other security factors.

Cadent Houses (3rd, 6th, 9th and 12th): An emphasis on my cadent houses indicates that the impact of the other person on my life will come chiefly through mental association. Learning, personal change, growth, and development will be strong orientations of the relationship. If I *willingly* learn from the person, his influence on me will be that I grow and develop through the *conscious* application to my own life of that which I learned from him, i.e., that I grow through consciously changing myself in ways stimulated by the other person. If so-called "malefics" fall in my cadent houses, stressfully aspected to my natal planets, I will experience the person as nagging, unaccepting, or manipulative. The relationship will endure primarily if I continue to learn from and to be stimulated by the other person.

We can now look at the individual houses, in four groups, depending upon whether the house is associated with a water, earth, air, or fire sign. I must point out that the meanings of the houses in chart comparison are often slightly different from the traditional meanings assigned them for the interpretation of a natal chart.

THE LIFE HOUSES OR HOUSES OF IDENTITY

These are the houses associated with the fire signs. Planets falling in those houses can encourage or oppress my sense of radiance and well-being; and they indicate a *sense of identity* that I feel for the other person. In other words, these planets ideally give me *spirit* and make me feel *alive!* And even when the interaction is more stressful, the other person still has a strong impact on shaping my identity and self-confidence.

First House: Planets falling in my first house stimulate me immediately and directly, and they give me a feeling of *identity* with that aspect of the other person symbolized by the planet (or planets) which falls here.

Fifth House: Planets falling in my fifth house affect my ability to communicate my emotions, to express myself freely and creatively, and to enjoy myself immediately. I identify emotionally with whatever aspect of the person is symbolized by the planet concerned; in other words, I can enjoy and express myself *through* the other person in whatever way is indicated by the planet. If, for example, another person's Saturn falls in my fifth house, my ability to enjoy myself may be limited or toned down, or I may greatly enjoy that person's seriousness and capability and hence enjoy myself through that person's qualities.

Ninth House: Planets falling in my ninth house affect my philosophical views, religious beliefs, my conscious aims for my own growth, and

—generally—things in which I find meaning, value, and philosophical significance. Planets in my ninth influence my *understanding* in a way that either promotes or inhibits my growth, development, and conscious orientation for changing myself. They can help or hinder my learning from experience.

THE RELATIVE OR ASSOCIATION HOUSES

These are the houses associated with the air signs. Planets falling in these houses stimulate intellectual interests and personal and social relations. In other words, planets in these houses bring me into contact with other *persons*, whom I see as individuals with whom I want to relate in a truly *personal* way.

Third House: Planets falling in my third house affect my way of communicating with others, chiefly through associative mental processes and speech. Planets here stimulate my growth, change, and learning in areas of mental development and intellectual expression; they can awaken my feelings of being a peer with the other person and show the ability to establish quick personal rapport with the other person.

Seventh House: Planets falling in my seventh house stimulate my feelings of partnership and of *particularly* close association toward the other person. These planets emphasize some aspects of true relatedness, a mutual give-and-take between us. This sort of relationship will tend to complement the view I have of myself, if the planets are "benefics;" or it will disrupt or force change in my self-concept through the effects of the interaction. This form of relationship tends to be felt as a specifically one-to-one balanced sharing of the persons' energies.

Eleventh House: Planets falling in my eleventh house will either promote or inhibit my attainment of friendly, congenial relationships and social stability. For example, if the other person's Jupiter or Venus falls in my eleventh, there is a strong likelihood that I will see him or her as a true friend, i.e., one who loves me and enhances my feelings of social acceptance and security. In addition, that person may help to clarify my real purpose in society and my future personal plans.

An *over-emphasis* on these two types of houses (i.e., "fire" or "air" houses) calls for caution in my approach to the relationship; for it could easily burn itself out in a short time if it has no deeper foundations in either emotional or practical considerations.

TEMPORAL OR POSSESSIVE HOUSES

These houses are associated with the earth signs and thus pertain to practical considerations. Planets falling in these houses show that those aspects of the other person indicated by those planets are *useful* to me, i.e., that they serve *my* purposes. The relationship thus could be a good, convenient arrangement (marriage, business, etc.) if our motives are openly accepted; or, if the other person is unwilling to be used for my ends, it could then develop into a manipulative, even destructive relationship, with my *using* the other person for purely selfish purposes.

Second House: Planets falling in my second house stimulate my desires to value, own, possess, or control the other person (or some aspect, quality, or ability of the person). What I do about these desires, i.e., my attitude toward them, will then create either a manipulative relationship (often in the name of "love") or an association in which I can appreciate and freely cherish the other person. If I can realize that the person is "mine" in the largest sense, without *owning* him or her, then a relationship of deep contentment can ensue. Planets in my second house can also indicate financial ties, an influence upon my possessions, or an impact on my business plans and activities.

Sixth House: Planets falling in my sixth house indicate an influence upon my habits and upon my efforts to change myself in basic down-to-earth ways. Planets here stimulate learning that leads to growth and change in my daily life. Such an influence can help or hinder me: it can undermine what I am and my own efforts to change *in my own way,* or it can provide me with support and comfort in my conscious attempts at self-development. I will thus experience a person whose planets or ascendant fall in my sixth house as strongly influencing me, in either a helpful or nagging way. An emphasis on my sixth house can also indicate positive stimulation of my productive work, or—in some cases—interference with my productivity and work goals.

Tenth House: Planets falling in my tenth house serve my ambitions and my hopes for worldly success, honor, reputation, and public approval. Planets here can also indicate a business or professional association, the satisfaction of ego-needs for recognition and power, or can have an important impact on shaping the kinds of social structures (e.g., marriage or career) I want to build. Whatever planet falls in my tenth shows that that function or quality in the other person relates to my sense of public approval, authority, or to the kind of ambition I am working toward. If the other's ascendant or Sun falls in my tenth house, I may be ambitious with regard to him; I may tend to utilize him and to have high hopes *for myself* through him. If I am able to transcend the selfish aspect of my feelings, I can then simply have hopes for the person freely, regardless of my own satisfaction. In other cases, I may see that person as an authority in his or her own right, and I may respect this ability and patiently learn from the person.

THE PSYCHIC HOUSES

These houses are associated with the water signs and thus have an impact on me in those areas where I am most psychic, sensitive, and vulnerable. Planets falling in these houses reveal those aspects or qualities of the other person that influence me emotionally, that can penetrate deeply into me. Thus, I will often be somewhat threatened by such a person because I am so vulnerable to him. Therefore, I can react to the other person by fearing or disliking him; or I can open up to him in the hope that we can develop a relationship at a deep, *soul* level. People whose planets or ascendant fall in my "water" houses are able to penetrate into the depths of my being, and to reveal my limitations, weaknesses, and deepest desires. Such deep contact between people can result in profound, intense, emotional ties; but there is often a tendency toward explosions, upheavals, instability, and constant irritability on my part. The future of the relationship will depend a great deal not only upon how *I* react to this threat (which is also a possibility for closeness), but also upon the other person's attitude toward the power that he has over me. A relationship with many ties in these houses will prosper mainly if the two people are emotionally at peace with themselves.

Fourth House: Planets falling in my fourth house affect my most personal, deep, vulnerable emotions in the roots of my being. The effect of planets in this house, therefore, is usually experienced as either comfortable and secure or as disturbing and frustrating. For example, Pluto falling in my fourth can represent a profoundly disturbing effect upon the emotional foundations of my existence, which may turn out to be either a positive or a negative experience. Planets here also effect domestic tranquility, and one's ability to totally relax in someone else's presence.

Eighth House: Planets falling in my eighth house stimulate deep, often sexual and erotic, *powerful* feelings in me. If the planets are stressfully aspected, there may be a power struggle; and I may find my efforts to exert power and control over the other person disrupted (Uranus in my eighth) or thwarted (Saturn in my eighth). This house in part represents my emotional search for values, which effort on my part can be helped or hindered by the other person. The eighth house also represents a test of my responsibility in the use of my power. Planets falling in this house can also have the effect of producing some type of spiritual awakening in me, as well as a powerful yearning for emotional peace and healing at a deep level.

Twelfth House: Planets falling in my twelfth house affect me emotionally in ways that can awaken me to the unknown, to that which is essentially beyond my understanding. Planets in my twelfth influence me through vague, usually-confusing emotions. Such influences often awaken fear in me, although planets here *can* also greatly influence my spiritual development. In other words, planets falling in the twelfth stimulate growth, development, and change in profoundly deep ways, affecting the very roots of the emotions at the spiritual level. Influences represented by planets falling in the twelfth house are essentially beyond my conscious understanding. Therefore, I often react to this aspect of the other person with distrust, worry, fear, or uneasiness. This is especially true if the planets falling in my twelfth are "malefics." If the planets are "benefics," then I can often sense some kind of hidden support from the other person. The twelfth house generally indicates the blind spot in ourselves, the influences from others of which we are only vaguely conscious. For example, if the other person's ascendant falls in my twelfth house, he is *essentially* beyond my understanding. He bewilders and confuses me. I feel overwhelmed by him. Thus, I can react to him by giving way to my irrational fears, or I can appreciate the sense of mystery and complexity that he inspires in me. The twelfth house is especially important in chart comparisons; for it can reveal the needs of a soul for future growth and give quite specific clues about karmic ties with the other person. For example, why am I so irrationally fearful of violence from Mr. M? Astrologically, his Mars falls in my twelfth house. Do these emotions come from nowhere? Or do they indicate, along with the astrological symbols, a past relationship in which I *ex-*

perienced the potential violence of Mr. M? These questions can be answered only in the personal experience of each of us. What I am emphasizing here is that the twelfth house indicates (both in the natal chart and in synastry) things that we have to come to terms with and integrate in our conscious spiritual-psychological growth. Therefore, an analysis of our close friends' (and enemies'!) charts in comparison with our own can reveal things that we all need to be aware of in order to live and relate more freely.

In a chart comparison, an *over-emphasis* on my possessive and psychic (or "earth" and "water") houses calls for caution in my approach to the relationship; for it could develop into a manipulative and emotionally-enslaving experience, i.e., a relationship that could be "negative" and even life-denying if both people insist on clinging to the past and to limited emotional and security patterns.

****

Note: Lois H. Sargent's book *How to Handle Your Human Relations* is an excellent work on Synastry, and its section on the interpretation of inter-chart aspects is without equal in subtlety and accuracy. Lois Sargent has a deep understanding of the *relative importance* of various aspects in comparisons. However, the book says very little about the interpretation of the houses in Synastry. Hence, this article is meant to fill that gap and is intended to be used in conjunction with Sargent's book. (The book is available from the AFA—its publisher—and from CRCS Publications, the publisher of this book.)

IV — Understanding Transits

The most important transits—and this is what I want to focus on in this workshop—are transits of the outer five planets—Jupiter, Saturn, Uranus, Neptune, and Pluto. They are usually the most important in indicating major life developments. When you pay attention to *all* of the transits going on in your chart, you'll often see things happening with Venus transits, Mars transits, and even Mercury transits; but they are usually very transitory types of experiences, with no lasting depth or significance. Conjunctions, squares, and oppositions are the aspects that *usually* correlate with the most important experiences. But I have begun to pay a lot of attention to the transiting semi-sextiles, semi-squares, and quincunxes also—*especially* the semi-sextiles. It's true that on certain days you will feel a certain flow and there will be a sort of harmonious feeling to your whole day. And you'll look up your transits and you'll find that Venus is trine your Sun or Venus is sextile your Mars or Jupiter is trine your Moon. So you can also look at trines and sextiles, but those are very minor things in most cases, especially if you *isolate* them; but a trine or sextile of a transiting outer planet to some natal chart planet can be quite significant if it occurs *at the same time* as a more challenging transiting aspect.

There's a whole approach to astrology that is just starting to develop and an approach to transits along with it that could be called the "holistic" or "cyclic" approach. Dane Rudhyar, of course, pioneered in developing and popularizing this approach. It's probably the best framework in which to view specific transits. Basically, you treat all transits in terms of the entire cyclic relationship between any two planets. There are a number of ways to do this, but—for example—say Saturn (or any of the outer planets) is conjunct your natal Venus right now. O.K. In about 7 years Saturn will square that Venus; in another 7 years or so, Saturn will oppose that Venus; in 7 more years Saturn will square it again and so on. Well, in this sort of holistic approach, if you really want to look at the whole thing and not just look at transits as isolated little blips of experience, you start out with the conjunction.

Say transiting Saturn right now is squaring your natal Venus (goes to board to draw example). Let's make a kind of natural chart here. Let's say you have Venus in 15° Cancer. O.K. Now say Saturn is in Libra. If transiting Saturn is at 15° Libra now and you have your natal Venus in 15° Cancer, there is obviously a square between those two planets. Whatever is going to be happening then, you can probably *interpret* it quite accurately, in a traditional sense, just by knowing what Saturn means, what Venus means, what houses are involved, etc. You don't *have* to look at the whole thing, the whole cycle. And you often won't have time to do so when you're doing other people's charts. But "interpretation" is often different from *understanding*. So, with your own chart or for people who are real close to you and whose inner experiences are fairly well known to you or for those few clients who *do* care about the deeper meanings of life, it may be worthwhile to look back 7 years and see what was happening when Saturn was conjunct the natal Venus. What was happening *then* is very often related to what is happening now, because both transits are part of one cycle that symbolizes the total interaction between Saturn and Venus. And if you look at transits that way, you can use the semi-squares, semi-sextiles, and so on much more practically and comprehensibly, because you'll then see those aspects as change or development periods within the context of an entire cycle, even if they don't coincide with striking "events." You'll just *understand* your current experiences more thoroughly. And in your own life—especially with Jupiter and Saturn transits—it's worth looking back a few years and seeing what was happening the last time Jupiter or Saturn hit the natal planet that it's now hitting. Because very often you can remember what was happening then and you can relate it to what is happening now, and you can see that developmental order and process and pattern in your life.

Q: Are you suggesting that we go back and look at the identical point or what? You were talking about Saturn and 7 years—you would have to go back 28 years to find the identical point, wouldn't you?

A: To find the identical aspect, yes. But that's not what I'm saying. I'm just saying that, especially with Jupiter and Saturn transits, just go back to the previous conjunction, square, or opposition. (This is also useful with Uranus transits, but then you should include semi-sextiles and other aspects as well.) In other words, say Saturn is hitting your Venus now by any of those three kinds of aspects, then go back seven years and see what was happening then, when Saturn was conjunct, square or opposite Venus at that time.

Q: And then try to find a common denominator between the two experiences?

A: Yes. Now sometimes you can relate it in a very obvious way. Say, seven years ago you got married and now you're reorganizing that marriage. In other cases it would be subtler, like now you're breaking up with so and so and seven years ago you were breaking up with someone else. It's showing you this pattern in your life and the fact that there are certain things that you were confronting seven years ago which you're still confronting now. By doing this, you can judge for yourself how much you have developed in those seven years. With Uranus transits, use all aspects that are multiples of 30°, and then you'll see that some transformation or awakening or clarified understanding has happened approximately every 7 years in some dimension of your life, as Uranus periodically made those aspects to a specific natal planet. The conjunctions, squares, and oppositions are naturally the most powerful (and often most dramatic) transits, but—especially with Uranus—the other aspects also often reveal some significant change taking place, although it may not be a major crisis and may not confront you so blatantly.

Since Jupiter goes through the whole zodiac in twelve years, about every three years Jupiter is conjunct, square, or opposite any major point in the chart. With Jupiter therefore, all you have to do is go back three years to find some significant pattern. And often, but not always, there will be a connection between those various periods. You can only go back in most cases to the last conjunction. Theoretically that is the beginning of that cycle. In other words, say you've got

Saturn square Venus now. Well, you can go back 7 years to when Saturn was conjunct Venus. Whether you can then go back 7 years further, whether that will show you much I don't know. I doubt if it would be that important.

Q: I know, with Sun and Saturn, if you go back 28 years you find some pretty major things.

A: Oh yes. I'm not saying major things won't be there every time or almost every time. I am saying that the specifics of each cycle are kind of different, especially with the Saturn cycle. First of all, if you look at the Saturn return at about age 29 or 30, that is the end of one complete life cycle in terms of your entire life structure, your ambitions, your priorities, your whole character. But you can also look at other Saturn cycles. Say Saturn is conjuncting Venus, conjuncting Mars, conjuncting anything, conjuncting the Ascendant too, which we'll talk about later. All of those Saturn conjunctions begin new cycles, essentially new 29 or 30 year cycles. They're cycles related to building different kinds of life structures, depending on what natal planet is being hit.

A FRAMEWORK FOR TRANSITS

Before going into more specifics, I want to mention some key ideas about transits that Donna Cunningham points out in her book *An Astrological Guide to Self-Awareness*.* In that book, she very concisely provides a good attitude and a constructive framework for using transits, in the chapter called "A Spiritual & Psychological Perspective on Transits." She says that transits are not isolated events over which you have no control but instead are part of an integral psychological process that you are participating in. O.K., that's one point that I'll try to make today, quite often I hope. Although in most cases you can pick a specific transit and say specific and accurate things about it based only on the nature of the planets involved, to make it really useful you have to look at the entire current *pattern* of transits; because in most cases, when there is one important transit, there are usually at least two and often three, four, or five other significant transits within a period of a very few months. And such complicated patterns are impossible to interpret in any rigid or dogmatic way, because all you can do is get a feeling for all the different transits and try intuitively to bring them together in the context of the person's entire life situation and present state of consciousness.

---

*Published by, and available from, CRCS Publications, the publishers of this book.

Another thing that Donna Cunningham points out is that one cannot fully understand a particular person's transits *without a deep knowledge of the natal chart.* She says, for example, if transiting Neptune is squaring your natal Mars, you have to take into account how both Mars and Neptune operate in your chart, according to sign, house, what houses they rule, what aspects they have, and their general strength. That is really, really true. That is why most books on transits are—well, *most* books on transits are almost worthless. Even the better books on transits are only useful as rudimentary guidelines to what may be experienced during certain periods. And that's because there is so much depth, so much subtlety and complexity in anybody's chart and in anybody's life. You can read all these books; most books on transits tend to be dogmatic and also tend to be rather negative. And yet if you test what those books say, in so many cases it won't jive with what people really *experience.* If you're an astrologer or into astrology and you read all these books and believe that all these negative things will happen, then very likely they will. But as long as you protect yourself from all those negative attitudes, then very often what will be happening to you will be much subtler than what these books describe. I used to be in terror of certain transits when I first got into astrology, because all the books I'd read told me how horrible all of them were: "Uranus will hit your Sun—sudden accidents or death or something; the Saturn return—all your teeth will fall out and you'll look horrible and be sick." But as I've lived through more and more of these so-called traumatic transits, I'm realizing that most of them are quite interesting. You can really learn a lot. And many of them are quite fun, even if they're also stressful at times. But it's only knowledge of the natal chart that can enable you—before the transits are actually happening—to tune into the meaning of the important transits with more depth than just using the basic principles.

Another thing she says is that transits are *processes:* "Too much attention is paid to events in astrology and not enough to the processes that bring about those events. Actually, events are more like sign posts, more visible than the processes naturally, but you don't jump from one town to the next. You've covered that distance gradually. Events may be the culmination of a process, or they may be the catalyst that starts a process. But they are most useful to study as outer indications of inner trends." I think that is a really good point. Any transit can manifest as an inner urge, as an inner feeling alone with no outer things happening, or it can manifest as an outer experience that pressures the person to confront something. And that often happens if you didn't know what you had to deal with then—something in the outer world often brings you into contact with it. Or it can be both inner and outer. In many cases it is both.

Q: What would determine which or how much of each of those qualities ...?

A: I know of no way of determining how much it's going to be inner and how much it's going to be outer. The only general rule I've seen that makes any sense to me is: the more self-knowledge you have and the more subtle your consciousness is, the more you pick up the inner meanings of your life and of the experiences in your life and the more likely the transits will manifest on a subtler level rather than on a gross level. Very extroverted people who don't like to reflect—their transits tend to manifest as events most of the time; maybe 75% of their major transits will manifest as events. But I don't have any way of telling what the trend will really be. If you approach the outer events as indications of what's happening on the inner levels, it doesn't really matter then whether you can predict an event; because you can just tell yourself, or someone else whose chart you're working with, that *whatever* is going to be happening at a certain time has a basic kind of meaning that you can understand.

Q: So whatever the individual has to work through, it could be something occurring inwardly or something occurring outwardly, but they'll still have to work through a similar kind of ...?

A: Yes. Especially the real stressful transits. Saturn, of course, is especially known for work. But with any major transit of the outer five planets, there's often effort required—especially if it's the opposition, square, or conjunction because those are the aspects that challenge people to work, to put in or to put out energy. The main thing is that the work can be done on an inner level, or you can work off that tension on an outer level, or a combination of both. Say Saturn squares your Mars, you may have to work extra hard then. On the outer level you may have a job where suddenly you have more responsibilities; the company may have a big contract or something and you may have to work overtime for a month. Some people—if they're hard workers anyway, if they're active people—they'll work off that tension through outer activities. If they're real passive people who just lay around and complain quite a bit and don't think about themselves very much in a positive way, then they will be in the worst shape because they aren't active enough to work off that tension in gross activities. So they're liable to feel the worst frustration of all and to get real angry and resentful and frustrated.

Another alternative is that you can get in touch on a *subtle* level with what Saturn square Mars means within yourself. Say you're feeling lots of frustration: Saturn may be defining the expression of the Mars energy and in some cases actually blocking it, or at least definitely slowing down the speed with which you get what you want, which is one of the Mars meanings. But if you're a fairly patient person—and Saturn aspects particularly deal with the need to be patient—you can go within yourself and realize that this is part of a necessary process and that this is a time period when you've got to *define* some things within yourself, and so maybe there's a point to that frustration which you feel. As a matter of fact, most people who have experience with different kinds of psychotherapy know that frustration is an effective therapeutic tool. If you frustrate someone enough, they're going to have to develop new ways of dealing with things—either that or just be incredibly miserable. If you frustrate them enough, you'll be applying pressure to them so that, hopefully, they will eventually explode or try something new. Transiting Saturn hitting Mars or the Ascendant or the Sun are very often times when you'll feel that pressure or frustration most acutely. And then you have to work with the natal chart. If you're an Aries Sun with the Moon in Aries with Sagittarius rising, then you won't like that frustration! You won't want to tolerate it. You'll try to act in new ways and try to work it off, to work off that tension. If you're a more passive person, say a Pisces Sun with Moon in Libra and Virgo rising, tending more toward passivity and not initiating things, then those kinds of transits may be a little harder to deal with, or you may just decide, "The way I can best deal with them is just to be patient," and so you then might develop more inner depth of understanding and more acceptance of your real nature.

In consultations with a client, I first try to get an idea from him or her what has been going on in the last year. This is something that I cannot overemphasize. When I first started doing transits years ago, I never did that. I was so fascinated by the whole idea that you could tell something about the nature of a certain time period just from one little planet in relation to another one, I didn't really think about the meaning of what I was doing, the ramifications of the kind of counseling I was giving either. But more and more, it became apparent through hundreds and hundreds of consultations that you've got to do what

Donna Cunningham says in her book—you have to always look to the past year and sometimes to the past two or three or four years, depending on what's happening. The reasons for that should be obvious, but one reason is that some transits last over two years. Pluto and Neptune transits usually last two years or more, and likewise with a real powerful Uranus transit.

It's hard to say which is a powerful transit and which isn't, but usually if it's a conjunction, square, or opposition of the outer five planets to any of the personal planets (Sun, Moon, Mercury, Venus, Mars) or to the Ascendant or Descendant, you've got a particularly powerful energy flow or blockage. So you've got seven different points right there. If Uranus conjuncts something you've got a tremendous change released in your life, a tremendous energy released also. And how long will it last? Often it will be about two years from the first transit, from some months before the first conjunction to some months after the last one. Everyone here knows about retrograde planets, right? Transits often happen three times. They can hit one point, then go retrograde and hit it again, and then go direct and hit it for the third time. It can also happen that Neptune and Pluto can hit the same point five times. That will last over two years, and often even three years. Outer planets—their transits are so important. So you have to look back as well as forward when doing someone's chart or consulting with them, to really put things in a clear and broad perspective.

Another example is transiting Saturn, which seems to have a wider orb than any other transiting planet. Many people can feel it as soon as Saturn gets into a certain sign—especially if their Sun (or sometimes their Moon or the Ascendant) is in that sign or in square or opposition to it. Say your natal Sun is in Pisces, and Saturn is now going into Virgo. Some Pisces people will feel Saturn going into Virgo even if their Sun is 28° Pisces, that is, even if Saturn will not exactly oppose their Sun for two years. They will often feel it as soon as Saturn gets into the sign that's square or opposite their Sun sign or Moon sign or *in* their Sun sign or Moon sign. Anyway, Saturn is in a sign for approximately two and a half years, so there's one more factor that can last about two and a half years.

As a matter of fact, two and a half years is a good handy orb of time that you can generally give to the transits of all the outer *four* planets. It's not just from the first transit to the last transit that takes two and a half years, although that's true sometimes; but what seems to be true as far as I see—if it's an important life change and therefore usually indicated by something involving Uranus, Neptune, Pluto, or Saturn or a combination of two or more—what will often happen is that it will take *at least* two and a half years to *assimilate* the meaning of that change. Say you have your Sun in one degree Leo and Saturn conjuncted your Sun last summer. So, maybe even before that, certain things happened then and something probably *started* then, because remember conjunctions are the beginning of a new cycle and of course the end of an old one. That's why the conjunctions are so powerful. Not only do you have two planets merging their energies, but you have simultaneously ended a whole phase of life and launched out on a whole new cycle. And it may take 2½ years to realize what you've started and what you've ended and the essential meaning of these changes.

Q: In other words, the conjunction could be the climax of one kind of cycle or it could be the initiation of another kind of cycle that is building up?

A: Or very often both. It's usually both, especially if it is a transit of the outer four planets (Saturn, Uranus, Neptune, Pluto) to the personal planets or sometimes to Jupiter or Saturn or to the Descendant, Ascendant, or Mid-heaven. In contrast to the conjunctions, the square aspects usually mark major *adjustments.* Say any of the outer planets squares your Sun or your Moon or Venus, I'm not saying that important things don't happen and that there's no realizations then, but that you're *adjusting* to something that's already going on. Sometimes you do completely stop doing something and you start doing something else, but it's much more common that you make an adjustment during the square aspects. The conjunction, on the other hand, very, very often correlates with the absolute end of a cycle—a very definite end and a very definite beginning. However, and this is another good thing to know about conjunctions, people will often sense the *end* of things but they won't immediately sense the beginning of a new long-range cycle. Take Saturn again, or Uranus or Pluto, these three transits (and even Neptune sometimes) will correspond with the end of something—some decision to terminate something, or circumstances which forcibly terminate something, as with a Saturn transit or with a Pluto transit where right before your eyes something just totally disappears, some big thing in your life is just totally gone. Or Uranus can just rip away the past very quickly and often seemingly quite violently. So what people often notice is, "Help! The past is gone." or "What I used to hold onto is gone, what used to be secure is gone." And they don't often notice the starting or beginning of new things, because they're not immediately obvious; they're still in seed form and have yet to fully manifest.

That's one of the values of astrology; if you know what to look for, it can make your life easier. You can know in advance that you're going to have to let go of certain things during certain cycles. And you can also know that you're going to be starting some new things then, that some new patterns of life and awareness will start to develop after the old patterns are radically altered. I guess it's a law of life that the old things have to be gotten rid of before the new can be born, so the new can have space to develop and grow. If you have a garden full of weeds, there's no place to plant things. You've got to weed out all the old junk to make room for some new plants, and the new plants—although you can't tell it while they're still seeds or sprouts—*may* be stronger and healthier and more beautiful than the old ones.

Today I'm mainly going to concentrate on the conjunctions, squares, and oppositions; and so when I'm talking about transits I'll be referring mainly to those aspects since the other aspects are usually very minor compared to those three. But, as I mentioned before, you should also keep an eye on semi-sextiles and a few other of the aspects, when formed by a transit of one of the outer four planets. The opposition aspect, somewhat like the conjunction, does often correlate with a fairly major decision—in other words, it's not always just an adjustment like the square; and you know that one of the common key words for the opposition is *awareness*. That's especially true for oppositions, but hopefully awareness should pervade your experience with all the aspects.

Q: If you're taking this as a holistic cycle, then the opposition has got to be the point where you're the most objective about that cycle.

A: Yes. That's what people mean, I think, about "awareness." At best, one's objectivity has peaked then. During the conjunction you have no objectivity—you're just such a part of this tremendous release of energy. One finds oneself more at the mercy of impulses during the conjunctions of the outer planets than during the oppositions.

We should also talk about the importance of getting some kind of feedback from someone before doing any kind of transit work for them, or at least getting the feedback while you're doing it. But if you're going to do it for someone by mail and you're not going to talk to them, you should always require some input from them before you say or do anything—mainly because it's practical. It will help you do a better job. Why should you use your energy for guessing games when you could ask the person for definite information? In fact, Donna Cunningham puts it very well. She says that, after you have got some feedback and have related the transits to what the person is experiencing, predictions made in this way may not be as spectacular as the shot in the dark variety but they are *more organically related to the client's life*. This is a very good point, I think, one which is so often ignored by doing traditional one-sided "readings." Sensational predictions may be impressive now and then and may be able to boost your ego, but they are rarely helpful to anybody!

Cunningham also talks in very positive ways about pain. The most important transits very often involve some kind of pain. But pain can be many things. She points out that in many cases pain is a cry for help. If we heed it, we can do something constructive about it, and then we could do something to prevent further complications and to enter a healthier time of life. She also points out that most of the pain associated with the important transits, thus with the transits of the outer planets, are what you can call growing pains. It's just growing up and out and in and requires that you stretch your mind and body and everything else, and often there's pain. She points out that pain often comes during the process of adjusting to a greater demand that is placed on us by life. But the organism grows (by organism she's not just talking about the physical organism but your mind and emotions too) and it can grow to accommodate the new demand. Soon the higher level of functioning, or the more comprehensive level, is no longer painful but actually feels normal to us.

That's a really good point and that's why I'm taking the time to give this sort of philosophical introduction to transits, because so much of astrology seems so complicated if you deal only with technicalities—and transits are the same way. Some people are doing transits of *the transiting mid-points* to natal planets! So much of astrology can be really, really complicated, unnecessarily complicated, if you don't have some kind of guiding philosophy for what you're doing. But once you have that, your work becomes—for yourself and for others—much more subtle, much more practical, much more helpful. As a matter of fact, I'm sure some of you have noticed that among astrological writers there tends to be one type who is the theoretician or technician whose writings may be very interesting but whose insights or discoveries you often cannot apply in any practical way to any human being's life. And that *is* a kind of astrology, but it's so often not related to what you might call astrological counseling or to something that is going to be specifically useful in an individual's life.

So this positive attitude toward pain, I think, is a really necessary one, especially when you have the transits of Saturn, Neptune, Pluto, and Uranus to the personal planets or to the Ascendant or Descendant. Not always but very often you'll have to go through some kind of pain then. Those cycles heighten the growth process. They speed it up or concentrate it in some way. We'll get into all that too. But you start growing fast, and therefore your growing pains come on rapidly too. In fact, one other thing about transits that is good to realize is that most transits don't bring about things out of the blue. They don't *cause* anything, really. *Transits simply correspond with certain times when you are ready to get in touch with something that you have been growing toward for a long time.* So many transits bring to your awareness what you've felt or intuited or wanted or needed for years. But you won't fully *confront* those desires or needs or emotions or whatever until certain transits happen. It's like we need this kind of cosmic prompting to get out of our ruts and to really try new things. Looked at from this point of view, a great deal of the pain of transits is, as Cunningham writes, no more than the side effect of the process of strengthening, healing and growing that can go along with any major transit. It doesn't *necessarily* go along with it; it depends upon your attitude and how you deal with it. We make a mistake in focusing our attention on the pain rather than the growth process and its potential.

And so many astrological textbooks and teachers tend to encourage that kind of negative thinking, focusing on the pain or catastrophic nature of so many things. I can't believe people live like that. I have Mercury conjunct Jupiter, so I like to be optimistic in my thinking. And usually it seems to work much better than the old school of negativity orientation. Once in a while someone will come back after a consultation and say, "You were a bit too optimistic about that Saturn transit because I really went through hell." But in most cases, even if they went through quite a bit of suffering, because of my optimism they were at least able to see *something* positive in what was happening. And my pointing out the positive, constructive side of that experience or time period may have tempered their suffering and given them *some* perspective on its long-range purpose. If someone had told them, "Saturn is going to be hitting your Moon for nine months and you'll be miserable; you'll get sick; if you get pregnant, the baby will die," and on .and on, just imagine what that does to someone's mind! And it's worse if they tend to be a little bit fearful anyway.

SATURN TRANSITS & RESPONSIBILITY

All right now, Donna Cunningham points out one way of looking at Saturn transits and how different approaches to Saturn transits would view the very same thing. For example, a Saturn transit might correspond with someone being sick, but the illness was not necessarily *caused* by Saturn. Illness is often the result of long term self-neglect, such as eating the wrong things, not taking care of yourself, not getting enough sleep, etc. In other words, one of the main features of the so-called Saturn influence by transit is that Saturn makes you take care of things that you've been neglecting or running away from. Saturn is the planet of duty and responsibility. It tunes you into what you are *responsible* for. In order to do that, it will sometimes discipline you— through illness or through having to work extra hard or whatever.

It's amazing the way astrology has been misused, where you start blaming everything on the planets. It is true that the transits often manifest in such an impersonal way that there's absolutely no way that you could have done anything or avoided anything that happened to you. Most of the time, probably, you couldn't have avoided it. Sometimes it's like these big cosmic hands that just reach down and just start tearing up your life. I feel that one can over-emphasize this bit— which is very faddish these days—about, "Oh, I'm responsible for everything, I make my own destiny," and all these faddish psychological jargon trips. Then you really build up your ego, only to have it crushed a few years later when you see that you're really not in control of everything. Wait till the big cosmic hands come in! One reason so many people are paranoid about astrology is that it often shows you quite clearly that you're *not* in control, as you'd like to think you are. I think the practice of astrology could benefit a great deal from taking more responsibility for things, rather than blaming everything on the planets. But, at the same time, it's true that the outer planets (because the further out you get with the planets, the more *impersonal* they become) do act very impersonally. And, when Saturn is sitting on your Sun and you feel rotten and you feel exhausted and you need 12 hours of sleep, no one can convince you that that is entirely a result of self-neglect. So you have to use a certain amount of moderation in everything, especially these little philosophical goodies about "you're responsible for everything." *Ultimately*, you are responsible, if the karmic law is a fact and therefore you only get what you put out. Ultimately you *are* responsible, but what is not pointed out most of the time—especially by people in different psychological fields who are really into this "take responsibility" business—is that many things that you initiated lifetimes ago, which you are only now confronting, also have their impact.

COMMENTS ON SPECIFIC TRANSITS

I should also elaborate on another point that Cunningham makes. She says, "Some of the emotional pain that we go through during transits is actually simply a kind of temper tantrum at not being given what we want when we want it." And you know, it's no doubt true. Uranus has been whacking all kinds of planets for me for almost two years now; and I've had more temper tantrums than I've had since I was about three years old. It's amazing. Of course, Uranus tends to make you impatient too. She also points out that much of the pain from transits comes from resistance to change. And that should be pretty obvious. This is a really good point about Uranus transits in particular. And I would say the same sort of thing is often true for Jupiter as well. In my experience, Uranus transits often correspond with actions that the person has thought about for a long time but has lacked the courage to pursue until the Uranus transit has prompted him or her to do so. Now to understand some of these things, you have to have some experience with transits. Some of these points might not be that meaningful to you until you start working with transits quite a bit. But it would probably be worthwhile to note down some of these fundamental things as the workshop progresses. What I mean here is that Uranus transits traditionally correspond with sudden events or unpredictable occurrences, and—in the *traditional* interpretation— these things just come out of the blue, there's no reason for them, no meaning to them, or anything.

So say some lady is married and her husband beats her up; she feels rotten about him. She's in a bad mood. All her friends apparently know that she's not satisfied with the marriage, but she seems to be sticking it out for some reason. Then all of a sudden, Uranus comes along and conjuncts or squares her Venus and she says, "I'm getting out of here!" And she splits with some younger man. And her friends say, "What a sudden event!" It's just that Uranus gave her the individuality and the individual push and the craving for something new and exciting and alive that she needed to force her to *act* on how she had been feeling for years. That's true with Uranus transits and sometimes with Jupiter too. You'll start doing things that you've thought about, or felt strong urges toward, for a long time. Uranus and Jupiter transits can give you *confidence*. Jupiter, especially, can expand your confidence. Uranus transits can give you confidence only if you act on the urge toward more independence. If you don't act on that urge toward more freedom that Uranus transits bring, you won't get the confidence that it could otherwise give you. In other words, you've got to tune in on it; you've got to manifest that energy in some way through action.

And really one might say a similar thing for Jupiter transits too. Say Jupiter is transiting your 1st house or your 10th house or any house for that matter, in that area of life there is the possibility of gaining more confidence. But you've got to experiment. Jupiter is known for adventure, right?—for expanding into new areas of activities; but you've got to act on it to take advantage of the opportunity for more confidence and more growth. Actually, transits are totally unpredictable things. What you *can* predict is the time period, basically, and the essential meaning and nature of that time period—and in some cases, the ramifications of what you do then. You can't always predict what *will* happen or what you *should* do. Sometimes it's obvious what you should do; in other cases, it's totally up to the individual's own value system. You know astrological counselors get so many questions about divorces and separations and couples breaking up, and that is always a heavy question, especially when there are children. So you can't tell them what to do. They've got to decide.

Also about Uranus: having smoldered a long time under restrictions, when a Uranus transit comes along you may need to break away from the past in a very extreme fashion at first, just because you *have* to be a bit of an extremist to break away from the past patterns that are very strong and that you're very tied in with. And there again I would say it often takes two or two and a half years to assimilate the meaning of a Uranus transit. But after that time you can get back on a more even keel, on a more balanced approach to things. You might even start corresponding with your spouse that you left 2½ years ago or some such cooperative action. But Uranus transits tend to mean that you're leaving something behind and that you are revolutionizing that area of your life. Quite often, the purpose of Neptune transits seems to be the loosening of ties with worldly things, and a drawing closer to the spiritual. The disillusionment and depression that often occur during Neptune transits are just the medium through which a yearning for the spiritual comes about.

Q: The mood of the Neptune transits . . . what was that?

A: In other words, very often one may be totally disillusioned with something or someone or with some part of yourself or your life while Neptune is conjuncting, squaring, or opposing one of your personal planets or Ascendant. And that disillusionment that you feel at first brings me to another law of transits: the hard stuff comes in first; you usually get hit with the hard stuff first. In other words, when the transit is just coming on or if it is going to be exact three times, the first time is usually the hardest. The first exact aspect is *usually but not always* the hardest. There are exceptions. But, it tends to be that way, because it's the first encounter with this new thing in your life, this new influence, this new urge, this new part of yourself. It's shocking; it jolts you sometimes, or it really feels heavy. But as you tune into it, you sort of get used to it and learn how to cope with this new life energy, so it gets easier and easier to live with. And also, the positive side of any transit can manifest more clearly as you learn to *accept* what is happening and learn how to deal with it. As long as you're feeling the heavy, negative part or dimension of a certain transit experience, it's very difficult and quite rare to see all the positive things that are going to come from it.

Q: Does it ever happen in reverse where you might feel the strong positive part first and then the negative?

A: Yes, it does—for sure! But I don't see that too often. But I've had that experience once myself. Have you ever felt like that? Or are you just speculating? (A: Just speculating.) The *usual* pattern is what I described, and I see that repeatedly. Recently I saw someone who has a Capricorn Venus. Transiting Pluto is squaring her natal Venus, and this is going to repeat *five times*. When it first happened, her whole marriage fell apart, just absolutely collapsed. One minute she was married and the next minute there was not only no marriage left, but her husband moved in with another woman and was trying to get custody of the children through court action. They had totally terminated any affection for each other, at least that's the way it appeared on the surface. Who knows how much affection was there to begin with—probably not a whole lot. But Venus in Capricorn is a dutiful sort of person and also even more than being dutiful, they look out for themselves in a material sense. They are very much in touch with financial and security values. Venus shows values and Capricorn is very conservative. And I've seen people with Venus in Capricorn endure unendurable marriages, because they are often very fearful people. They're fearful of taking risks; they're fearful of getting hurt; and they are very fearful of financial hardship. But anyway the heavy stuff for her is coming at the beginning of this period. And she was just in shock. She was saying, "I can't believe he's doing this." Not that she was sad to see him go. What really jolted her was his action to try to get the kids—that's what really upset her. That put the finishing touches (Pluto) on any love feelings she might have still had for him. Both children are girls anyways; and they're both fairly young and she is not a bad mother. That was pretty heavy. But as this change process develops, I can just watch what is happening to her, and she's getting above it more and more and getting used to it and in fact gaining strength from it.

Q: Was that the only major transit she was having?

A: Oh no. She had others too. But that was by far the most important transit she was having. I don't remember all the others offhand. But that's why I wanted people here to bring their charts, so toward the end of the workshop we can use some examples from the class and see some of the complexities of multiple transits as well as just looking at isolated transits.

STEPS & APPROACHES FOR PERSONALIZING THE MEANING OF TRANSITS

One last thing from Donna Cunningham's material on transits. She says these are good steps to know for making better use of your so-called hard transits. One is: get to know the planets well. Get to know exactly what they mean. Shortly we'll go through each of the five outer planets and give a definition of their transiting influence. Step two is: get to know your chart in real depth. Understand your own chart, and what you're really saying there is *understand your own self*; the more you know your self, the more you're going to know what kind of things you can tune in on during certain transits. So step three is to know yourself. Step four is: learn to respect yourself. In other words, whatever is happening during transits, don't put unnecessary value judgments on it. Don't say, "This is bad the way I'm dealing with this." You're feeling like that, so you're feeling like it! There's something meaningful in that feeling or in that experience. You can't just judge it or you won't be able to learn from it. Step five is perhaps the most important: take the long view of things. Don't get hung up in one event or one experience, or in one transit for that matter. They're all just cycles in this gigantic drama. One of my favorite analogies is to see life as a play, you know, and everybody is on the stage. There are various acts, and within these acts there are various scenes. And in some plays you're the leading character; you're probably the leading character in all your individual plays—the character sometimes changes costumes, ages, situations, and develops different aspects of character. If you can think of that analogy or keep it in mind, say Pluto is hitting your Venus and your marriage is falling to pieces—O.K., maybe that's just the end of act I or the middle of act II. It's not your whole life! It's nice to keep things in perspective because then you don't get thrown off balance so easily.

Step six: discard old notions in judging the effects of transits. Step seven is: when you have a lemon, make lemonade. If you're having a so-called hard transit, try to develop the positive potential of the aspect. In other words, say Pluto is squaring Venus, emphasize then the positive manifestation of that; put energy into transforming Venus—your values, your love needs, etc. Step eight is: avoid escapism; and Step nine is: find out where the pain is coming from and do something about it. Being an Aries rising, I'm very prejudiced in favor of action, but it seems to me that action is a fantastic way of dealing with the so-called hard transits. Sometimes, naturally, you can tend to act too much. You can act rather impulsively, especially if it's a Uranus transit. Doing something to confront that part of yourself that is being stirred up by that transit is important, really important because otherwise you just sit there and feel that stress—which eventually takes it's toll on your body, on your physical health, on your family life, love life, everything.

There are a few more introductory things to mention and then we can get into the specifics of the individual planets. And I brought my notes on this so I could just read it. It's a really important concept if you want to use transits in a simple, synthesized way, and not rely on a textbook wherein only isolated bits of information are given. Astrology basically is very simple. It deals primarily with the four energies called the elements: air, fire, water, earth. And all life experiences except the highest spiritual experiences are manifestations of these different energies playing in different ways. Each planetary principle, in other words each planet in your chart, shows how that energy flows or how it is *regulated*. All transits merely stimulate certain energies to flow in a certain way and with a certain rhythm, and we'll get into those ways and which rhythm is related to each planet. In a way, all transits are the same in that they simply activate things in the natal chart. They simply stir up parts of yourself or dimensions of your own life. No matter what the transiting planet is, when it hits Venus for example, it's going to do something to Venus, so to speak. It's going to affect that dimension of your life represented by Venus—your marriage, your values, your attitudes toward love, sexual things, and so forth. So all transits—especially of the outer planets to any particular natal planet—simply *activate* that natal factor, but each transiting planet activates it in a different way and we'll spend quite a bit of time on the individual planets and what kind of energy release and rhythms they correlate with. All transits of the outer planets (and you can include Jupiter and Saturn, too) are so important because they stir up the unconscious. They bring you into touch with the essence of your natal chart or the essence of yourself which is represented in the natal chart. But all of them work by a different method.

One example, here, take transits to natal Mars; just look at your natal Mars, then suppose transiting Uranus or Pluto was hitting your natal Mars by conjunction, square, or opposition. They tend to stir things up, bring things to the surface from the unconscious, possibly making you much more "Martian." They may tend to increase your strength or your desire to express your particular Mars energy and attunement. Uranus revolutionizes things, Pluto transforms things, so Uranus or Pluto hitting Mars could revolutionize or transform the way you express your strength, your sexuality, your power, your assertiveness in general. And then look at Saturn, for example, conjuncting, squaring, or opposing Mars. This also will affect Mars and all those things about Mars that we mentioned. However, it will do it in a different way. It will make you more realistic about the way you assert yourself. It may tone down or slow down your aggressiveness or your activities for awhile. Even your physical energy flow may be slowed down and you might be tired for awhile, for a month or two. It all depends on the natal chart. *All transits* are affecting some basic factor in you in your life, rather than being something up in the sky or something out of the blue. Who knows what you're going to do? Look at your natal chart and see what Mars is all about. What is Mars *for you*? What are your big activities now that are exciting you (Mars)? What's your sex life like (Mars)? What are your ambitions that have to do with Mars? How are you living everyday? How much physical energy do you have? If you tune in on the natal chart and your true nature in its present state of development, then you can deal with the transits. If you don't tune in on the natal chart, it's primarily only a general kind of outline interpretation that you can give to transits.

One other thing that occurred to me and it's not a real clear-cut rule or law, but it seems so often that Saturn and Pluto transits are very specific *harvesting* times—in other words, when you harvest a kind of karma, when you encounter things that are the obvious results of things you've done in the past. And I don't want to make this any kind of rigid "rule" because you can harvest or begin new karma at any time; but so often, when Saturn or Pluto is transiting the natal chart, it seems that people encounter things that they cannot control, obviously destined things. And it seems that Jupiter and Uranus aspects by transit are very often what you might call "seeding times," when you start new things, when you plant new seeds which will sprout and bear fruit later. They tend to be times when you launch out into new things, new experimentation, new adventure. I hesitate to mention that; it's only something you can use very cautiously. It's not a rigid law, and certainly you can't arbitrarily divide such transits in all cases into just these two categories. Transits show *how* the energy is released. It does not show *what* is released. It does not show *what will happen*. It shows how the *energy* is released. And so much of it depends on you and how you use that energy, and how you *want* to use it.

THE BASIC RHYTHM & FUNCTION
OF THE TRANSITING PLANETS

Here I'll mainly focus on the outer planets, but I'll also briefly mention other planets. Let's start with Venus. Venus tends to harmonize and smooth out whatever it touches. Venus transits are only rarely important, no matter what the aspect. Once in a while, if Venus is activating something in your natal chart, during that day or at most for two days, you might feel particularly social or be in a pleasant mood or get some good news or feel some relief of tension. If Venus is conjunct one of the natal planets, there may be some pleasant sort of experience, not too important by itself though.

Mars tends to speed up things, tends to activate things rather aggressively. In other words, say Mars is hitting your Sun or Venus or is conjunct your Ascendant, there's an influx of energy. How that manifests depends on the person. Sometimes the person will absorb it and use it and do things and be particularly active for a period of two to three days or be extra assertive during that time. If Mars hits Mercury, you'll often be more aggressive in your speech, very irritable too because Mars will stir up the nervous system and put you on edge. In other cases when Mars aspects the Ascendant, Sun, or Moon, you're not in control of the energy and it's often experienced just as a fever. You get hot and have a fever for a few days. During most fevers, Mars is in a very close aspect to one of the personal planets or the Ascendant. In fact, it's especially useful to look at Mars transits in the case of feverish illnesses, especially in young kids; because if it's a simple rapidly passing Mars transit happening, you don't have to be too worried. But if someone's got a high fever and other symptoms that are quite serious and there's no Mars transit going on, then their condition might be pretty serious. If it's a Mars transit alone, it's understandable and it will pass quickly as soon as the Mars aspect fades off.

When one of my kids had transiting Mars conjunct his Moon, he got a real high fever; and since his Moon is in Aries, he gets high fevers fast. The fever went up so fast that he started having convulsions, and that kind of convulsion comes not so much from how high the fever is but from it coming on too rapidly. The kid does everything rapidly, with Moon in Aries. His temperature went from normal to about 105° in a very few minutes. I knew that he was having this transit anyway and I was kind of expecting something to happen, expecting him perhaps to get kind of irritable for a while or something like that. But anyway, he went into all these fits and his jaw locked up and he started turning blue. It was pretty weird. Eventually we got him breathing, forced his jaw open and pulled his tongue out. But still I wasn't too worried because I knew there was this tremendous influx of Mars energy and that in about two days he would be fine. I'd seen it before with him and with other kids, although he had never had convulsions before. So we called this doctor, just to get another diagnosis. And the doctor says, "You should really have him checked for spinal meningitis because these kinds of symptoms could indicate spinal meningitis and that would be really serious. You should have him checked. The tests are real involved and painful, and there are spinal taps. If indeed it is meningitis, the child should be treated immediately." Although the doctor said that, she did not feel it was meningitis. And interestingly, the way she described his situation physically was that there was a release of energy so intense that his body couldn't handle it, and his nervous system was overwhelmed by it! And therefore his nervous system went into a spasm. And that would jive perfectly with the astrological indicators: *Too much energy*—it over-amped his nervous system, which then started trembling and shaking. So, to make a long story short, I didn't really care if he got the tests or not because I was confident that he would be fine, but due to various pressures he got the tests; it was a real messy ordeal at the hospital for a whole day. In two days his fever was gone, and he was fine. If it had been up to me, I wouldn't even have taken him for the tests because I was pretty sure about what was happening.

Jupiter transits expand whatever they touch. They often open doors for various opportunities and increase your energy with most aspects. They also can give you a much more comprehensive understanding of whatever area of life is being influenced by them, mainly by the house position of transiting Jupiter or by the natal planet that Jupiter is aspecting. We're going to go through these in much more detail too. This now is just a brief thing on each planet.

Saturn transits, by house position or by the planet that is being aspected, slow down the rhythm of nature and concentrate it, in fact concentrate your experience at that time. It delays the rhythm of nature and slows down your energy flow. It tends to restrict and condense your energy field. Jupiter, on the other hand, expands your energy field, and you feel more buoyant, more expansive, more optimistic. That's one thing I meant before when I was saying that this whole fad about "I'm responsible for everything" is taken a bit far. Sometimes when you have these various cycles, you can tangibly feel this change in your energy field, and you can't control it at all. Say Jupiter is conjuncting your Sun, you just feel this *faith*. When I was 23 and Jupiter was conjunct my Sun, I was hitch hiking in Europe and I didn't care if I got a ride! I was so happy, just sitting contentedly by the road I didn't care if anyone ever picked me up! But of course, with Jupiter conjunct my Sun, I got a ride to exactly where I was going. I didn't even hold my thumb out. Now with Saturn you feel constricted, and you don't feel much faith—you've got to *work* for what you get. I remember when Saturn was squaring my Sun. (And you know, aspects to the Sun are really powerful; aspects to the Moon are real important;

aspects to the Ascendant are important and aspects to the ruler of the Ascendant also—all have a great impact on your physical being, your physical energy.) I could not believe Saturn on my Sun—this was Saturn square my Sun—it was amazing. I actually felt like there was this big heavy load on my shoulders that I had to carry around. And if you look at Capricorns—I can often spot a Capricorn from quite a distance away. They often stand like this. Their head is drawn down and their shoulders are somewhat hunched forward and drawn up as if they have been carrying the weight of the world. And that's how I felt when Saturn was hitting my Sun.

And as a matter of fact, people who tend to be rather malleable and rather sensitive will often take on certain qualities of the transiting planets—sometimes to the point where their appearance will radically change and people will tell them how different they look. And when Saturn started hitting my Sun, people actually started guessing me as a Capricorn! I was quite flattered actually, because I don't have any earth sign emphasis at all. But I could see how they were guessing that, because I was walking around hunched over and I couldn't smile for about nine months! Everything was real serious—I really felt like a Capricorn.

Uranus speeds up the rhythm of life. It speeds up the usual pace of your development and growth. It hastens change. And by "speeding up," I don't mean like 2 or 3% but about 500%! It really goes fast. Oftentimes, things will happen so hot and heavy when Uranus is aspecting the personal planets or the Ascendant or sometimes also when it's hitting Saturn or natal Uranus, things will be going so fast and developing so quickly and you'll go through so many changes that you'll feel like you're just spinning. You'll often have insomnia too, under Uranus transits, because Uranus energy is too much for the nervous system. Your body cannot handle Uranus in concentrated doses for very long.

Q: How is that speeding up different than that from Mars?

A: Mars is much grosser physical energy. It's a more muscular, visceral kind of energy. Uranus is totally a nervous-system kind of energy, a mental energy. The Uranus energy itself is much more electrical, much faster, much more subtle than Mars.

Q: Are you saying that when you look at Uranus transits, it's kind of like looking at a catalyst? As Uranus would refer back to another cycle? In other words, you would see a bunch of events, but they would be happening not in a Uranus cycle but in another cycle. And Uranus is coming along and acting sort of like a catalyst, say, in a Saturn cycle or whatever?

A: It is definitely a catalyst type of thing, and it's *experienced* that way! And if Uranus is a catalyst, you could say that Pluto is a catharsis. Pluto is more like a purging of the past. Occasionally certain other things will act as a catalyst too; but if you're going to use that term, Uranus is the most appropriate transit to use that term with. Uranus things do tend to come on suddenly, very actively, very powerfully. And almost always it's a catalyst in the sense that things that you were *somewhat* in touch with before or constantly dwelling on or strongly feeling tend to be activated very quickly. I would say that using the term "catalyst" is quite accurate. Uranus tends to revolutionize whatever it touches.

By the way, with Uranus, Neptune, and Pluto, the house positions of those transiting planets don't matter that much. They're in a house too long to matter that much. In other words, whatever they mean in a house, you get used to it. However, any transits over the four angles of the chart are important. Say Uranus hits the Ascendant, Descendant, Mid-heaven, or fourth house cusp, it's generally felt—especially with the Ascendant or Descendant, it's always felt—as a speeding up of your whole life and as a very rapid series of changes in most cases. In some cases it manifests on a very subtle level. I remember I had got into the habit a few years ago of correlating Uranus as it conjuncts the Ascendant with big, rather obvious changes since that is so often true. But then within about two weeks, I saw two people who supposedly were having Uranus transiting the Ascendant and who could not identify with what I was saying. But I was talking about it on too gross a level; it turned out that both of them got into astrology during that transit, and that totally *revolutionized* their orientation toward life and their way of understanding themselves. The Ascendant, you know, is your personal approach to life. But until I was reminded of the fact that Uranus is traditionally the planet of astrology, I just wasn't tuning in on that.

O.K., so Uranus speeds things up and also brings to the surface things that are just below the threshold; it awakens you to whatever you are ready to grow into or to start developing or to face very directly and honestly. And a Uranus transit will often bring it into being. One example of what I mean is that so many people will wait to make a big change in career or life direction or marriage or something like that until Uranus prompts them to. Uranus, when it comes along, just hits you over the head like a sledge-hammer, but it's an *electrical* sledge-hammer. And your whole being just gets jolted, you get speeded up, and generally you're inundated by new ideas. Some source of new excitement comes into your life. That can be a person, a study, a new event, it can be moving across country; it can be any number of things. We're going to get into Uranus some more later.

Neptune is the hardest planet to talk about, with Pluto a close second. The further out the planets get, the further out their meanings are and the subtler their meanings are. But basically, Neptune transits tremendously sensitize whatever they touch. They also tend to dissolve it; they tend to dissolve the old form of that dimension of your life, shown by the natal planet being transited. Say Neptune is transiting your Venus, it will very much dissolve or at least *refine*—that's another key word for Neptune transits—that area of your life. With Neptune transiting your Venus, you may have the opportunity to refine your approach to love. Some relationship you have may dissolve totally, or your attitude toward it may become much more refined and much more subtle and sensitive. For example, if you're a real jealous person and Neptune hits your Venus, at first you may be more jealous; it may stir up all that stuff because Neptune also has the influence of making things more confusing. Neptune transits often put you in a fog where you're vaguely feeling all these different emotions and don't quite know what direction to go in. But if you honestly face what's happening then, Neptune hitting your Venus may enable you to refine your attitude toward love or marriage or your partner or whatever. And by the time it's over, you may be much less jealous; you may be much more understanding of the partner's needs and your own needs.

And sometimes Neptune has the impact of *spiritualizing* things, in the sense that it attunes you to intangibles, to subtleties. It's not always going to be a spiritual thing. The majority of the people in the world are not spiritually oriented, so naturally when they have Neptune transits they're not going to become super spiritual. But if one tends toward that or is open to it, often when Neptune hits certain planets in the natal chart by transit, the person will become more attuned to subtleties, more attuned to spiritual truths or to some of the forces in life which can be called "spiritual." If you're particularly Neptunian or Piscean and have not learned how to protect yourself and to maintain your concentration and the integrity of your own energy field, you may be inundated by spiritual entities and you may get overwhelmed by these forces. Now this is not true for all Pisces people, but it's quite common—Pisces *is* the Neptune sign.

The main thing with Neptune transits is that, during a Neptune transit, your life opens up in the area indicated. If Neptune is aspecting Mercury, your mind can open up to much more subtle perceptions. You may be much more confused at first. You may be unable to concentrate effectively. All your old rigid opinions and what you thought was "knowledge" may dissolve to the point where you may think you don't know anything anymore. But something positive is happening behind all of that confusion, because it's opening you up to a much subtler form of knowledge.

If Neptune hits your Sun—I'll give you two quick examples of transiting Neptune aspecting the Sun. One person, a woman thirty-some years old—when Neptune just started squaring her Sun, her husband moved out. Although it's an unpopular idea with some women today, the Sun in fact in many women's charts, especially those who are living a fairly traditional marriage-type structure, does relate to the husband as well as to their own individuality. It tends to relate to their husband especially when they are younger. As they get more and more individualized, it tends to be more and more symbolic of themselves. Neptune was in Sagittarius, Neptune squared her Sun in Pisces, the husband moved out, and the whole thing was up in the air for about a year and a half. This was a triple whammy—Neptune went retrograde, hit her Sun again and so forth. The marriage was up in the air and totally uncertain because he wouldn't commit himself to wanting a divorce or moving back in. It was just all up in the air. And she's a Pisces Sun and fairly used to being somewhat passive throughout her whole life and letting him take the lead. During that time, she was quite miserable at first. She got into astrology at that time and into reincarnation and into lots of things that gave her a much better perspective on her life and which gave her a lot of strength to take the steps to divorce him. It was a pretty amazing thing to watch because, within a fairly short time—a year and a half, she really developed rapidly. When I first saw her when Neptune was first hitting her Sun, she was a real bundle of confusion. She was in the whole Pisces trip in a negative way, you know, complaining and whining and the whole bit. She got a lot stronger fast!

This past summer, there was another interesting revelation about Neptune. Now, not every time Neptune hits somebody's Sun will there be a dramatic-type thing like getting a divorce or like the next example, but it's a time to keep your eyes open. O.K., so what happened last summer—there was this kid with natal Sun in Sagittarius. Neptune was conjuncting his Sun. Transiting Jupiter was also opposite his natal Jupiter, and he took a trip to England with his mother. He's only five years old. He went to England, and Jupiter is traditionally known for long journeys and foreign travel; and it was quite educational for him (Jupiter) because he went around to all these museums. But also, while he was there, he met this spiritual master. And I don't know all the details; but essentially, this Master was initiating some people, was tuning them in to powerful spiritual experiences. This little kid was sitting in the back of the room at a reception where all these people were talking to this spiritual master, and all of a sudden this kid jumps down and runs to the front of the room and confronts this Master and says, "I want you to initiate me." Ordinarily it's required that you must be 22 or 23 years old even to be considered for initiation into this spiritual path. But this kid was a Sagittarius and is quite adamant when he wants something; he really knows his mind. He just said, "I want it," and he got it. So this master touched his forehead and the kid just about left his body immediately. He was just flying and totally spaced out. Seemingly, he was having all kinds of amazing visions because he was so affected by it that he couldn't talk for quite awhile.

Anyway that's an example of Neptune, too—contacting spiritual things. Whether it's purely an inner experience or a person or place or book that has a spiritual influence on you, Neptune can attune you to spiritual things. This is one thing that books on transits do not clarify at all, and that's the positive aspect of Neptune. You can also say that Neptune, at another level, is discontent. You feel discontented, you feel the need to escape, you're beseiged by uncertainty and confusion, you want to get out of this fog. But on a higher level, Neptune is refinement and spiritualization of whatever it is touching.

Likewise, you can do a kind of positive/negative thing with the other planets too. Uranus at the lower level, or the negative manifestation you might say, might just be restlessness or craving change just for the sake of variety or just for the sake of change with no point to it—extreme selfishness. And Uranus is a planet of selfishness, by the way. There are different kinds of selfishness, but when you have Uranus hitting your Sun or Mars or Venus, the tendency is to say, "the hell with everybody else, I'm doing my thing." And cooperation is not at all easy for you when Uranus is hitting you. However, positively, Uranus is *awakening* to a new kind of clarification. And at the best, at the highest level I suppose, Uranus can show a kind of *inner liberation* coming through understanding, coming through a tremendous clarification. Say Uranus hits your Venus—in spite of all the other things that may accompany that transit, and you may go through many different changes then, it's also possible to experience a tremendous liberation in your attitudes toward love, toward emotional involvements with other people, toward marriage relationships, all Venus things. There can be a kind of inner freedom that develops then through clarification. But usually, that comes only after experimentation too. In other words, Uranus, like the sign Aquarius, stands for *experimenting.* You try all these things, including things that might have been forbidden or at least unconventional. Through experimentation, you also gain much more experience and often a better perspective on what you really want to do and what you really need.

Pluto functions *negatively* mainly as compulsion, often kind of dragging you under. All these forces come into your life and there's an urge to do all these things compulsively without any conscious reason. Also, you will often notice that when transiting Pluto hits certain planets in the natal chart, the personal planets particularly, there's a tendency to get much more ruthless. But ruthlessness can be good. It depends on how you're using that ruthlessness. It can sometimes be good to be ruthless with yourself. And it can even be good to be ruthless in reorganizing your life if you're not satisfied with how it is. Negatively, Pluto can be excessively ruthless. But on a higher level, it can be a positive kind of ruthlessness and a conscious dedication to the transformation of yourself or some aspect of your life.

And Saturn is probably pretty obvious to most of you. On the negative level, Saturn manifests as depression, anxiety, and so on. I wrote a whole chapter on Saturn in *Astrology, Karma & Transformation* and I think it was about 30 pages long, with a lot of dense type on each page. So there's only so much we can do with Saturn today, but we will get into some things about Saturn. To me one of the most important things about Saturn is that when transiting Saturn aspects natal planets, it's a time to *face your fears.* Negatively, it can manifest as fear. The positive way of dealing with it is to face your fears.

And if you don't consciously accept the fact that you have to face those fears, you'll probably be forced to face them anyway. "That which I have feared has come upon me," or whatever that old saying is in the Bible. That's Saturn for you. If you don't confront the fears, then they'll grow and grow and grow because you're refusing to look at them, and pretty soon they'll jump into your life full blown or full grown. Saturn, positively, concentrates your attention. You may feel less energy, but your energy will be more concentrated. Your awareness will be much deeper. Also, a positive way of dealing with Saturn transits is to resolve to confront those things and to accept the responsibility that you feel you should take on, in whatever area of life is indicated by the house position of Saturn and/or by the planet that it is aspecting. With Jupiter transits, positively, it's pretty simple—optimism, confidence, expansion, the urge to *improve* your life in some way. Then negatively, it's just going to excesses, blowing a lot of money, blowing a lot of your energy, trying to do too much at once, and wasting money, energy, and time.

Q: Pluto positive was conscious . . . ?

A: Well, one of the meanings is a conscious dedication toward reforming yourself or some dimension of your life.

Q: Does that come out as some unconscious thing you are doing? Is it some type of thing that is occurring and you have to kind of think it out or . . . ?

A: What I mean by "conscious dedication" is that one of the best ways of dealing with a Pluto transit is to dedicate yourself energetically, like, "I'm going to start transforming my life in this area." Because if you don't consciously do it, then the Pluto transits tend to come on unconsciously and manifest more compulsively. It's kind of like: when Pluto transits a natal planet, whatever that planet signifies is going to be deeply changed within the next two years as Pluto goes back and forth aspecting that planet. One way or another, it's going to be changed. So the best thing to do in many cases is to say, "Yes, this is going to change; it has to change; therefore I better start doing it myself." And then you can use that Pluto energy, take it into your life and use it as part of yourself, consciously use it to transform things. Because if you don't accept it as part of you, then it acts as what Jung calls an "autonomous psychic force," an autonomous complex—something that has a life of its own, totally separate from your consciousness.

What often happens with so many of these transits—the Pluto transits, the Uranus transits, the Saturn transits—is that at first you won't recognize what's happening, and you won't recognize what's necessary either and what changes you have to make or undergo. But these pressures will build up—from outside sometimes, from inside, or from both—and you feel like you're just squeezed to do something. But, you know, the logical mind is so stupid. The logical mind is usually so out of touch with the reality of life processes because it tends to see things in little blocks, in very rigid ways. So what often happens is that the hardest stuff tends to come first during most transit periods. What tends to happen is that this pressure builds up and finally you start getting desperate to do something, or finally all these pressures just almost push you bodily into some new phase of life.

What happened to me recently is a good example; and I'm supposed to know better, or so some people think. All these transits have been happening to me—Pluto, Uranus, and Saturn. All of them were showing radical changes, and I knew that I could no longer function in my old office. I used to have a little closet about half as big as this front room here. It was a horrible, horrible place—no windows, fresh air, or anything. And I had all this work I had to do and I was always miserable, because the pressure of all that work just kept building and building—and people calling all the time and the demands put on me were just insane. And aesthetically the place was hideous. I didn't see that it was the right time to go to this bigger place because I would have to pay about three times the rent. But eventually, everything just pressured me into signing a lease for this place here, although I had no idea how I was going to pay for it. It just became *necessary*. But now it's easy to see that the whole thing was just ready to happen, and there's no question of paying for it or anything because everything works better. When there's more room, everything works better and it's more efficient. So it's more economically efficient too. And I didn't see the coming radical changes in my work or how popular my books would become. Moving out of that tiny office nicely symbolizes a lot of inner changes, especially my sloughing off (Pluto!) the old restrictions of my former work structure. Now I have *room* and *space*! All these transits were telling me "Make changes, leave behind this and that, start out into new things," but I was still unsure and hesitant. That's the usual reaction, especially if you have many planets in fixed signs like I do. You tend to wait till the last minute to make the necessary changes because you want to hold on to your security.

JUPITER & SATURN THROUGH THE HOUSES

When Uranus, Neptune, or Pluto first goes into a house, there is often a noticeable change in your life corresponding with that planet and the house it's going into. But that feeling of change does not tend to be dominant during the whole period that the planet is in that house. Whereas with transiting Saturn and Jupiter, while they are in a particular house they tend to signify important developments related to that house in that person's life throughout that entire time period. Now Jupiter has a twelve year cycle. It averages out to be about one year in each house, unless your chart is the kind where some houses are real big and others real tiny; that would also depend to some extent on the house system you use. In most cases, Jupiter would be in one house for about one year. Saturn will be in a particular house about 2½ years. But that will vary from about 2 to 3 years, depending on your particular chart and how large or small certain houses are and also on when Saturn goes retrograde.

Let's just divide up the circle here (going to blackboard) into houses and totally ignore the signs right now. Just watching transiting Saturn and Jupiter in the houses is such a useful tool! Really, you could throw out all the rest of astrology and, just using Jupiter and Saturn passing through or "transiting" your natal houses, you would have such a practical tool that it would be better than any other method I know of for understanding the cyclic and regular nature of important developments, changes, and growth periods in your life. So what we can do now is to take Jupiter and Saturn simultaneously through all the houses. Naturally the influence of Jupiter and that of Saturn are polar opposites. Jupiter tends to be expansion and Saturn tends to be contraction or constriction.

Wherever Jupiter is, you'll want to improve things, to expand things. Whatever house Jupiter is in shows that you can gain a more *comprehensive* understanding of that area of life through wider experience, through adventure, and just generally through expansion. Whatever house Jupiter is in shows that it is in that area of life where you either want to improve things—you have an urge to improve things—or at least, even if you don't have the urge then, an opportunity comes to you that enables you to improve that area of your life. But that's not to say that you'll take advantage of the opportunity. You may not even see it as opportunity. Just because Jupiter is in a certain house, it's not—as many books would imply—that you'll automatically do all kinds of wonderful things and have such great things happen to you. It still will require a certain amount of *action* and the capacity to be open to a broad view of things and a wide vista of new possibilities. And, by the way, all these things can be applied to Jupiter aspecting a particular natal planet too, as well as transiting a particular house. I'll give you an idea of what I mean by that in a second. Another important factor is that Jupiter gives you an urge to act in a way that has *future ramifications*. Jupiter, Sagittarius, and the ninth house constitute what is known as the ninth letter of the astrological alphabet. And all of them have a connection with the *future*. For example, Sagittarius is traditionally known as the sign of "prophecy." You often find Sagittarian people like William Blake, the English visionary poet, being prophets of the future. Many of them have a sense of *what is going to be* in the future. Likewise then, when you have Jupiter aspecting any natal planet or in any particular house, there's often something going on that gives you a feeling of future developments, future possibilities in that area of your life. And usually it's not just a *thought*. It's usually some kind of vision of the future—how things could eventually be improved to be like an envisioned ideal or you often get some kind of inner knowledge or faith. So those are some of the basic meanings of Jupiter transits, and we'll go through some examples in a minute.

Saturn transiting in a particular house or aspecting a natal planet also gives you the opportunity to understand something better. But instead of understanding more broadly and widely and comprehensively like Jupiter does, it's an opportunity to understand it more deeply, in a very specialized *immediately* practical, in-depth way. Saturn always brings the possibility of deepening your consciousness. And naturally, wherever Saturn is, you have the need to define things, to live in the present, to learn patience, to be more certain, and also to build. One of the key phrases for Saturn is *building through effort*. You build in whatever area of life is shown by the house where Saturn is, or in whatever dimension of experience is shown by the planet being aspected.

I'll also put the planets here. (Draws in the planetary symbols associated with each house, using a simple chart of equal houses.) These are the planets that are traditionally associated with these various houses, and with the signs that correspond to those houses. So we'll put Mars in the first house, Venus in the second house (the Taurus house), Mercury in the Gemini house (the third house), and so forth.

The reason I'm also putting the planets up here should be more apparent shortly; but basically, Saturn—for example—going through the third house is in many ways similar to Saturn aspecting Mercury. As we go through these things, it would be good if people would look at their charts to know where transiting Jupiter and Saturn are now. Some of you know that automatically; but if you don't, it would be good to find out what house Jupiter is in now and what house Saturn is in, to see if you can relate to what we'll be saying. And also especially notice if transiting Jupiter or Saturn is conjuncting, squaring, or opposing any natal planet. You should also keep an eye on any quincunxes or semi-sextiles being formed.

JUPITER & SATURN TRANSITING THE 1ST HOUSE

The first house deals with your spontaneous self-expression and action in the world. It correlates with Mars. The first house, then, is a very active house. It's an outgoing house, and it characterizes *you personally doing your independent thing.* So when Jupiter goes into the first house, *or when Jupiter aspects natal Mars,* there's an expansion or increase in the urge to assert yourself. There's generally much more physical energy, generally more confidence, and often weight gain when Jupiter goes into the first house. When Saturn goes into the first house, there's often a weight loss. You know, Jupiter likes to do things in a big way. When Jupiter went through my first house last time, my energy and appetite about tripled. I gained about 20 pounds, which I really needed to gain because I was real skinny—because of Saturn. I lost about 30 pounds when Saturn went through my first house.

Anyway, Jupiter in the first house or Saturn in the first house is really an important period because the first house is the beginning of a whole new cycle. It's the beginning of new developments you're going to initiate through definite action and commitment. So Jupiter gives you the confidence to initiate things that maybe you have thought about or intuited for a long time. And it's generally experienced by most people as a fairly positive time that gives them a lot of optimism about the future. Naturally, these are general trends, and if you look at a particular chart you may find that Saturn is squaring someone's Sun and opposing the Moon at the same time that Jupiter is going over the Ascendant. It may not be experienced as all so optimistic in that case, but it's undoubtedly a really important and decisive time—if they have that many transits of Jupiter and Saturn simultaneously. Does anybody have Jupiter going through their first house now? (No response from audience.) I guess everyone with Jupiter in the first house is outside playing or they're too busy doing things to sit and listen to anyone, right?

One thing that is quite common with Jupiter transits, especially as it approaches the Ascendant and goes into the early part of the first house, (and it's also experienced when Jupiter aspects Mercury, or occasionally the Sun or Moon) is that one has insights into the future. They'll sometimes have visions of the future or precognitive dreams. That might be one thing that you could check if you go back into your past, if you've ever had that sort of thing. It's not always a big sensational thing. It's often a kind of feeling or hunch. Even business people, stock brokers, and real skeptical, materialistic people talk about how they've "got this hunch." They don't think of it as psychic or visionary or prophecy or anything. It's just "a hunch." So what's a hunch? It's a sense of how current *trends* are going, and if those trends keep going in the same basic way, they'll lead to a certain future situation. And Jupiter can tune you in to that kind of flow into the future. We don't have time to go into lots of examples, but there are a number of people I know who—especially when Jupiter crossed the Ascendant—had a flash on something they could start now that would develop and grow into the future, and which was proven later to be true. Their vision of the future or precognitive dream came true exactly to the letter. Not always will precognitive dreams come true literally. But, if you have such experiences when Jupiter is active, the chances are good that it will work out fairly accurately.

Saturn in the first house is a period of less confidence at first. This is the *usual* thing. It may be different with different people now and then. But the usual thing is that people have less confidence because they notice their faults more, and their desires to act independently (shown by Mars and the first house) are often somewhat frustrated. And of course this also goes for certain Saturn transits of natal Mars. It's often a period of some heaviness; many people really notice their faults then, their failings and their weaknesses. The best thing that one can do at that time is to tune into what realistically is really wrong with them *and what is really right with them,* and then start to build the kind of *being* they want to be through some kind of effort. Saturn in the first house—the best way to characterize that time is: it's a period of "getting it together." It's a period of finding out about yourself. It's a time when people really need feedback, really honest and realistic feedback about themselves. And it's a time to put effort into *coalescing* a lot of different parts of *you*, integrating yourself into some kind of rather new and much more solid personality. The first house, of course, is *yourself* and the *image* of your personality that other people see. Does anybody have Saturn in the first house now? Three people here have Saturn in the first house now. Did anyone have any comments to make about this?

Audience: I felt tremendously relieved when Saturn went into my first house after it had been in my 12th house.

After the confusion, yes. That's common too. Saturn in the first at least gives you something definite, a more definite sense of direction. It may require work or effort and it may even tune you in to the fact that things may be hard or demanding for awhile, but it often feels more secure because it's more definite. Again, it depends a lot on the person. Now you're real fiery. (Addresses person in the audience.) You would like *action*, more like the first house. Somebody who is real spacey and Neptunean and *comfortable with that*, might like Saturn in the 12th better. Again, you have to relate it to the individual chart. Another fairly common pattern is that, when Saturn first goes into the first house, there's often some heavy thing or some seriousness or even depression; but as soon as people really start working at themselves in some way or changing their diet or starting an exercise program or something that organizes their lives or bodies, they start feeling much more comfortable. When Saturn is in the first, you can build a tremendous amount of inner strength—physical as well as emotional and mental strength. But it doesn't come free. You've got to work at it. Whereas when Jupiter is in the first house, Jupiter is kind of free. It gives you strength, energy, confidence, and you don't have to really *work* for it. You do, however, have to be open to it and *accept* it. You might waste it, but at least it comes rather easily. Does anybody else have Saturn in the first now?

Audience: Yes. I didn't realize it when it was first happening; but when it went over my Ascendant, I went on a diet and lost 12 pounds, and I also started exercising and I don't even like to exercise.

It's really different for everybody, depending on how attuned you are to the planet or planets involved. I don't know if I've pointed it out before, but the natal chart shows how you are attuned to a particular vibration. For example, just take Saturn, how you experience Saturn transits will depend very much upon how Saturn is situated in your natal chart. In other words, if you have all kinds of difficulties with Saturn in your everyday life—as shown in most cases by Saturn's placement or aspects—then the transits tend to be harder. That's something that is so individualized that you can't put it in a book and you can't generalize about it. Individual people, by studying their own charts, get to know how they get along, so to speak, with certain planetary energies. If you get along with Saturn, then Saturn transits often mark a positive culmination of important developments and sometimes public recognition or worldly success. The people who hate Saturn are usually the lazy people, really. But I should emphasize that how you "get along" with a certain planet is not always and reliably self-evident in the natal chart. Someone could grow to do so, even if the natal aspects to that planet were all squares.

Saturn hitting Mars is somewhat similar to Saturn in the first house. There's often a toning down of their energies, sometimes a markedly different energy level. I got a letter yesterday from someone whose whole complaint was, "God, I'm so tired and I've been to all these doctors and I still just feel exhausted all the time, etc., etc., etc." So I looked in her chart, and Saturn is crossing the early part of her first house. And Saturn hitting Mars will also often be that way. But again, it's so unpredictable. The main thing is to understand the basic principles. What is the essential meaning of Jupiter or Saturn in a particular house? Once you have a feeling for *that*, then you can relate it to the individual cases. I know someone who was really weak and had incredibly low energy for being only 25, and I thought, "When Saturn hits her first house, unless she really works hard at it, she's just really going to be a wreck; her body is just going to fall apart." So when Saturn hit her Ascendant, she started jogging everyday. Her physical strength is now about double what it was a year ago. It's rather amazing; I can still hardly believe it. But part of it is discipline too. Saturn is the planet of discipline. She really disciplined herself to do it every morning, every week day morning. She gives herself weekends off.

Q: Most of the time then, in the physical sense, unless you discipline yourself, to keep up some kind of physical activity, you might experience some loss of strength or loss of energy?

A: I would say so. That would definitely be the tendency if Saturn's in the first or aspecting Mars by various angles.

JUPITER & SATURN TRANSITING THE 2ND HOUSE

When Jupiter or Saturn is in the second house, it invariably puts an emphasis on second house activities: money or getting training or education to make money, improving your material security, learning about investments, it could be a million things; but it's usually related to something material and practical. It often has correlations with work and career too. As a matter of fact, all the earth houses—the 2nd, 6th, and 10th houses that correlate with the earth signs—when Jupiter or Saturn goes into those houses, it often affects your work or your attitude toward the kind of work you want to do. With Jupiter in the second, some books say, "You'll get rich;" well, occasionally that might happen, but you can't at all count on it. What's more likely is that there's an urge to *improve* your financial situation. And usually by the time that period is half over, the person has more confidence about their ability to handle money or to make enough money, or at least to have access to the kind of resources that they feel they need. Saturn in the second also often manifests as the person having an urge to make more money. But the tendency is for things to be much slower. Saturn is slower. Jupiter tends to be rather quick and easy, or at least considerably more enjoyable than Saturn. However, it's not unheard of for people to make large sums of money or to get inheritances or to win contests when *Saturn* is in the second house. It can happen; I've seen it happen, not often but a few times.

Q: When Saturn or Jupiter is in the second house?

A: Actually, when either one is there, but I was referring to Saturn. It's more common to have someone get some money easily when Jupiter is there. But Saturn does not stop it. See, Saturn *consolidates* things; it brings things down to earth. And very often, with Saturn in the second house, your financial situation will be consolidated; it will be made more definite. Your way of earning money will become more defined. One thing I've seen repeatedly which I've never seen in any book—all these books contend that Saturn in the second house is going to cause all sorts of anxiety about money and perhaps even dire poverty or bankruptcy. Anxiety *is* often felt, especially when Saturn just approaches and goes into the second house; but this by no means shows poverty or financial catastrophe but rather that you just feel pressure to define how you're going to take care of your body in this material world, that is, how you're going to make money to buy food and shelter and all this. The thing that I've seen so often is that, first of all, many people change jobs then. And part of the motivation is to get into something that will ultimately give them more financial security. But in many cases too, people will start training (when Saturn is in the second house) or schooling of some kind that eventually will give them a skill with which they can earn more money. So, while Saturn is in the second house, if the money is not flowing in in great batches, it doesn't mean it's never going to; you can't be rigid about it. Astrology shows the inner motivations rather than the outer manifestations. The inner is shown *more accurately* than the outer. So even if someone is going to school when Saturn is in the second house, Saturn in the second may symbolize the *motivation* for their going to school, to do something that is going to help them make more money or have a more secure existence in the material world. A rigid type of astrologer might say, "Oh gee, you shouldn't be going to school; there's nothing in your third house or ninth house now."

And by the way, when Saturn or Jupiter hits Venus by conjunction, square, semi-sextile, quincunx, opposition, or even occasionally by trine, there are often experiences like those we've been relating to the second house. They tend to be shorter, however, than the period when Jupiter or Saturn is in a house. And you have to keep in mind that these things we've been mentioning are specifically focused on the second house, whereas a transit of natal Venus can manifest as either the second house or the seventh house side of Venus' nature (or both). So sometimes a transit to natal Venus will focus entirely on close relationships, marriage, and other seventh house matters, with no correlation to the practical affairs of the second house. Other times, a transit to Venus will manifest very similarly to the same planet passing through the second house.

Q: In my chart right now Saturn is in the second house, conjunct the Moon, and all things are changing, occupation changing to art rather than an intellectual pursuit; with my possessions, all I've been doing for five or six months now is taking things and giving them away.

A: Restructuring. That's another key word for Saturn—*structure* or *restructuring* as it's transiting. You're also probably defining what you need and what you really value. It's so different with everybody, though. It's such an individual thing that the most you can do in general conceptual treatments of astrology is outline some basic principles and hope you'll penetrate into some of the essential stuff. With every person it's so different.

JUPITER & SATURN TRANSITING THE 3RD HOUSE

The third house then, and this applies also when Saturn or Jupiter is aspecting natal Mercury—there's always a development of some kind in the way that you express your ideas and in the way that you think and even in the way that you perceive things. Jupiter hitting Mercury or in the third house tends to make you more optimistic-minded or positive-thinking oriented. Saturn hitting Mercury or in the third house tends more towards serious thinking and sometimes toward pessimistic thinking, in some cases even depression or worry or anxiety. But again, it depends on the person so much, their nature, openness, attitudes, and level of understanding. For example, you can see the transiting planets as cosmic beings that give you messages, and particularly so when a transiting planet aspects your natal planet real closely. It's like you can get messages from them; it's like they're talking to you or their vibrations filter through from the unconscious. It's hard to put it into words, but some people might know what I mean.

The best example I know of and I didn't even know about transits at that time—happened just after I graduated from college. I was working in the college library. Saturn was transiting opposite my natal Mercury, and I was going through this amazing reorganizing and restructuring of my thinking. The whole way that I had thought in the past was being restructured in a much more realistic way. Saturn also pressures you to be realistic. It was like I was getting some *heavy* instructions from some Saturn being on how I should think and look at things from now on. Pages and pages of notes on the things Saturn told me resulted from this period, which lasted for weeks. It was real interesting. To most modern people, talking about getting messages and instructions from the planets sounds like you're either a UFO freak or totally batty. But nevertheless, it's a useful metaphor and it's as true as any other way of describing what you experience or what you *can* experience when certain transits are happening. For another example, when Jupiter is in your first house, you can get these messages like an inner voice saying, "You can do it, you can do it, have confidence— go on and try it"—that sort of thing. When Saturn is transiting something, the message may be, "You better look at this carefully, pay attention to yourself, know your limits, don't hurry, be practicable." When Uranus is transiting, you get this constant message: "Oh the hell with it! Get rid of all those restraints!" God knows what Neptune says. Neptune doesn't even speak in languages, except maybe in poetry or song. Neptune just goes in nuances. Pluto is just, "I don't care any more! It's all over!" It always likes to be drastic.

So anyway, Jupiter or Saturn in the third house or hitting Mercury—by itself it's not usually felt to be a real critical time, but it can be used later as a period of learning that you'll be glad you went through. Especially with Saturn there! With Saturn hitting Mercury or in the third house, you can really deepen your understanding of things and you can become much more certain of what you think, of what opinions and ideas and concepts and facts have value to you. The tendency is, when Saturn is hitting Mercury or in the third house, to test those concepts, to test those ideas and see if they measure up in some practical way. Does anybody have Saturn or Jupiter in the third now?

Audience: I have Jupiter in the third. It's conjuncting my Mars-Jupiter conjunction in the third.

You were born with Mars conjunct Jupiter in the third? And transiting Jupiter is conjunct those two now? (Yes.) The entire process shown by the Jupiter transit started quite a few months ago and will continue for a while more. What have you been doing?

Audience: Well, beginning in January I started an MBA program in college.

Of course we're talking about the Jupiter return here too. Every twelve years Jupiter returns to its natal place. So you must be about twenty-four. The Jupiter return is a very common time for people to expand their educational activities, especially the second return in the early twenties. But also at the first one, at about age twelve, there's a definite change in the young person's educational interests. Also you're getting into an astrology class. That must be part of it too. So there's the Jupiter return in effect, in addition to the third house transit by Jupiter—all in all, a strong emphasis on learning and broadening your skills and interests.

JUPITER, SATURN & MARS RETURNS

Q: Are you going to talk about returns?

A: Well, since you brought it up, I might as well mention three of them. The Jupiter return every 12 or so years is experienced by almost everybody as a pretty positive time—new plans, new possibilities, new aspirations start to take form, a lot of optimism and a lot of clear perceptions of future opportunities. Often there are rapid changes then too. But usually, no matter what other aspects you're having then, if the Jupiter return is happening the tendency is for there to be at least an *overall* tone of "progress," whether it's getting a better job, getting into a graduate program, or something else that to you signifies progress and improvement.

You can write a book about the Saturn return. In fact, there are complete books written about it and the Saturn cycle. In a way, it's a bit overemphasized (to the neglect of other transits); but it is important because your childhood is still going on until your first Saturn return—at about age 29 to 30. Many people don't get a really clear feeling for what they really want to do or *have* to do until their first Saturn return. Before your first Saturn return, your life is made up of random attempts at all these different directions, but many or all of them are misguided experiments. Whereas the Saturn return often marks your destiny taking *form*. Saturn is a kind of destiny planet. That's why so many seemingly destined things happen under Saturn aspects, not just the Saturn return but with Saturn aspects to other planets too. And often you then get a better feel for what you're destined to do. Sometimes you're just pressured into it, even if you resist it. Other times, even though people often say that Saturn is restriction, the Saturn return is experienced as tremendously *liberating*; because suddenly you know what you're supposed to do, whereas before that there was always the feeling that, "I'm not quite sure what I'm supposed to be doing." So on the surface you may have seemed free, but in your inner experience you may have been really frustrated. After the Saturn return, you may have an obvious lack of freedom on the outside, but you may be much freer within. And there is also a shift in your sense of freedom and responsibilities at the second Saturn return at about age 58-60.

Also, the Mars return is occasionally important. The Mars return is every two years. It's often experienced as renewal of energy or new plans, but usually it's just new plans related to what you're *already* doing. Rarely does it by itself indicate some major new step. But say you run a business or something and you have your Mars return, you may start a new line of products or a new advertising gimmick. However, if your Mars return occurs when a lot of other things are happening (real important things like Saturn, Uranus, or Jupiter transiting aspects), it's all the more likely that you'll act dynamically or start something new. Also, Mars opposite Mars—which happens every two years—is something to keep an eye on because it's often a period of blockage or frustration. It hardly lasts but a few days, but some people feel really screwed up for those few days. It's like one Mars is over here and the other Mars is over there, and the person just can't seem to mobilize his energy. There may be people who don't experience that, but I've seen it repeatedly with myself and with other people. It's hardly ever a big deal unless you're trying to do some big project at that time—like within two or three days of the exact aspect—but then the project seems to meet with all these frustrations. I would never want to take on any big project with Mars opposite Mars.

Q: You know when you were talking about the Jupiter return and that there was sort of a key for the first one, then the second one, and really there's about five or more Jupiter returns in one lifetime. Are there key things associated with the other Jupiter returns?

A: Well, the third one is pretty easy to characterize. It happens at about age 35, and that's a kind of magic number for a lot of people—especially women. Many women seem to really take off on their third Jupiter return. It's often more important for them than the second one if in their 20's they had kids and parental duties. In terms of their personal ambitions and educational plans and all that, the third one then often marks an important time. But for everybody, the Jupiter return really means new possibilities. It's tuning oneself to the fact that there are new opportunities now, that you can do new and promising things—things that you may never have thought of before. But as to the fourth, fifth, and sixth ones, I don't really know how to especially characterize them. I've seen a lot of people go through them, but generally I just describe them to clients in a general way so they can identify with them.

The other return that we might mention is the Uranus return, even though many people don't live to experience it. It happens about age 84 or so. And I don't know what it means except that I would think if you lived that long, you might experience some new sense of freedom or become super rebellious after possibly outgrowing all social restrictions. More than most transits, the Uranus return would probably be unpredictable and totally an individual thing.

Q: Now this may not relate to what we're talking about, but there was this old man in Florida who was 110 who started taking reading lessons because he was going to start learning the Bible. He was a farmer who was 110.

A: Yes, that doesn't relate at all. (laughter) That idea could have been born, though, at his 9th Jupiter return (at about age 108). People often get not only a strong urge to learn and improve themselves, but also often experience a new religious faith at the Jupiter return.

Q: What happens on your second Saturn return?

A: It depends mainly on what you learned at the first one, and on how effectively you put your learning into practice. Sometimes it's accompanied by feelings of tremendous frustration, if you find you haven't lived in accord with your true nature.

Comment from audience: A lot of people commit suicide around that age.

A: Which follows from what I just said then. It depends on how much you feel you've fulfilled yourself and done what you were meant to do. Actually, most of the clients I've had have been of the age of the first Saturn return (plus or minus a few years), or they've been of the age when Saturn was opposite natal Saturn. I guess I've done a few dozen charts when the second Saturn return was happening. Usually the personal life is fairly organized by then; the person is usually committed to or resigned to their marriage or lifestyle, although there are exceptions. Every once in a while someone will take off and split from their spouse at that time, but more often people are thinking of planning security for the future, retirement, etc. One lady I saw last month—her second Saturn return was happening and she has to decide some important things. Saturn returns are almost always decision times. Grant Lewi points out that it's a time when you're really tremendously free. It's one of the few times when you can really choose, "Yes, I'm going to stay married to so and so; yes, I'm going to do this career or take off on a totally new trip." This woman has to decide, along with her husband, who is going through the same thing, whether or not they should sell their business and do something else for the rest of their lives or whether they should hold onto the business as a security blanket; but that would also mean that they have to keep working every day. *She* works pretty long hours at the business. He doesn't; he mainly plays golf. He's therefore more inclined to keep the business. He just does a bit of bookkeeping because he's an accountant. But she does all the hard physical work, and she's now about 60. So they haven't decided exactly what they're going to do. But that's what it very often is—a very practical decision about arranging your life and security things. That's the essence of it for *most* people, but of course more inward, contemplative people can also experience a renewed sense of inner purpose at that time.

I know a man whose second Saturn return is approaching. It won't be exact for two years. He has natal Saturn and Jupiter conjunct in the 8th house in Virgo and Mars at the beginning of the 8th house in late Leo. Transiting Saturn is conjuncting his natal Mars, and it's approaching Saturn and Jupiter, and he just sold the business that he put his whole life into. He put all his energy into his business since his first Saturn return. At the age of 29 he quit working for the company he was working for and started his own business; and he worked at it and worked at it and worked at it, made it a big success and now—with the second Saturn return coming—he's selling it, at a tremendous price, millions of dollars. All he has to do is go fishing and hunting for the rest of his life. It's a great relief to him, a big load off his back.

I should also mention something else about the Uranus cycle. Even though the Uranus return doesn't apply to many people, other parts of its cycle do apply to most people. If you consider the Uranus cycle as an 84 year cycle, then when you're about 21, transiting Uranus is squaring natal Uranus—although at times it is exact when the person is only 19. Around 19, 20, or 21 though, there's often that rebellious trip of, "I've got to get away from Mommy and Daddy and make my own living." Then there's the opposition we talked about as happening around age 42 or a little before—sometimes it's felt as early as age 38. There's usually radical changes and a break with the past at that time— also new and exciting activities. Then again in another 20 years or so, in the late fifties or early sixties, transiting Uranus is squaring natal Uranus again. And that is very common at the retirement age of 60-65. Often, a lot of creativity and originality (as well as eccentricity) starts to be expressed more actively then than was possible before. It can be and probably *should* be a period of pronounced personal freedom, social awareness, and revitalized creative interests.

JUPITER & SATURN TRANSITING THE 4TH HOUSE

If you put transiting Jupiter or Saturn in the fourth house, you've got on one level a very common indication (either one of them can be an indication) of moving or of improving your property or your home or of dealing with your *roots*. Jupiter particularly, in the fourth house, gives an urge to make your home more comfortable. And people then have the urge to have more space, to expand or improve their home or home environment. This sometimes means that they move to a more spacious house. Sometimes it manifests as their building on to their present house. They may add on another bedroom or make the basement into a recreation room, all kinds of things. I was talking about this recently in a class, and several people spoke up and said, "We just added on to our house, and Jupiter is now in my fourth." But with Saturn in the fourth too, you'll often improve your property, not so much because you want more space but because you want your place to be more *solid*. So you'll then often put more effort or energy or money into your home or yard to make it feel more solid or permanent. In any case, with either Jupiter or Saturn in the fourth, the emphasis is on the private life and sometimes the inner life.

When Saturn went into my fourth house, I started building brick walls, with bricks and mortar, stones and cement. I never finished any of them because I don't have any planets in my natal fourth house. There was no lasting energy to get it done. All I did was to lay the foundation (Saturn) and only about two tiers of bricks, and finally I hired someone else who didn't know what he was doing to finish it. It's the funniest brick wall you've ever seen. It looks like a mortar wall with a few bricks in it. Also, when Jupiter goes into the fourth, it's quite common for people to move, or to start contemplating a large-scale future move. In every case I've seen, if they move then, they really like their new place, their new location. It feels really comfortable. And once in awhile, they'll move into a place with less square footage—in other words, the actual living area is not bigger—but it will be an environment that feels so much more comfortable that they'll really like it.

Q: Because it would be more airy, like a country setting or something?

A: It depends on the person's taste. Some people would like moving to New York City. For example, one guy I know was living in Santa Ana in Southern California, in the smog which was horrible. He had a pretty nice apartment, very large for the money; it was a good deal, but he couldn't stand the area. The smog was horrible and when Jupiter went into his fourth, he moved to Laguna Beach. He got a real tiny place, about half the square footage that he had before, and he had to pay more because the rents are high there. But he was much more comfortable in the new place just because he's a Pisces, and he loves being near the ocean and the air is better there too. Anyway, transiting Jupiter and Saturn can indicate very similar things, but there's a slight distinction. The main distinction is in the motivation—what's *motivating* your behaviour. With Saturn in the fourth, you may improve your house because you want it to be solid, you want it to be secure, or you want to invest in it because it's a good investment. With Jupiter, the motivation tends more to be simply *enjoyment*. On a more subtle level, these transits through the fourth house, or when Saturn or Jupiter aspect your natal Moon, can correlate with a change or reassessment of your self-image or a change in your inner confidence.

Q: These also apply the same to natal charts too. Because my husband has Saturn in the fourth house in the natal and I have Jupiter there, and we've moved 17 or 18 times in the last 20 years. And he himself has moved something like 48 times. It really works that way.

A: The basic principles work in the natal chart too. But I'm not focusing on that now. As a matter of fact, that's even harder to talk about because there are even more manifestations of the natal planet placements than of the transiting planets. But even with transits, we're by no means mentioning all the possibilities.

JUPITER & SATURN TRANSITING THE 5TH HOUSE

Transits of the fifth house or when Saturn or Jupiter hits the Sun—it affects your creative energy and the whole mode of expressing your energy creatively. Saturn tends to be heavy. In fact, Saturn in the fifth or aspecting the Sun is one of the harder transits, but also often one of the most rewarding. Saturn in the fifth house, I would say, is second only to Saturn in the first house as a time when people often feel real heavy, because it's in the Sun's house—the life force! Saturn in the fifth or in the first is often felt as kind of a heavy time and often a time of low physical energy and not particularly a lot of optimism. However, again you have to be careful with it. Saturn going into the fifth, the early part of the fifth, is often experienced as much heavier than Saturn at the end of the fifth house. With Saturn in the early part of the house, you'll often realize the state of your creativity, the state of your ability to create, the state of your love life too—how capable you are of giving your love energy, and you also get realistic about how much you're getting. And if you feel really unloved, unwanted, and unappreciated then, that's an important message too! As Saturn gets into the later part of the fifth house, you can do something about it . . . hopefully. At least you can adapt yourself to accept how things are. Hopefully, you can take steps and make an *effort* to express your affection and creativity much more definitely. Saturn in the fifth or hitting the Sun is a time to discipline and structure and define the way that you express your creative energy. By creative energy, I mean that in the broadest sense, whether you express your creativity and vitality in a love relationship or through some kind of work or with children or all three. The main thing is that the fifth house Saturn position is—in the early stages—often felt as rather frustrating, but it gets easier as you get used to it and learn the lessons of that time period. That's also true of some transiting Saturn aspects to the Sun.

Sometimes the transiting aspects to the Sun for women are a little different from the aspects to the Sun for men. Lots of times, aspects to the Moon for women will be big experiences, big decisions and so forth.

Q: Can you say more about transiting Saturn conjunct the natal Moon?

A: First of all, there could be all that fourth house stuff thrown in there too: there could be moves, there could be decisions about the home, the environment, etc. And for most people it's a period of being thrown back upon themselves. They get more realistic or at least they have the opportunity to get more realistic about what they really are. The Moon symbolizes, among many other things, how you feel about yourself, how comfortable you are with yourself. And Saturn hitting the Moon—a lot of people go through pretty heavy numbers then. A lot of depression too is common. I think that is also partly because the Moon is a passive planet. The Moon represents an unconscious or semi-conscious part of yourself and how you *feel*. It's not something you can grab onto tangibly. Very often, people make important decisions then. They'll get thrown back on themselves, and they'll be forced by something outer or inner to re-evaluate what they're doing. I'll give you two examples real quickly.

One guy, when Saturn conjuncted his Moon, had applied to about 10 medical schools, and all of them turned him down; and the final one turned him down when that aspect happened. And he was real depressed for about three or four days and really grumpy. During that time, he had to reevaluate whether he was really *meant* to be a doctor, and whether he really still *wanted* to be one. He had to face the fact that if he really wanted to be, he would have to move out of this country to go to medical school, because his grades weren't good enough to go anywhere in this country. So that's what he's doing. He's almost finished with medical school in France now. But he had to come to grips with that. One of the best phrases for transits is "coming to terms with things." Another guy, when Saturn conjuncted his Moon in his sixth house, got evicted from his house, and then he started really looking around desperately for some kind of work—which he couldn't find. Then he decided, "My only hope is to get my rich girlfriend to marry me." So he asked this girl that he used to live with if she would like to get married, because she's a hard-working Capricorn and he thought at least there would be someone to support him then. And she told him to get out! And he was quite depressed for at least a couple of weeks. All these things he had tried to run away from kept confronting him. So he had to face the fact that some day he might have to start earning a living for himself. And he had to face realistically what the true situation was with the woman (Moon) in his life, and face what his real feelings and needs were.

Jupiter in the fifth is very different from Saturn in the fifth. Jupiter in the fifth usually gives you abundant creative energy. In fact, a lady just showed up at my office the other day saying, "Well, Jupiter is in my fifth, and I've got this abundant creative energy!" She's producing all this art work. Many creatively-inclined people really expand their efforts when Jupiter is in the fifth house. They'll often branch out into other things too. When I was 20 years old and Jupiter was in my fifth, I was making movies, writing plays, writing poetry, and getting into astrology simultaneously—also having a big love affair. The Jupiter transit of the fifth house the next time around took a totally different form—not nearly so much carefree fun! Jupiter in the fifth is a very common time for love affairs or love experiences that you tend to enjoy. Saturn in the fifth is a time when a love affair may be a little heavy or sometimes you don't get one at all, although you're looking all the time. When Saturn goes into your fifth house, you also might be especially attracted to Saturnian or Capricorn types of people. And when Jupiter goes into your fifth house, you might be attracted to Jupiter-type people, optimistic people. Jupiter in the fifth for most people is a pretty happy time. Saturn in the fifth is not indicative of a total lack of creativity, but you don't have the abundant creative energy which is typified by Jupiter in the first or fifth. Your energy is more limited. So when Saturn is in the fifth, it's a good time to discipline the way that you do your creative work. Say you're a writer, a painter, or whatever. Saturn in the fifth is a good time to learn how to just *do it*, almost mechanically; everyday just do it for a certain length of time. With Jupiter in the fifth, you can rely more on inspiration and still get things done. With Saturn in the fifth, however, you'll never accomplish anything unless you discipline your creative methods.

JUPITER & SATURN TRANSITING THE 6TH HOUSE

Then we get into the sixth house, with Jupiter and Saturn there, obviously it's often a time of making changes in job, work, often in health habits too, everything from diet habits to sleep habits. And you often ask yourself, "What *use* are you?" Remember the sixth house is the Virgo house, somewhat self-critical at times: Saturn in the sixth is commonly a time of being hard on yourself or criticizing yourself too much. Sometimes there are annoying chronic health problems then too. The main thing is, with either Jupiter or Saturn there, you should put energy into doing things about your health and daily habits. Jupiter in the sixth, especially, inclines the person to want to improve their job situation, either the kind of job, the job environment, or the kind of people they work with. With Saturn going through the sixth, sometimes they'll feel a lot of hassles in those areas, and that will prompt the person to make a decision about whether or not they're going to keep that job. Does anyone have Jupiter or Saturn in the 6th house now?

Q: I have Saturn in the sixth.

A: How long has Saturn been in your sixth?

Q: Since 24° Cancer.

A: Oh, quite a while then. . . . Do you have a job?

Q: No. I've been unemployed since about September. Then I began school.

A: So you stopped working at some job while Saturn was in your sixth house?

Q: Yes. And the jobs between January and September were very erratic. I ended a very successful job as Saturn went into my sixth. So, since December of '75 I've really been reevaluating that whole area.

A: Have you done anything about health things?

Q: I've been focusing on health. I've been reading more and more books on health. I've been very interested in vegetarianism and things like that.

JUPITER & SATURN TRANSITING THE 7TH HOUSE

With Jupiter and Saturn in the 7th, it should be rather obvious. And this is somewhat similar to transiting Jupiter or Saturn hitting Venus—a focus on relationships. The funny thing is that a lot of marriages will have more difficulty when Jupiter is going through the 7th than when Saturn is going through the 7th. And one of the reasons seems to be that, when Jupiter is in your 7th house, you have an urge to improve your relationships, or to expand the scope of your relationships; and if you're with someone who is dead or if the marriage is basically dead or unimprovable, there will often be an urge to expand the scope of your relationships beyond that marriage. Whereas Saturn in the 7th makes you confront very realistically what the marriage is and take a look at it very seriously. A lot of relationships go through big changes and a lot of marriages end when Jupiter or Saturn go into the 7th house; and if the marriage has ended then, when the planet that was in the 7th goes into the 8th, then you have all the settlement, all the money things, and all the joint financial hassles. Sometimes that gets to be quite a mess. Time is getting short. I think we can just briefly go through the other houses because there are some other things I still want to do.

JUPITER & SATURN TRANSITING
THE 8TH & 9TH HOUSES

Does anyone have Jupiter or Saturn in their 8th house now?

A: Transiting Jupiter is in my 8th now.

Q: And have you expanded your astrological studies?

A: I'm concerned not only with astrology but other kinds of occult studies too, and also with most of the things people relate to the 8th house.

Q: Just since Jupiter has been in the 8th or before that?

A: Especially since Jupiter's gone into the 8th.

The 8th house is a hard one to talk about because everything related to it and to Pluto and Scorpio is somewhat underground, or unconscious. But usually Jupiter or Saturn in the 8th house will put an emphasis on deeper things, whether it's your psychological state of mind, your emotions, or other kinds of deep "soul-security." Often times there's an emphasis on power and sexuality too. Jupiter tends to expand one's interest in sex or in sexual adventure. Saturn in the 8th is very often a period of emotional and sexual frustration, although there are often a lot of really good lessons then too. It's not always that you're frustrated by *circumstances.* In other cases, you'll decide to define or discipline your use of all kinds of power, sexual energy, financial power, and other things while Saturn is in the 8th house.

As one might expect, transiting Jupiter or Saturn going through the ninth house is often a period of truth-seeking, the essence of which is *learning who you are.* It is a great period for learning, especially a time of broadening one's philosophical or religious horizons while Jupiter is going through its own house—it's therefore a bit like the Jupiter return . . . renewed faith, new educational activities, often travel, and so on. With Saturn in the ninth, your source of faith is often contracted, at least for a while; you may have doubts about everything you used to believe in or that you thought you *knew*. But again, Saturn's pressure is not for nothing; by going through this period you can build a deeper, more solid foundation for your religious or inspirational life. That part of your life can be thereafter more based on personal experience than upon tradition or past training. There can be interest at this time in any kind of vast system of thought or in any kind of ideas that purport to give your life a purposeful direction. There are also lots of career planning activities (*related to your ideals*) that people get into at this time, rather as preparation for the on-coming tenth house period.

JUPITER & SATURN TRANSITING THE 10TH, 11TH, & 12TH HOUSES

In addition to the usual things correlated with Jupiter or Saturn going through the tenth house, you can elaborate on its meaning by remembering that the tenth house is a Saturn house—hence, all forms of life structure, responsibility, and long-term plans may be emphasized. And these transits are quite similar to Jupiter or Saturn aspecting natal Saturn. It's a useful counseling tool too, like if someone's unemployed and they're really looking for a *better* job; keep an eye on Jupiter or Saturn hitting natal Saturn, especially by conjunction, or especially Jupiter going into the 10th, 6th, or 2nd houses. Those transits tend to help you get jobs that you really like or to improve your work situation in some noticeable way. It doesn't always mean immediate fantastic pay. Some people, as Jupiter or Saturn passes into the 10th house, quit jobs that were real secure or that paid fairly well simply to have more options in their lives and to have the opportunity to do what they wanted as a vocation. So it doesn't always mean money when Jupiter is in the 10th, but you may get into something you like better and that has a *future* in it, since you know Jupiter is known for future things.

The 11th house is probably, more than any other house, poorly explained in most books. And I don't have the time to explain it much better now. But it does deal—among other things—with your sense of purpose in society, how you fit into society. The last chapter of my book on the elements* goes into some detail on each of the houses. When Jupiter or Saturn goes into the 11th, very often you'll participate in more group activities; and you do that partly because you have a better sense of what your role is in society, what *you* can do that other people need or just how you fit into the world as a whole—not vocationally but *personally*. One lady I know, when Saturn went into her 11th, rapidly became the head organizer for this group of about 60 or 70 single people; and she started being in charge of organizing this group's activities. Saturn in the 11th house was just a perfect symbol for what she was doing. Like Aquarius the Water Bearer (which is associated with this house), you'll often *pour out* your energies to others at this time.

The 12th house is a doozie and it's also—like Neptune—quite hard to verbalize. But especially Saturn in the 12th house tends to be a really important time. Either Jupiter or Saturn in the 12th house tends to space you out a little bit. But the "space-out" is not particularly disturbing in most cases when Jupiter is in the 12th. But when Saturn's there, there's often a considerable feeling of being lost or having no direction. That's often how people explain it when Saturn is in the 12th house—"I've got no direction, I don't know what's happening next." The old structures symbolized by Saturn tend to dissolve rather quickly when Saturn is in the 12th house. In other words, what used to be meaningful to you or used to give you some energy or support tends to fall apart; and you often feel real *empty*. So you start looking around and you say, "Gee, I've got to find something to hold onto." The 12th house—like Neptune and Pisces—is very intangible. So there's nothing you can do when Saturn or Jupiter is in the 12th house *except* to tune in on intangibles, tune in on spiritual things and ideals, tune in on subtleties or on artistry—some kind of art or poetry or music. But there's no way that the 12th house phase can be made to fit into your ambitions and desires in the practical world. What it is for is to develop in inner ways, or in subtle or aesthetic ways. There is considerable disorientation felt by many people when Saturn is in the 12th house, and how disoriented, pleasant, or unpleasant it is depends on your openness to the infinite. Does anybody have Saturn in the 12th now? (Several people raised their hands.) What's happened with you?

---

*C.f. *Astrology, Psychology & the Four Elements*, available from the publishers of this book.

A: I've really enjoyed it. Just because there has been quite a bit coming up from the past and knowing that I should tune into it now . . . and I've developed a confidence to face life and anxiety . . . and dealing with avoidance tendencies is really a big thing right now.

Neptune you know, 12th house, Pisces—*avoidance, escape.* But when Saturn hits Neptune by transit *or* is in the 12th, one of the keynotes of that time period is facing up to what you've been avoiding. That happens too when transiting Pluto hits Neptune; many people have had Pluto hitting the natal Neptune in Libra during the past few years. With Saturn in the 12th house, of course one has to keep in mind that this is the absolute end of a cycle. It's the end of an entire life cycle, and many people experience that it's the end not just of their overall life structure but even of their old personality structure. Old attitudes and ideals and priorities and ambitions just fall apart then, but falling apart can be kind of inspiring too; if you know what's happening, then you can flow with it. But it's a preparation time; it's kind of a clearing the decks for the building of a whole new lifestyle and a whole new personality structure which can start as Saturn approaches and goes into the first house.

Q: Could you talk about Jupiter in the 11th house a little bit more? I have Jupiter there.

A: And here you are sitting in a group—a group educational effort.

Q: Well, of course I have Mars conjunct Jupiter in the same place.

A: What, you were born with Jupiter conjunct Mars in the 11th house?

Q: Yes.

A: What sign are they in?

Q: Gemini.

A: You've been a teacher or something, huh?

Q: Yes. I've been teaching.

A: Languages or English?

Q: Sciences, biology, botany and also language.

A: Gemini tends to be scientific or verbal or into manual skills.

Q: Well, I studied and semi-taught foreign languages and writing for a while. I've been involved with languages all my life really, but only as a hobby.

A: So Jupiter has recently returned to its natal place in the 11th house. So you're probably expanding into some new phase of activity that will eventually be directed into group activities. When you have all that Gemini stuff in an air house—11th, 3rd, or 7th—there's got to be direct contact with people. In the 11th, it tends towards groups—like maybe five or more people at a time as a focus of a lot of energy.

Q: Well, that's always been true. I've been involved in teaching and many kinds of educational and group activities.

A: The 11th house does have the Aquarius and Uranus connotations of not just group work but also politics, science of all kinds, social change and revolutionary types of activities. Almost everyone I've ever seen with the *Sun* in the 11th—which is something that no textbooks ever seem to mention—is really attuned to political changes or trends. That doesn't mean that they'll necessarily do anything about it, but they understand such things naturally and easily. And often they're quite fascinated by them, even if they don't actively participate. But anyway, there's usually some need to pour out your energy to the masses in some way if there's an 11th house emphasis.

Q: (The same person—with Mars conjunct Jupiter in Gemini in the 11th—resumes his questions, etc.) At the first Jupiter return, I made a decision to go into the seminary, to be a priest, but I got out of that. And now it's the third Jupiter return, and I've again been involved with another church and with teaching.

A: The only person I know with Jupiter conjunct Mars in Gemini has been in graduate school now for about 10 years!

Q: Yes, well, I've been in school now for about 15 years.

A: All these people with strong Gemini have to try out all sorts of new things.

Q: And I have Sun in the 9th house, which makes it even worse.

A: Oh, yes, no kidding. So what sign is your Sun in then?

Q: Aries. And my Moon is in Leo.

A: Maybe you should start your own school.

Q: Oh, good idea!

A: A radical, innovative school for the new age.

SOME DETAILS OF URANUS TRANSITS

One thing about Uranus transits that I want to mention briefly is that Uranus transits have so much to do with *outgrowing* things. They are often signals that you have outgrown old patterns and that you are ready to change—even if you don't know you are. It's kind of like people aren't aware of their own growth. They're always changing and hopefully they're always learning, but they don't always realize how much they've learned and how much they've grown. But when Uranus comes around and bops you, or zaps you with its electrical current, so often it's brought to your attention rather rapidly how different you are in essence from the role you're currently living. Your real nature, now surfacing from all this new growth, is probably not compatible with certain old habit patterns in your lifestyle, so you're uneasy and restless. And it's sometimes kind of frightening, because there are often powerful urges to make radical changes. Uranus transits can of course be dealt with on a number of different levels. On a subtle level, you can revolutionize your understanding of or approach to whatever dimension of life is indicated by the planet being aspected by Uranus. Whereas on a grosser level, there's the urge to do something totally different, totally outrageous in some cases, just for the sake of excitement. I've got two little examples here.

Transiting Uranus squaring natal Mercury—O.K., this happened to someone who has Gemini rising; therefore she has Mercury as her ruling planet. Any transit to the Ascendant or to the ruler of the Ascendant is really very powerful. It affects your whole being. It's not just some compartment of your life. It affects your appearance in many cases, your physical health, your physical energy, and your whole approach to life. So with Gemini rising, she naturally has a very mental and intellectual approach to life. She reads a whole lot, she is really curious, quite interested in a lot of other people, although with a Cancer Sun she's also somewhat of a recluse. She hides from people while simultaneously longing to talk to them. So how it works out is that she stays home and talks on the phone all day! She gets her Cancer security and still talks (Gemini & Mercury). Anyway, Mercury in her chart is in Leo and was recently squared by transiting Uranus in Scorpio. These are some of the things that were going on at that time. First of all, she realized that she had outgrown all of her old ways of thinking *and acting*, because you know the Ascendant has to do with action, how you act in the world; it's the cusp of the *Aries* house. Geminis act through their tongue or through their hands! She also realized that she had outgrown her appearance. So she cut her hair real short. By the way, when you see people making radical changes in their appearance, it's very often a Uranus transit. This realization that she had outgrown her old ways of thinking and old ways of perceiving things—that realization had been coming on for at least one or two years, manifesting as considerable discontent and a strong desire to change, but the changes weren't right to be acted on for a long time. And those urges toward change weren't given any form or direction until the transit got real close. And when the transit got real close, she took a leave of absence from her job and went on a trip to Nepal all by herself. She went with a group, but she didn't know anybody else in the group. And now she's applying for different kinds of jobs too, because she's getting very cramped in her old job. That's often an experience that you get at the early stages of a Uranus transit—you feel cramped and you just want to explode beyond the restrictions.

In another case, when transiting Uranus squared *Saturn,* there was a realization of a need to be free in the way the person was doing their work, a need to feel excited about some kind of work that they were doing. In other words, all the old work structures shown by Saturn were jolted by Uranus, kind of shaken up and radically changed. Also, Uranus squaring Saturn brought about a *freedom* from what used to be oppressive duties, from what used to be felt as very serious obligations and a lot of fears. A lot of those things were just wiped out. It's kind of like Uranus helped the person become liberated from what used to really hold them down—the Saturn things. Uranus transits at best are very liberating and it's a very exciting, interesting time. One thing I've noticed that is bad about Uranus transits is that, on the psychological level, it does tend toward desperate extremes and getting really really headstrong and very selfish too, very self-centered. And then the other thing is physically; a Uranus transit is a very hard energy for your body to handle. It really tests your nervous system, and it will often be a time when there will be nervous ailments, twitches, skin rashes, insomnia, and all kinds of weird things that can hardly ever be treated effectively. But when the transit passes, the symptoms often pass or at least decrease in severity.

FINAL COMMENTS

With Jupiter and Saturn transits, you should keep in mind what they're doing in your chart *by sign*, and not just by close aspects. When the aspects are real close, that's probably when things will come to a specific focus. But say you've got your Sun in Leo in the 5th house, and Saturn now is in Leo. From the time Saturn entered Leo until the time it leaves Leo, it's an important time; it's a Saturnian time for you. But as Saturn closely aspects that Sun, probably three times, those exact aspects will mark very distinct chapters in your development and in your assimilation of Saturn's lessons. *Probably* the first transit of the three will be the most noticeable and have the strongest impact. But in general, I would say the orb should be kept small with Saturn. Personally, I didn't even notice Saturn square my Sun until it was exact to the minute, and then everything went crazy, everything was going wild. But I noticed it from that minute—I couldn't help but notice it—for the next nine months until the transit was exact 2 more times. Then it slowly faded out. Jupiter transits are kind of like Saturn; they can be given a kind of general orb *by sign* if Jupiter is in your Sun sign or in your Moon sign or your rising sign—all those things may be positive types of feelings and confidence that you'll notice. But the orbs on the *exact* aspects to angles or to natal planets should probably be kept to just a few degrees, and that's when specific things will often be happening. I used to think that all transits should be given an orb of 1 degree, because all of mine were so exact. With many people, however, it seems that you have to use a little larger orb, 2 or 3 degrees or sometimes even more. I would think 5 or 6 degrees would be the absolute maximum in most cases, especially with Pluto and Uranus transits.

Also included in the topic of transits are lunations. Some people look at the transiting Sun and Moon independently, which I hardly ever do. It's not too important, especially the transiting Moon which zips through your chart about every 28 days. The transiting Sun you can look at somewhat, and it might occasionally be a little significant. The main thing with the Sun and Moon is the *New Moon,* when the Sun and Moon are conjunct, which is sometimes called a lunation. You can judge it by the house position to some extent, that is what natal house it falls in. Those "Celestial Influences" calendars put out by Jim Maynard are very useful, because they list the New Moons by zodiacal position and time. You can also use Full Moons too, and those calendars give all the information on them also. The main thing with the New Moon is: is it going to closely conjunct, square, or oppose a natal planet? The New Moon might then activate or energize that planet. In most cases, the lunation merely energizes whatever is shown as potential in your natal chart. It's not positive or negative or hard or easy, it's just *activating.* The main thing with the lunations is to see if it conjuncts, squares, or opposes a natal planet. And then keep an eye on it. It won't always do something. But my experience makes me think that the conjunction is by far the most reliable of the aspects with the lunations. In other words, if you ever have the New Moon conjuncting *any* planet in your chart, maybe even within a half a degree of exact, definitely if it's within 15 minutes of exact, it's going to activate that planet. The activating might start as much as 3 or 4 days before the New Moon is exact. In other words, as the Sun and Moon get closer and closer together on that natal point, so to speak, you're going to feel it before the exact New Moon is formed. And then that influence often continues until the next New Moon. The most powerful manifestation is usually in the first 14 days, the first 2 weeks—in other words, from New Moon to Full Moon. That's usually the big energy release. After that, it does tend to taper off. Some people say that if the New Moon is a Solar Eclipse, then it may even be stronger and may even last for many months then. I personally am not convinced that that is true, that the eclipse is that much stronger than the lunations; they may be, but I haven't seen anything to make me think that. And I have paid attention to them for years. However, if you use all the 30°- multiple aspects,* you'll often find a whole series of lunations

---

*Since this workshop took place, I have increasingly recognized the importance of all the aspects that are multiples of 30 degrees, both in natal charts and in transits. While I still feel that the conjunction, square, and opposition aspects are the strongest aspects by transit, I have come to believe that all 30°- multiple aspects formed by the transiting outer five planets can in many cases be important. In particular, it seems that the semi-sextiles and quincunx (or inconjunct) aspects formed by transiting planets are almost always neglected and their importance underestimated. In many ways and in many cases, a transit of one of the outer five planets in semi-sextile or quincunx to a natal planet will be *experienced* as more significant and noticeable than the same combination of planets forming a trine or sextile! The semi-sextiles and quincunxes of the transiting outer five planets seem to refine attitudes, reinforce or alter recent decisions or plans, or at times even to mark especially significant periods of change that far exceed the intensity and importance of the things that happen during the trine and sextile periods. It should be emphasized, however, that such periods are usually quite a bit less important, dramatic, and decisive than the conjunction, square, and opposition periods, and that they are noticeably less filled with pressure and obvious problems of a crisis magnitude.

I have particularly noticed that the semi-sextiles formed by transiting Saturn or Uranus to any natal planet often coincide with periods of stress, change, or realization, or with events that are somewhat reminiscent of what one regularly finds with the conjunctions, squares, and oppositions. For example, transiting Uranus in semi-sextile to natal Sun may well correlate with a period of rapid changes in one's identity and entire sense of self. Creativity of a new type may begin to flourish. Radical ideas and an interest in social welfare may become especially appealing. And, of course, the house where one's natal Sun is located (as well as the house ruled by the Sun) will be brought forcefully into play, and a great deal of energy will be focused into that field of activity. I suggest that the reader refer to his or her own experience of Uranus in semi-sextile to the natal Sun to corroborate this idea. Likewise, a semi-sextile of transiting Saturn to the natal Sun will usually be felt as a period of significant alterations in attitudes and practical realizations, although without most of the feelings of depletion and exhaustion so often found when the aspect is the conjunction, square, or opposition.

tripping off a certain natal planet, month after month for maybe four or five months.

Q: What does the transiting Sun do? Energizing? And what about the nodes in transits?

A: I doubt that the Sun's transit is very *important*. It's never been very important for me. Neither have the nodes been important for me. Some people will do transits to the nodes or transiting nodes to natal planets. They may be good techniques for some people, but they have never meant anything to me. Transiting Sun or Moon by themselves I don't use at all in consultations. I just look at the New Moons, and occasionally the Full Moon will trip off something too. Say you have your natal Sun at 13° Aries, and there is a Full Moon between 13° Aries and 13° Libra—in other words, if the transiting Sun is at 13° Libra and the transiting Moon is at 13° Aries, then this Full Moon will activate that natal Sun. Sometimes it will be real noticeable; other times you just have a little something or other happening, or you notice nothing at all. The New Moons and Full Moons are not easy to interpret. The only way you can do it is to really understand that factor in the natal chart that is being activated; otherwise you'll be totally lost.

Q: You mentioned something about Saturn going into the 11th house and participating in group activities or something. I've had Saturn in the 11th for the last year, and I've been roped into organizing some activities involving people and have had to work with lots of people getting them to do something.

A: The fact that you said "roped into" sounds like Saturn! It sounds like responsibility—those cosmic hands coming into your life! Well, thank you for coming.

V — Some Thoughts on Astrological Counseling

Since astrology deals most significantly and most immediately with the *inner* world (i.e., the world of the *psyche*, the world of personal *experience*), one must therefore assume that astrology is composed of certain laws and principles which transcend the material world's more obvious and more provable laws. Hence, any astrologer, while perceiving the reality of a client's situation in symbolic form (or, one might say, in its essential *energy form*), is also challenged in the counseling situation to *interpret* those abstract perceptions into plain English that the client can relate to. The client's level of awareness and degree of openness will in large measure dictate not only how the astrologer attempts to phrase his or her "interpretations" and perceptions but also how easy it will be to communicate something significant to the client and yet still retain the essential truth abstractly represented by the astrological configurations.

By "how easy it will be," I'm mainly referring to the fact that the astrologer has to "step-down" his or her consciousness any number of levels before real contact can be made with most clients. It is as if the astrologer is a *transformer* (in the sense of electrical transformers), stepping down the energy current to more immediately useful levels. No doubt most astrologers breath a sigh of relief when they first meet with a client who is able to tune in directly on the astrologer's highest perspective, for in such cases the counseling appointment can not only be less work for the astrologer but in fact often energizing and inspiring. However, in my experience, the vast majority of clients cannot make that kind of connection with the astrologer; they are what they are, and their consciousness is limited to a certain range of understanding and to a set pattern of thought. And in those cases, the astrologer has to "descend" from the purity of abstract perceptions and symbols, which in themselves are so intriguing and invigorating, to the dull and rather complex level of everyday life, with all its considerations, reservations, limitations, and frustrations. Therefore, one question that must be asked is: How does one make this transition from the heights of elevated perception to the depths of involvement in the material world? In other words, how does one give form to the invisible, intangible realities of life in such a way that the client can relate to one's explanations and yet still not lose the inspiring, refreshing, and strengthening qualities inherent in astrology's essential beauty and simplicity?

One way to approach this subject is to view astrology as a language, as has so often been stated. Astrology *is* a language of life, a cosmic language, a language of energy, and—as I repeat whenever I get the chance—an *experiential language*. The astrologer often serves not so much as "interpreter" (in the usual astrological sense of the word) but as a *translator*. So often, when we see a particular complex or configuration in an individual's chart, we don't *know* what it means. Surely we can develop all sorts of theories about its probable meaning in the abstract, the potential which it *may* represent, and so on. But we don't *know* what it means in many cases! And therefore, *undirected* attempts to "interpret" such factors by superimposing various theories is often a poor counseling method, for by doing so we unnecessarily place limits on the possible meanings the client might be able to relate to.

In such cases, I have often found myself playing the role of translator, i.e., simply attempting to explain to the client as clearly and simply as I can what the astrological language is saying to him or her. In some cases, as I systematically explain this abstraction in concrete terms, I'll often get a clearer insight into the reality of its meaning for this particular person. In other cases, the client will have some insight tripped off by this simple, systematic effort at translation. A sort of "free association" on the client's part is therefore made possible and encouraged, and the likelihood of the client gaining knowledge of real value and usefulness is thereby increased. In fact, I feel that by-passing this translation phase of astrological work too often leads the astrologer to play "know-it-all" and the client to either distrust the astrologer or to put too much value on specific statements which are then viewed as *facts* rather than accurately as *interpretations*. After all, the *cosmos* is speaking to the person through the birthchart! Can we improve on that with our limited theories?

I suppose it is my Aquarius Moon and strong Uranus attunement that leads me so often to emphasize the objectivity and "scientific" approach which I feel that a good astrological counselor must have. By "scientific," I don't mean the material sciences or a knowledge of statistics. Rather I mean *scientific* in the true sense of the word: from *scio*—I KNOW. I feel it is absolutely important for the astrological counselor to be able to differentiate between 1) what "I know" and 2) what "I think" or what "Some part of me knows." In many cases, we will get a feeling that something or other is the case with a given person; that may take the form of hunches, past life intuitions, anticipations of future events, etc. These feelings or intuitions are no doubt interesting, but—if *I* don't know for sure that the particular intuition is true—it is often better counseling practice to leave it unsaid. In cases where the specific intuition has a strong bearing on a particular problem that the person is encountering, it *may* at times be profitable to express the idea, but putting it forth only as a feeling or possibility rather than as a statement of fact.

Many of us have noticed the increasing use of terms like "karmic astrology," "past-life astrology," etc. And it is in this kind of astrological work that the Aquarian "I know" so often gets lost in vague, hypothetical guesswork. As I explained at length in my book *Astrology, Karma & Transformation,* if the law of karma is a true universal law, then all astrology is "karmic astrology" and every birthchart factor is related to karma. If karmic law is not a true universal principle, then "karma" should not be mentioned at all in relation to anything, let alone astrology! One can't have it both ways . . . although many seem to be trying! To have it both ways is equivalent to saying, on one hand, "You should go out and get that new job because Jupiter is conjuncting your natal Saturn, and this shows opportunities for rapid advancement which may be missed if you don't act now!" and then stating in the next sentence, "But of course Saturn is aspecting your Venus which means there is some karmic adjustment in your financial or love picture which just has to be accepted and waited out." (Note that, for some "karmic astrologers," the supposed "karmic" situations merely have to be endured, with no trace of initiative or change of attitude.)

Many astrologers who emphasize the *counseling* value of astrology, myself included, are dismayed and even angered (because their profession is being devalued) when references to karma are *unnecessarily* interjected into astrological work. There is a kind of astrological practitioner and writer who mis-uses the spiritual and esoteric traditions which are based upon karmic law and reincarnation theory. I am not referring here to genuine psychics who can and do give accurate past life readings, perhaps intermingled with some astrology, although these are fewer in number than many think. This kind of person is often not doing counseling, does not pretend to do counseling, and is often not particularly interested in counseling. Doing psychic "readings" is their work, and their clients go to them expecting that very sort of service.

If one is not a practicing psychic, however, and holds oneself out to the public simply as an astrologer, I feel it is imperative that he or she either entirely refrain from references to karma (if the astrologer *or the client* does not believe in it) or that karmic theory be established as the framework through which the entire substance of the birthchart will be understood (when both astrologer and client really understand and accept what karma is!). In other words, karma—if used at all in astrological counseling—should be a background which sheds light and meaning on the specific life-situation, not reducing everything to a "karmic cop-out" level of understanding but rather providing encouragement to grow and acceptance of one's lot in life.

But even in this latter arrangement, in which there is a mutual understanding between astrologer and client based on their shared faith in the truth of karmic law, the astrologer needs to remain grounded in the present, dealing with immediate circumstances, feelings, and realistic alternatives. For, although on an ultimate level and from a very high state of consciousness, perhaps everything is subject to karmic law, the fact that most of us are not developed spiritually to that state of awareness should prompt us to accept the limitations of our perceptions and therefore to deal with life based on our immediate experience. In other words, although it is comforting and strengthening to put faith in absolute abstractions, we have to live our lives and make our decisions using our relative, concrete consciousness—limited though it may be.

Along the same lines, it is a rare astrologer who is sufficiently evolved to act as a true *guru*, i.e., a true spiritual teacher and guide. In fact, although some astrologers like to play this role, I wonder if any astrologer is really capable of providing to another person the real gift that a *guru* has to offer: liberation of the soul from all bonds and limitations. Again, we have to think of the client's *long-term* welfare and spiritual well-being, not the glorification of our egos. By too enthusiastically taking on more spiritual responsibility than we can capably handle, an astrologer may be assuming a tremendous karmic burden for himself, as well as misleading some struggling soul who is seeking any trace of light and hope he or she can find. My feeling is that, while the astrologer is not a true *guru*, he or she *can* help to lead people toward a more refined and spiritual direction in their lives by acquainting them with the power, beauty, and truth of the Oneness of the entire universe and the higher order of all manifestations of life. In this sense, astrology serves a "spiritual" purpose by elevating and refining the mind of those who use or study it.

TRUST IN THE COUNSELING SITUATION

I mentioned above the possibility of mistrust arising in the mind of the client if the astrologer plays the "know-it-all" role that is so often seen in consultations where the emphasis is on a "reading" rather than on a counseling dialogue. But another factor related to trust is the need for the astrologer to feel comfortable with and to accept his or her own feelings—not only the general intuitions one might get during a particular consultation but also the "vibrations" one gets from the client. This doesn't necessarily mean that one should *express* all such feelings to the client, but "Trust your vibes" might be a good motto for all counselors, especially those just beginning a professional practice. Since so much in a counseling situation depends on the *rapport* (or sympathetic resonance) between the counselor and client, it is extremely important to be able to evaluate one's feelings and "vibes" toward a client with some objectivity. Naturally, a comparison of the two charts may well be useful for this kind of understanding. In some cases, when one finds that poor rapport does not get any better after one or two appointments with a person and that the communication is therefore quite awkward and limited, the best thing one could do for the client would be to refer him or her to another astrologer/counselor.

No matter how much astrology one knows and no matter what clever interpretations and predictions one is able to make, all of one's abilities can be quite effectively blocked with a particular person with whom one has either no rapport or even some degree of hostility. I'm confident that many astrologers have noticed how easily they open up and do their best work with certain types of clients, and—on the other hand—how working with other types of clients is like "pulling teeth" to draw out from within oneself even an obvious insight or to elicit even a moderately authentic response from the client. I strongly feel that referral is a more ethical practice than persisting in doing what psychologists/psychiatrists often do: that is, denying the reality of the lack of energy-harmony with a given client and insisting on extensive analysis *of the relationship itself*—at the client's expense!! My feeling is: if it doesn't flow with ease, at least consider the possibility that that client may be better off with someone more attuned to his/her nature.

PROBLEMS OF PSYCHOTHERAPY
& COUNSELING TODAY

As more and more astrologers commit themselves to doing in-depth counseling, and as some are getting formal training in psychotherapy, there is an increasing possibility that the problems inherent in modern-day counseling and therapy methods will begin to infiltrate the work of astrologers as well. Therefore, I think it may be of some value to point out what I see as some of the weaknesses or faults of the counseling/therapeutic methods, attitudes, and philosophies currently in vogue.

First, *most counselors can't leave well enough alone!* They are trained in analyzing every little tidbit of information, every gesture, every desire to the point where their minds are completely saturated with intellectual theories and thus no longer open to perceiving *what is.* The simple and the obvious are ignored or not even noticed. Naturally, it is financially profitable to seize upon every possible "clue to the real cause behind your problem," and to drag out this sort of analysis indefinitely. The fact is, the mind can always find more details to analyze. It can always create more theories to fit any and every pattern of behavior.

The question the counselor must consider is: Has this client reached a point where he or she can live a relatively autonomous, relatively happy life in which his or her functioning and self-expression is not unduly encumbered? If so, it may well be time for the counselor to step out of that person's life and to let the client stand on his own two feet once again. None of us is perfect, and the chances of any of us becoming perfect in this lifetime are rather dim. Therefore, we should not persist in demanding (as all too many therapists seem to do nowadays) that the client reach some idealized state of perfection that we ourselves have in fact not achieved. And anyway, what gives us the idea that we are the ones who can lead that person to that exalted state of "wholeness" if we ourselves do not embody that ideal already? "The blind leading the blind" is a cliché that accurately applies to such cases of therapeutic hypocracy.

Second, *analytical reduction of one's problems to a sexual cause and/or methods of evaluating and treating sexual disfunction are overemphasized and often misdirected.* Ever since Freudian theory became widely known, there has been a school of thought in counseling and therapy circles which overemphasizes the role of sex. Modern American life's obsession with sex has renewed this trend, which many thought had died off as psychotherapeutic theory matured, but it is now under a new garb (laboratory "scientific" studies of sexual functions) and with a new jargon. One cannot read through the workshop descriptions in a symposium for marriage counselors, psychologists, or even ministers without being struck with what appears to be a renewed obsession with sex's role in our psychic life. Even the conservative publishing companies run by churches now churn out dozens of books each year that deal with sexual problems, frustrations, and incompatibility.

Jung attempted to rectify the overemphasis on sexual theory in psychology by showing that there are deeper and more comprehensive forces motivating human behavior; and this compensatory work was also developed by many other psychologists. But now the swing back in the other direction has occurred once again, perhaps an inevitable trend in a culture that is increasingly dominated by machines, economic pressures, sensual fixation, urban concrete jungles and the loneliness and inner emptiness that accompany them.

I see many positive aspects of this increased recognition of the importance of sex in human life. In some ways, the early ideas of Freud are only now filtering down into the mass-culture and becoming influential in the everyday life decisions of tens of millions of people. Indeed, since most of us live more on concrete than on the earth itself, it is only natural that our resultant lack of grounding *in the earth* would eventually necessitate a compensatory groping toward the physical roots of our being. What utterly bewilders me is the fact that most counselors and sex-therapists have only a random batch of cleverly devised theories to support their work. Most completely ignore the insights into the sex energy and its interchange with another person that can be found in yoga and in astrology.

It became painfully apparent to me, through contact with hundreds of clients who had previously been to counselors and therapists who were not familiar with astrology, that so many sexual problems were merely a case of simple, old-fashioned incompatibility. This includes many cases of sexual "disfunction," such as impotence, frigidity, premature ejaculation, etc. To be sure, many cases of sexual incompatibility can be worked with, adjusted to, and lived with. But this is not to say that the fundamental lack of harmony *on the level of sexual energy* has been changed or "cured." It is simply acknowledging the fact that very few couples are completely compatible on the sexual level, and in fact—from my experience—I'd have to estimate that the vast majority of couples live with some degree of sexual/emotional incompatibility.

The point is that sexual compatibility or incompatibility essentially emanates from the energy attunement of the individuals involved. Such a view, of course, is quite incomprehensible to the therapists and "researchers" who insist on viewing sex as a primarily mechanical function (although they do admit it has some emotional overtones). This depersonalization of sex, and the accompanying separation of sex from the cosmic dance of life which should be seen as a *religious* experience, naturally leads to human beings who have sexual problems being treated in a mechanical way, and often with an overlay of extraneous intellectual analysis. The saddest part of this practice is that such treatment often tends in the long run to aggravate the original problem, for the person is encouraged to become even more of a *disembodied self.*

Third, *so many psychological/emotional problems today are at least partially due to environmental factors that a counselor now needs a broader knowledge than ever before of life itself, of various other fields of study, and of a multitude of therapeutic techniques and healing methods.* Among the trends in modern, technological civilization which contribute to "psychological problems" are:

a) The fact that so many people live their lives as a "disembodied self," out of touch with the physical body, the world of nature, and their archetypal roots. There is already an excess of mental gymnastics and pointless intellectualization promoted by schools, government bureaucrats, and government-funded studies. When funds get tight in a school district, for example, physical education classes and sports programs are the first to be cut, followed immediately by cutbacks in music and art curricula. This trend toward self-destructive overreliance on intellect is the cause of much of our modern psychological suffering; and so often counselors of various types (astrologers included) simply perpetuate this trend through their overly-analytical approach to human difficulties. I feel that a suggestion to a client to begin a definite exercise program or perhaps jogging, yoga postures, or swimming would often be more beneficial than all of the intellectual hyperbole that counselors so often engage in.

b) We live in an electronic age, a milieu that wires us in to raucous music, schizophrenic "art," and the endless idiocy of television and advertizing. The pace of life has become a rat-race in which there is no trace of tranquility, no sense of calm—and of course this is much worse in urban areas than elsewhere. Technology has gone wild, and we are letting it rip us to pieces daily. While we obviously can't change the entire culture overnight, we can at least take steps to find our *own* method of staying centered amidst the whirlpool of cultural madness. And it follows that, for many people, the practice of yoga, meditation, Polarity Therapy and other kinds of "body work" is a more useful means of *coping* with our environment than is an overly-analytical type of counseling (whether astrological or otherwise).

c) The state of environmental pollution is so bad that not only is a good portion of the food we eat contaminated by toxic materials, but the rate of genetic defects among the newborn is climbing at a rate which must be considered extremely alarming. As high as 10% of newborn children in some areas of the world are now born with genetic defects of one type or another. In other words, whereas the air, water, and earth are severely polluted already, the increasing use of nuclear materials is quickly ensuring that the fourth element, fire (the radiant life-force itself), is also becoming altered in significant ways.

When all of these things are considered, I think we must admit that a "counselor" today needs a great breadth of knowledge and experience to serve his or her clientel properly. Purely intellectual knowledge (and this includes *abstract* astrological knowledge bearing no trace of human wisdom or common sense) is not sufficient. Naturally, an astrological counselor can't be all things to all people. We must know ourselves and trust ourselves. This self-knowledge and trust in self is even more important now since it is increasingly difficult to obtain any sort of "authoritative" knowledge in any field. One can get a Ph.D. "expert" to say almost anything, no matter how obvious or how absurd. If we can't trust the "experts," who can we trust? We can trust the best that is within us, and we can trust the awareness that develops from a genuine, gut-level dialogue in a counseling situation. This person-to-person exchange, if pursued with true authenticity and sincerity, and if permitted by the openness of both counselor and client, is bound to produce useful results. As a great spiritual teacher has said, "It is sincerity of heart that matters."

A final thought: It occurred to me recently that astrology is really just an extension and broadening of our everyday reality. It simply deals with time and planetary cycles (including *earth cycles*). Everyone experiences the reality of a day (the earth's revolution about its axis), a month (approximating a complete lunar cycle), and a year (a complete revolution of the earth around the sun). Everyone sees (and in fact cannot fail to see) the obvious correlations of our everyday experience with these solar system cycles. In order to be able to relate to the fundamental basis of astrology, therefore, one simply has to extend the boundary of his consciousness beyond the orbit of the earth and its moon, into other dimensions of life. One has only to tune in on the *other* cycles within our solar system by realizing their place in the functional ecology of this entire system.

Admittedly, the earth, moon, and sun cycles and rhythms have the most *obvious* links with experiences that are common to all human beings. But is it not reasonable to assume that the other planets as well might have similar links with our lives, albeit more subtle and harder to perceive with the physical senses? Everyone today has a clock in the home, and we have only to point out to people the celestial motions on which clock time is based to begin to relate to them what astrology is and to show them that astrology is not something "out there" but instead is *right here now*. This might be a first step in expressing the abstraction of astrology in concrete terms, especially to the general public or to clients who are unfamiliar with astrology, and the simplicity of this approach has much to recommend it. If we want more people to *understand* what astrology is rather than rejecting it outright, it is incumbent upon us to develop a way of defining astrology which is ultimately simple. And, by keeping astrology as essentially simple as possible, we not only make it intellectually accessible to many others but we also bring it down to earth for the beneficial use of human beings.